CONVERSATIONAL SPANISH
for the
MEDICAL AND HEALTH PROFESSIONS

CONVERSATIONAL SPANISH for the MEDICAL AND HEALTH PROFESSIONS

Cynthia Ann Teed

Harold C. Raley

Jeffrey B. Barber

HOLT, RINEHART AND WINSTON

New York   Chicago   San Francisco   Philadelphia
Montreal   Toronto   London   Sydney
Tokyo   Mexico City   Rio de Janeiro   Madrid

Photo credits (by page number): Cynthia Teed: 1, 7, 14, 39, 69, 74, 84, 94, 110, 129, 141, 142, 178; Jan Lukas, Photo Researchers, Inc.: 55; Beryl Goldberg: 148, 188; Erika Stone, Peter Arnold, Inc.: 158, 168.

Cover photograph by Beryl Goldberg.

Library of Congress Cataloging in Publication Data

Teed, Cynthia Ann.
  Conversational Spanish for the medical and health professions.

  1. Spanish language—Conversation and phrase books (for medical personnel). I. Raley, Harold C. II. Barber, Jeffrey B. III. Title. [DNLM: 1. Medicine—Phrases—Spanish. W 15 T258c]
  PC4120.M3T4   1983   468.3′421′08861   82-15719
  ISBN 0-03-059287-9

CBS COLLEGE PUBLISHING
Holt, Rinehart and Winston
The Dryden Press
Saunders College Publishing

To John

CONTENTS

PREFACE

In the spring of 1979, Jeffrey Barber, Director of Personnel Administration at St. Joseph's Hospital in Houston, asked Harold Raley and me to teach conversational medical Spanish to his hospital personnel. Classes were provided for over 400 employees from seventeen different departments of the hospital. Our challenge was to develop a text that would teach pertinent, practical, and authentic Spanish and would appeal to both medically trained personnel and related personnel not directly involved with the healing arts.

We polled our classes to determine what our students wanted us to teach them, and we designed the course around their requests. The experience of successfully meeting the communicating needs of highly trained medical personnel while they were performing their skills in a hospital setting prompted us to write this text.

CONVERSATIONAL SPANISH FOR THE MEDICAL AND HEALTH PROFESSIONS was written from material gathered while teaching the pilot course at St. Joseph's. In addition, although the original text was used for that course, several changes were made during subsequent classes for over 1,000 persons (doctors, nurses, technicians, and administrators from seventeen different departments of the hospital including the emergency room, clinic, laboratory, and cafeteria) at the following hospitals in the Houston area: Jefferson Davis Hospital, Twelve Oaks Hospital, Westbury Hospital, and The Woman's Hospital. Finally, the text has also been used as a reference tool by medical personnel waiting to take the class and by those who already know Spanish but who needed a reference book to give alternate vocabulary items when dealing with patients from different Hispanic cultures.

Due to the attraction that the Houston Medical Center has for patients of every nationality, we felt a responsibility to produce a standard Spanish with variations (in the form of footnotes) for regional as well as national differences. A committee of teachers representing Chile, Cuba, the Dominican Republic, Guatemala, Mexico, Puerto Rico, and Spain was formed to revise the medical vocabulary in order to avoid any confusion in meaning or redundancy.

Conversational and medical vocabulary are taught in the text through the emphasis of cognate words. Where possible, all medical terminology has been organized into words with endings that are equivalent to the endings in English.

As the basic presentation of material is given in dialogue form followed by oral exercises, the authors feel that the use of the conversational approach is facilitated by this emphasis on cognates. It is our belief that most medical personnel are "visual learners" and prefer to "see" first rather than to "hear." This is in keeping with the nature of the healing professions, which require a tremendous skill in recognizing visual clues that are symptoms of physical illnesses, for example. Words such as *expectoration* can quickly be learned in Spanish (**expectoración**), for the medical student has already "seen" the word and knows the meaning. The instructor can concentrate on the pronunication and orthographical differences, while cautioning the students about potential problems such as false cognates.

CHAPTER ELEMENTS

The *Diálogos* are written with the intent to stress authenticity of setting and language. The level of grammatical Spanish is kept simple, direct, and practical, and pronunciation exercises have been included in the dialogues for all sounds of Spanish. The content of the conversations forms the main body of the text of each lesson. The *Diálogos* are intended to be read aloud by the instructor with choral response from the class or to be enacted by the students. We have found that the information in the text is so absorbing that most students, regardless of their level of Spanish or medical knowledge, become very interested in the easy fluidity of the material as well as its practical and realistic nature. Most phrases have already been heard around the hospital or are of such pertinent nature to the student's work that they are easily remembered. The dialogues are followed by *Frases útiles*, which include related vocabulary items, provide alternate ways of saying the same thing, and allow a creative teacher yet another opportunity to provide additional related vocabulary from varied nationalistic origins.

The next chapter element, the *Ejercicios de conversación*, is designed to stimulate conversation after the original conversational models have been drilled. Alternate forms of syntax (questions, commands, etc.) are also tested in this section. For an advanced class, these exercises offer a point of departure and allow the students to discuss the variations in hospital procedures.

To allow the instructor the time and opportunity to use his or her creative efforts more easily, we offer the *Situación y simulación* section. This chapter element encourages the student to formulate original sentences based on everyday hospital life. In addition, the *Situación y simulación*, along with the *Juegos* section, allows the more advanced students to compare notes and levels of skill in Spanish while learning from each other in a conversational exchange. Both of these sections can be omitted on the beginning level or if class time is limited.

Sections of evaluation or tests (*Pruebas*) are provided after every four lessons. These evaluations can be used as a form of review, as homework assignments, or they may be omitted completely if time is limited. A sample test for the first four lessons is provided in the *Primera Prueba*.

The topics that arise in conversational medical Spanish are so complex and varied that each chapter could conceivably be expanded threefold. With advanced classes we have found that these students will add a great deal of additional material that they have gathered from work, field trips, patients, medi-clinics, and public health departments in the city. The *Vocabulario* section is adequate for a beginning-level class, and it should be emphasized that cognate words have not been included. For more advanced classes, a standard dictionary should be chosen.

HOW TO USE THIS BOOK

Most class meetings consist of two 45-minute segments weekly. We have learned to vary activities and to *review* in order to protect our work and that of our students against lack of progress. Most learning will be achieved by classroom participation rather than by home study. A typical class period in a beginning class may follow this progression:

   a. Preliminary discussion on activity in hospital, current event in an Hispanic country, *Dicho* for the day, etc. This period may be used to prepare the students for the transition they must make into the mental framework of learning a language.
   b. Pronunication exercise—repetition of dialogue in choral response
   c. Presentation of new material (*Frases útiles* or *Ejercicios*)
   d. Re-entry of Dialogue—role-play form, memorized, or in chain form
   e. Choice—*Juego* or *Situación*
   f. Re-entry of dialogue and practice with variations of dialogue using slot-filler technique
   g. Re-entry of new material
   h. Request time

We have always allowed a small segment of time in each class in order to fulfill student requests for additional vocabulary, additional explanations of grammar, etc. Sometimes we discuss the basic syndromes (macho, madonna, etc.) indigenous to the Hispanic cultures, using the *Notas culturales* as a point of departure. A great deal of time may be devoted to cultural discussions during the advanced classes.

Additional suggestions for teaching this text:

   1. *Numbers* (ordinal, roman, cardinal, etc.) are crucial to medical Spanish. We teach these in beginning classes through *Bingo* played with a complete game of cards including prizes for the winners.

2. Since no homework is required, we depend on oral review to cement the learning process. We prefer not to assign material to be studied or ask the students to read aloud content that has not already been introduced in class.

3. If a class has a very difficult time pronouncing a particularly long or complex sentence, the instructor should break the sentence in parts and begin choral response with the *end* of the sentence working forward to the beginning.

In any class, students must be made to feel that the course (text) is geared toward their personal career needs and goals. This requires a good knowledge of the text on the instructor's part rather than native ability in Spanish or professional knowledge of health care.

ACKNOWLEDGMENTS

We are grateful to the following reviewers whose comments, both positive and critical, were instrumental in the shaping of this text:

Olivia López Carter, Metropolitan State College; Irma Blanco Casey, Marist College; Rochelle Kelz, North Park College; Edgar Metzger, New York University; Carmen Parr, Los Angeles Valley College; and Stephen Stryker, University of Arizona.

Cynthia Ann Teed

October 1982

CONVERSATIONAL SPANISH
for the
MEDICAL AND HEALTH PROFESSIONS

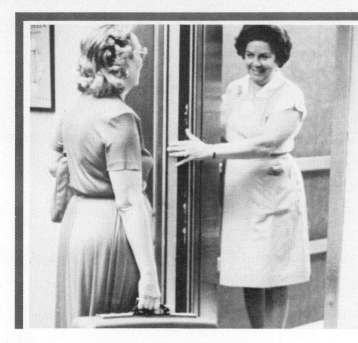

EL HOSPITAL

DIÁLOGO

Pidiendo direcciones

La Sra. Ramírez, una paciente, le pide direcciones al Sr. Jackson, un técnico.

Repita:

Sra. Ramírez	Sr. Jackson
Buenos días, señor.	Buenos días, señora.
¿Sabe usted dónde está la oficina de admisiones?[1]	Sí, sí, claro. Pase usted por el pasillo; y doble a la derecha; y la oficina está enfrente del cafetín.[2]
Muchas gracias, señor.	Para servirle, señora. No hay de qué.

1. or **oficina de admisión**

2. In the Southwest, **la lonchería** (*cafeteria*) is often used instead of **el cafetín. La cafetería** is also widely used and is considered less vulgar than **la lonchería. El comedor** is less frequently used and can be confused with the physicians' dining room.

Asking Directions

Mrs. Ramírez, a patient, asks directions from Mr. Jackson, a technician.

Mrs. Ramírez	Mr. Jackson
Good morning, sir.	Good morning, ma'am.
Do you know where the admitting office is?	Yes, of course. Go (pass) through the hallway; turn to the right; the office is in front of the cafeteria.
Thanks a lot.	(Glad) to be of service, ma'am. Don't mention it.

FRASES ÚTILES

Sustituya:

¿Dónde está la oficina de admisión?[1]	*Where is the admissions office?*
¿————— la oficina de pagos?[2]	*————— business (payment) office?*
¿————— la sala de recepción?[3]	*————— reception room?*
¿————— la sala de espera?	*————— waiting room?*
¿————— el departamento de personal?	*————— personnel department?*
¿————— el baño?[4]	*————— bathroom?*
¿————— la tienda de regalos?	*————— gift shop?*
¿————— el cajero?[5]	*————— cashier?*
¿————— el cuarto de vestir?[6]	*————— dressing room?*
¿————— el departamento de archivo clínico?	*————— medical records department?*

1. **admisiones** in some areas of the United States.

2. business office; the cashier's station (window) may be located here.

3. also, **el zaguán** (*entrance hall*) or *el lobby*, which is prevalent in the Southwest and Mexico. **El vestíbulo** may be used.

4. **El baño** refers to the area that contains the toilet and bathing facilities. **El servicio público, el servicio sanitario** (also known as **el servicio**), which refer to public restroom facilities (generally without bathtub or shower), may also be used. **El excusado** (*toilet*) and **el toilet** are Southwest regionalisms and refer to the toilet facility only. **El W.C. (el water closet)** also refers to toilet, and is of European (Spain) origin.

5. **La caja** refers to the place where payment is made. **El cajero, la cajera** refers to the person.

6. Also, **el vestuario** or **el vestidor.**

Está enfrente del edificio Wilson.
____ aquí.
____ allí.
____ detrás _____.

____ delante _____.

Doble usted a la derecha.
_____ la izquierda.
Siga usted derecho.
_____ por el pasillo.

Busco la unidad de cuidados
intensivos.[7]
_____ la sala de emergencia.
_____ el laboratorio.
_____ la sala de alumbramiento.[8]
_____ el cunero.[9]
_____ el departamento de
enfermería.
_____ el banco de sangre.

Está en el primer piso.
_____ segundo ____.
_____ tercer ____.
_____ cuarto ____.
_____ quinto ____.
_____ sexto ____.
Cruce la calle y está allí.

¿Sabe usted dónde está el
departamento de ortopedia?
¿_____ de enfermedades
mentales?
¿_____ de anestesiología?

It is opposite the Wilson building.
_____ here.
_____ there.
_____ in back of
_____.
_____ in front of
_____.

Turn to the right.
_____ the left.
Continue straight ahead.
_____ down the hallway.

I'm looking for the intensive care
unit.
_____ the emergency room.
_____ the laboratory.
_____ the delivery room.
_____ the nursery.
_____ the nursing
department.
_____ the blood bank.

It's on the first floor.
_____ second ____.
_____ third ____.
_____ fourth ____.
_____ fifth ____.
_____ sixth ____.
Cross the street, and there it is.

Do you know where the orthopedic
department is?
_____ mental
health __?
_____
anesthesiology __?

7. La unidad de cuidados intensivos (intensive care unit) is also called la unidad de terapéutica intensiva.

8. Also, la sala de partos.

9. From cuna (cradle), or la sala de niños.

¿_____ de cardiología?   _____ cardiology ___?

¿_____ de radiografía?[10]   _____ X-ray ___?

¿_____ de cirugía?   _____ surgery ___?

¿_____ de personal?   _____ personnel ___?

¿_____ de pediatría?   _____ pediatrics ___?

Sí, sí, claro. Está en la planta baja.   Yes, of course. It's on the ground floor.

_____ el sótano.   _____ in the basement.

Suba en el ascensor.   Go up in the elevator.

_____ por la escalera.   _____ the stairs.

_____ al segundo piso.[11]   _____ to the second floor.

Baje en el ascensor.   Go down in the elevator.

_____ por la escalera.   _____ the stairs.

_____ al primer piso.   _____ to the first floor.

¿Puede usted decirme dónde está la clínica paciente-ambulante?   Can you tell me where is the outpatient clinic?

¿_____ el departamento de archivo clínico?   _____ the medical records department?

¿_____ el departamento de servicio social?   _____ the social services department?

¿_____ la sala de operaciones?   _____ the operating room?

¿_____ la farmacia?   _____ the pharmacy?

Está enfrente del edificio Wilson.   It's opposite the Wilson Building.

___ detrás _____.   ___ behind _____.

___ al través _____.   ___ across from _____.

___ delante _____.   ___ in front of _____.

Está aquí. Sígame, por favor.   It's here. Follow me, please.

---

10. **El departamento de radiografía** (*X-ray department*) is also called **el departamento de X-ray** or **el departamento de rayos-X**.

11. **La planta baja** indicates ground floor or first floor. Therefore, **el primer piso** can mean either first *or* second floor.

NOTA CULTURAL

1. Directions

Hispanics are polite people and will often preface their requests with "polite phrases" that will tend to confuse the novice speaker of Spanish. It is advisable to pay attention to the following:

¿Dónde está? *where is?* and not the superfluous phrases such as:
¿Sería usted tan amable de . . . (Mexico) *Would you be so kind as to . . .*
Perdone la interrupción pero . . . (Cuba, España) *Forgive the interruption, but . . .*
Perdone la molestia, pero . . . *I'm sorry to bother (you), but . . .*

Ejercicios de conversación

A. *Conteste en español.*

1. ¿Dónde está la oficina de admisión?
2. ¿Sabe usted dónde está la sala de emergencia?
3. ¿Dónde está la sala de cuidados intensivos?
4. ¿Está la tienda de regalos en el primer o en el segundo piso?
5. ¿Está el departamento de personal en la planta baja o en el sótano?
6. ¿Dónde está el banco de sangre?
7. ¿Dónde está la farmacia?
8. ¿Sabe usted dónde está la sala de espera?
9. ¿Dónde está la oficina de pagos?
10. ¿En qué piso está el departamento de rayos-X?

B. *Traduzca al español.*

1. Turn to the left and go down the stairs.
2. Follow me, please.
3. Go up to the third floor. It's there in front of the pharmacy.
4. It's on the fifth floor.
5. Go down the hall. Thanks. Don't mention it.
6. Go down in the elevator to the basement.
7. Do you know where the blood bank is?
8. Follow the *signs* (**señales**) in the hallway.
9. Turn to the left; the dressing room is on the right.
10. Continue straight ahead. At the stairway, turn left.

C. *Escoja la respuesta correcta para completer cada frase.*

1. El técnico de radiografía está en _____
2. La enfermera está en _____
3. Los técnicos de sangre están en _____
4. La secretaria está en _____
5. Los psiquiatras están en _____
6. Los cirujanos están en _____
7. Los niños están en _____
8. La familia de la paciente está en _____
9. La farmacia está en _____
10. El hospital está _____

a. la sala de espera.
b. el sótano.
c. enfrente del edificio Wilson.
d. el banco de sangre.
e. la unidad de terapéutica intensiva.
f. la oficina de admisión.
g. el departamento de enfermedades mentales.
h. la sala de operaciones.
i. la sala de rayos-X.
j. el departamento de pediatría.

D. *Escriba una oración usando las siguientes palabras, recordando las reglas de concordancia.*

Modelo: estar / tercer / radiografía / departamento / piso
El departamento de radiografía está en el tercer piso.

1. comprar / tienda de regalos / flores / querer
2. hambre / porque / cafetería / tener / ir
3. saber / laboratorio / estar / donde
4. paciente / buscar / sótano / baño
5. sangre / necesitar / banco / sangre
6. estar / servicio / dónde / saber / público
7. pasillo / derecha / teléfono / estar
8. paciente / sala / emergencia / estar
9. favor / subir / piso / por / ascensor / tercero
10. izquierda / estar / sótano / farmacia / escalera / enfrente

Situación y simulación

You are working on the main floor of a large hospital where the Spanish-speaking patients or their families are frequently seeking directions. Write out the directions you would give them to find each of the following areas:

la cafetería
la tienda de regalos
la sala de emergencia
la oficina de pagos

el teléfono
el servicio público
la sala de espera

Modelo: ¿Sabe usted dondé está la cafetería?
Sí, claro. Está en este edificio en el primer
piso. Doble a la izquierda y está allí enfrente.

Juegos

A. Write the names and exact locations of at least twenty areas of the hospital on separate slips of paper (i.e., *pharmacy—third floor, across from the elevator* or *gift shop—basement, behind the laboratory*). Fold the slips and mix them up in a container. Each person picks two slips and explains in Spanish how to get from the first location to the second.

B. One person picks an area of the hospital, *without saying its name aloud*, and gives specific directions for how to get to that area, starting from the main entrance. The first person to correctly name the area to which directions are being given gets to pick the next area and give the next set of directions.

PALABRAS COGNADAS

Read through the hospital floor plan description on page 8 and the chart showing the organization of a typical hospital on page 9 and note the cognate words, which are numerous. The words which have no English cognates are listed in the *Vocabulario* at the back of the book.

¿Sabe usted dónde está la oficina de admisiones?

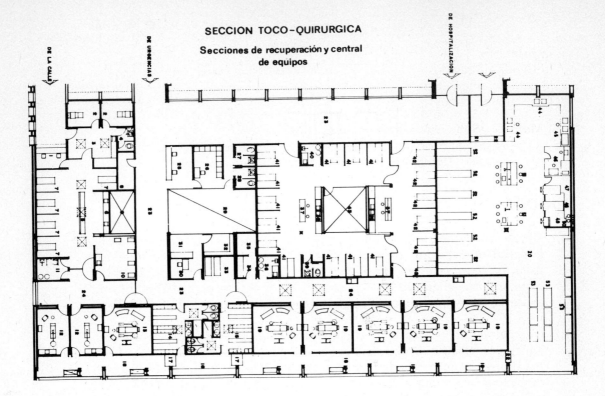

SECCION TOCO-QUIRURGICA

Secciones de recuperación y central de equipos

DE LA CALLE · DE URGENCIAS · DE HOSPITALIZACION

INDICE DE LOCALES

1. Recepción y control de pacientes
2. Cubículo para examen médico
3. Area de trabajo
4. Baño
5. Central de enfermeras
6. Area de trabajo
7. Cubículo para trabajo de parto
8. Bodega y guarda de baterías
9. Ducto de instalaciones
10. Atención inmediata de niños
11. Cuarto séptico y cuarto de aseo
12. Sala de expulsión
13. Sala de operaciones
14. Sanitarios y baños, vestidor de enfermeras
15. Sanitarios y baños, vestidor de médicos cirujanos
16. Cambio de zapatos y ropa estéril
17. Tapetes sanitarios
18. Circulación (área blanca)
18-1. Lavabos para cirujanos

19. Sala de operaciones
20. Central de equipos y esterilización
21. Recibo de material
22. Entrega de material estéril
23. Circulación (área negra)
24. Circulación (área gris)
25. Control de personal, pacientes, equipo y ropa
26. Descanso de médicos y enfermeras
27. Sanitario de hombres
28. Sanitario de mujeres
29. Terraza (de iluminación)
30. Oficina del anestesiólogo
31. Taller del anestesiólogo
32. Guarda de anestésicos
33. Estación de camillas
34. Guarda de rayos X portátil
35. Cuarto obscuro para revelado
36. Cuarto séptico
37. Central de enfermeras, de monitoreo

38. Area de trabajo
39. Sanatorio de enfermeras
40. Cuarto séptico
41. Cubículos de terapéutica intensiva
42. Cubículos de recuperación posoperatoria
43. Terraza (de iluminación)
44. Lavado de material y equipo con fregaderos dobles
45. Lavado de instrumental con aparato de ultrasonido
46. Sección de guantes: probadora, lavadora y encaladora
47. Esterilizador cilíndrico de 20'' × 36''
48. Esterilizador rectangular de 30'' × 42'' × 84''
49. Esterilizador de aire caliente de 19'' × 14'' × 19''
50. Tanques de gas esterilizador
51. Mesas de ensamble con guarda superior e inferior; cortadoras de gasa y guillotina
52. Estantería metálica para guarda no estéril
53. Vitrinas metálicas para material estéril

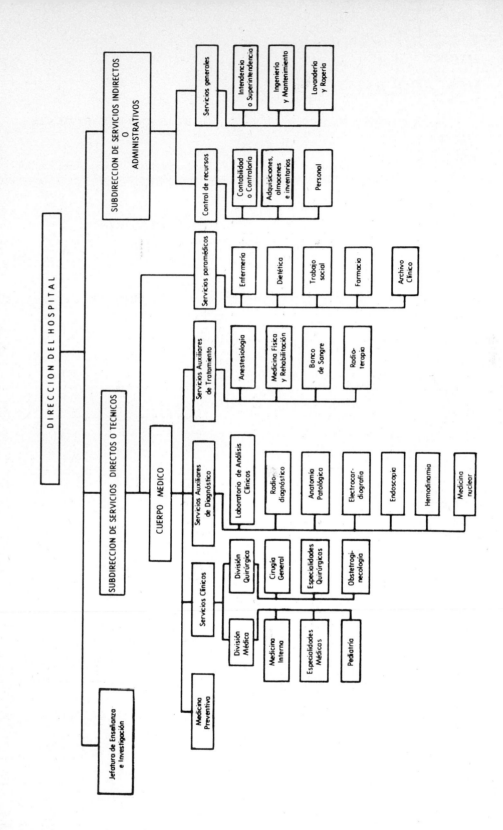

VOCABULARIO

AREAS Y DEPARTAMENTOS	AREAS AND DEPARTMENTS
el banco de sangre	blood bank
el baño; Damas—Caballeros	bathroom; Ladies' room—Men's room
la bodega	warehouse
la cafetería	cafeteria
el cafetín	cafeteria
la caja; el cajero	cashier (window); (person)
la clínica paciente-ambulante	outpatient clinic
el comedor	dining room
el cuarto de baño	bathroom
_____ vestir	dressing room
el cunero	nursery
el departamento	department
el departamento de anestesiología	anesthesiology department
_____ archivo clínico	medical records _____
_____ cirugía	surgery _____
_____ enfermedades mentales	mental health _____
_____ enfermería	nursing _____
_____ ortopedia	orthopedics _____
_____ pediatría	pediatrics _____
_____ personal	personnel _____
_____ radiografía	X-ray _____
_____ rayos-X	X-ray _____
_____ servicio social	social services _____
_____ X-ray(s)	X-ray(s) _____
el descanso	rest area
el excusado	bathroom
la farmacia	pharmacy
el laboratorio	laboratory
la lavandería	laundry
el lobby	lobby
la oficina	office
la oficina de admisión	admissions office
_____ pagos	payment _____
el pasillo	hallway
el piso	floor
la planta baja	ground floor
la sala	room
la sala de alumbramientos	delivery room
_____ emergencia	emergency _____
_____ espera	waiting _____
_____ operaciones	operating _____
_____ recepción	reception _____, lobby
el servicio	bathroom
los servicios públicos	bathroom, public restrooms

los servicios sanitarios	*bathroom, public restroom*
el sótano	*basement*
la tienda	*store*
la tienda de regalos	*gift shop*
la unidad	*unit*
la unidad de cuidados intensivos; terapéutica intensiva	*intensive care unit*
el vestíbulo	*vestibule, lobby*
el vestidor, vestuario	*dressing room*
el WC	*bathroom*
el zaguán	*lobby, hallway, entry*

SUSTANTIVOS

NOUNS

el alumbramiento	*delivery (baby)*
el archivo	*records*
el ascensor	*elevator*
la calle	*street*
el cáncer	*cancer*
la cirugía	*surgery*
el cuidado	*care*
la derecha	*right (direction)*
las direcciones	*directions*
el edificio	*building*
la enfermedad	*illness*
la enfermería	*nursing*
el equipo	*equipment, team*
la escalera	*stairway*
las flores	*flowers*
la gente	*people*
el hambre	*hunger*
el hospital	*hospital*
la izquierda	*left (direction)*
los niños	*children*
la operación	*operation*
el/la paciente	*patient*
el/la paciente-ambulante	*outpatient*
los pagos	*payment*
el pasillo	*hallway*
el personal	*personnel*
el piso	*floor*
el psiquiatra[1]	*psychiatrist*
el recurso	*resource*
los regalos	*gifts*
la sala	*room*
la sangre	*blood*
el señor; Sr.	*man, gentleman; Mr., Sir*

1. Alternate spelling: **el siquiatra.**

SUSTANTIVOS

la señora; Sra.
la señorita; Srta.
el tapete
el técnico
el teléfono
la terapéutica
el tratamiento

VERBOS

bajar
cruzar
decir
doblar
estar
haber; hay

pasar
pedir
poder
querer
repetir
saber
seguir
ser
servir
subir
tener
trabajar

CONJUNCIONES

porque
si
y (*e* before words beginning with
   i- or *hi-*)

PRONOMBRE

usted

PREPOSICIONES

a
al través de
con

NOUNS

woman, lady; Mrs., Ma'am
(unmarried) woman, lady; Miss
table cover
technician
telephone
therapy
treatment

VERBS

to go down, descend
to cross
to tell, say
to turn, bend
to be (location, condition)
to have; there is, there are (impersonal
   subject)
to pass
to ask for
to be able to, can
to want, love
to repeat
to know
to follow, continue
to be (permanency)
to serve
to go up, ascend
to have
to work

CONJUNCTIONS

because
if
and

PRONOUN

you (formal or polite form)

PREPOSITIONS

to, towards
across; over
with

de	from, of
delante de	in front of
detrás de	in back of
en	in, into
enfrente de	across from
para	for
por	for, through

ADVERBIOS

ADVERBS

a la derecha	to the right
a la izquierda	to the left
allí	there
aquí	here
claro	of course, certainly, clear
derecho	straight ahead
donde	where
no	no
sí	yes

ADJETIVOS

ADJECTIVES

claro	clear, sure
clínico	clinical
cuarto	fourth
primer[2]	first
que	what
quinto	fifth
segundo	second
sexto	sixth
tercer[2]	third

FRASES ÚTILES

EXPRESSIONS

buenas noches	good evening; good night
buenas tardes	good afternoon
buenos días	good morning, hello
muchas gracias	thank you, thanks
no hay de qué	don't mention it
para servirle	to serve you
por favor	please
sentirse; lo siento	to feel sorry for; I'm sorry
tener hambre	to be hungry

2. **Primero** and **tercero** drop **-o** before a masculine singular noun; e.g., **el primer piso**, the first floor; **el piso primero**, the first floor.

ADMISIONES

DIÁLOGO

Llenando el formulario de admisión

El Sr. Jiménez, un paciente, le dice a la Sra. Johnson, una enfermera, que él tiene que llenar un formulario de admisión. Por lo tanto, la Sra. Johnson le presenta a la Srta. Martínez, una secretaria que trabaja en la oficina de admisiones del hospital.

Repita:

Sra. Johnson

Buenos días, señor. ¿En qué puedo servirle?

Sr. Jiménez

Buenos días, señora. Necesito llenar un formulario de admisión.

Muy bien, señor. Le presento a la Srta. Martínez. Ella le ayuda inmediatamente.

Muchas gracias.

Srta. Martínez

Tanto gusto en conocerle, señor.

Tome este formulario y llénelo, por favor.

Más tarde . . .

¿Tiene una pregunta?

Se refiere al número de su seguro de hospitalización.

Sí, claro. Siga por este pasillo y el teléfono está allí a la derecha.
De nada.

Sr. Jiménez

Encantado. El gusto es mío, Srta. Martínez.

Muchas gracias.

Sí. En este formulario, ¿Qué quiere decir «Número de Póliza»?

Ah, sí. Pues, no me acuerdo del número. ¿Puedo llamar a mi esposa para preguntárselo?

Muchísimas gracias, señorita.

Filling Out an Admissions Form

Mr. Jiménez, a patient, tells Mrs. Johnson, a nurse, that he has to fill out an admissions form. Therefore, Mrs. Johnson introduces him to Miss Martínez, a secretary who works in the admissions office of the hospital.

Repeat:

Mrs. Johnson

Good morning, sir. May I help you?

All right, sir. Let me introduce you to Miss Martínez. She (will) help you right away.

Miss Martínez

A pleasure to meet you, sir.

Take this form and fill it out, please.

Mr. Jiménez

Good morning, ma'am. I need to fill out an admissions form.

Thank you.

Mr. Jiménez

Delighted. The pleasure is mine, Miss Martínez.
Thank you.

Later...

Do you have a question?

That refers to the number of your hospital's insurance.

Yes, of course. Continue down this hallway, and the phone is there on the right.
Don't mention it.

Yes. On this form, what does "Policy Number" mean?

Oh, yes. Well, I don't remember the number. May I call my wife and ask her?

Many thanks, miss.

FRASES ÚTILES

Sustituya:

¿Es usted el paciente?
¿_____ la paciente?
¿_____ el padre?

Are you the patient?
_____ the patient?
_____ the father?

¿Quién es el paciente? ¿Usted?

Who is the patient? You?

Sí, soy el paciente.
_____ la paciente.
_____ el padre.

Yes, I'm the patient.
_____ the patient.
_____ the father.

No, mi hermana Inez es la paciente.
_____ hija Carmen _____.

_____ abuela Sra. Ortega _____.

No, my sister Inez is the patient.
_____ daughter Carmen _____.

_____ grandmother Mrs. Ortega _____.

Dígame, ¿cómo se llama used?
_____ su hijo?
_____ el paciente?

Tell me, what is your name?
_____ your son's _____?
_____ the patient's _____?

Me llamo Antonio Quintero.

El se llama _____.

Ella se llama Marta.

My name is Antonio Quintero.

His name is _____.

Her name is Martha.

¿Cuál es su nombre?

Mi nombre es Pablo.

_____ María.

What is your first name?

My first name is Pablo.

_____ María.

¿Y su apellido?

Mi apellido es Ramírez.

_____ Bermúdez.

And your last name?

My last name is Ramírez.

_____ Bermúdez.

¿Qué es de usted? ¿Es su hijo?

Sí, es mi hijo.

No, es mi sobrino.

_____ primo.

_____ hijastro.

What (relationship) is he to you?
Your son?

Yes, he's my son.

No, he's my nephew.

_____ cousin.

_____ stepson.

¿Qué parentesco tiene la paciente
con usted?

Es mi hija.

_____ suegra.

_____ nieta.

What is the patient's relationship to
you?

She is my daughter.

_____ mother-in-law.

_____ granddaughter.

¿Habla usted inglés?

Sí, mucho.

No, muy poco.

Do you speak English?

Yes, a lot.

No, very little.

¿Por qué viene usted al hospital?

¿_____ su hijo _____?

¿_____ su nieta
_____?

Why do you come to the hospital?

____ does your son
_____?

____ does your granddaughter
_____?

Me van a operar.

Le _____.

Le _____.

They're going to operate on me.

_____ him.

_____ her.

¿Qué le pasa a su hijo?   What's wrong with your son?
¿_____ usted?   _____ you?

Siente un dolor de cabeza.   He has (feels) a headache.
Siento _____.   I have (feel) _____.

¿Qué siente usted?   What are you feeling?
¿_____ su prima?   _____ is your cousin _____?

Un dolor[1] en el brazo.   A pain in my arm.
_____ la pierna.   _____ her leg.

¿Es la primera vez en el hospital?   Is this your first time in the hospital?

Sí, señora.   Yes, ma'am.
__ señorita.   ___ miss.
__ señor.   ___ sir.

¿Cuál es la dirección de su casa?   What is the address of your house?
¿Dónde vive usted?   Where do you live?

Mi dirección es, calle Westheimer 1919.[2]   My address is 1919 Westheimer Street.
Vivo en _____.   I live at _____.

¿Qué número tiene su casa?   What is the number of your house?
¿_____ domicilio?   _____

    domicile?

¿_____ apartamento?   _____

    apartment?

---

1. Physical pain is described by using **el dolor** (*the pain*), emotional pain or embarrassment by the use of **la pena** (*the penalty, grief, worry, hardship, etc.*).

2. See appendix for use of numbers. In Spanish, the most frequent usage for giving numerical addresses is the two-digit form: 1919 Westheimer (Nineteen-nineteen): **diez y nueve, diez y nueve**.

El número es 4256.

———————— 143.

———————— 57-B.

The number is 4256.

———————— 143.

———————— 57-B.

¿Cuál es su zona postal?

¿———————— número de teléfono?

What is your zip code?

———————— phone number?

El número es 77002.

———————— 459-2073.

The number is 77002.

———————— 459-2073.

¿De dónde es usted?

Soy de México.

——— Puerto Rico.

——— Cuba.

Where are you from?

I'm from Mexico.

——— Puerto Rico.

——— Cuba.

¿Dónde nació usted?

¿———————— su sobrina?

Where were you born?

——— was your niece ———?

Nací en México, D.F.

Nació ———————— .

I was born in Mexico City.

She was born ———————— .

¿Es usted soltero?

¿——— soltera?

Are you single?

——— single?

No, soy casado.

——— casada.

No, I'm married.

——— married.

¿Cuál es su religión?

Soy católico(-a).

—— protestante.

What is your religion?

I'm Catholic.

—— Protestant.

Dígame, ¿tiene usted familia aquí?

Sí, tengo familia aquí. Raúl es mi hijo.

———————— Ana ———

tía.

Tell me, do you have family here?

Yes, I have family here. Raúl is my son.

———————— Ana ———

aunt.

¿Cuál es la fecha de su
nacimiento?

What is the date of your (or his,
her) birth?

Yo nací el 6 de julio de 1948.

I was born on July 6, 1948.

Mi hijo nació _____.

My son was born _____.

¿Cuándo nació usted?

When were you born?

¿_____ su esposa?

_____ was your wife _____?

Nací el 9 de marzo de 1933.

I was born on March 9, 1933.

Nació _____.

She was born _____.

¿Qué edad tiene usted?

What is your age?

¿_____ el paciente?

_____ the patient's ___?

¿_____ su padre?

_____ your father's ___?

Tengo 83 años.

I'm 83.

Tiene _____.

He's ___.

Tiene _____.

She's ___.

¿Cuál es su ocupación?

What is your occupation?

Soy abogado.

I'm a lawyer.

___ carpintero.

_____ carpenter.

___ mecánico.

_____ mechanic.

___ hombre de negocios.

_____ businessman.

¿Qué trabajo hace usted?

What work do you do?

Trabajo en una fábrica.

I work in a factory.

_____ oficina.

_____ an office.

_____ tienda.

_____ a store.

¿Qué trabajo tiene³ su esposa?

What work does your wife do?

Es comerciante.

She's a merchant.

__ ama de casa.

_____ housewife.

__ gerente.

_____ manager.

__ maestra.

_____ teacher.

3. From **tener** (*to have*); literally, "What work does your wife have?"

¿Cuál es la dirección de su trabajo?	What is your work address (the address of your work)?
¿_____ donde trabaja?	_____ the address where you work?

Calle San Jacinto 5678.	5678 San Jacinto Street.

¿Cuál es el número de su seguro social?	What is your Social Security number?
¿_____ licencia de manejar?	_____ driver's license _____?
¿_____ póliza de seguro?	_____ insurance policy _____?

El número es 243-00-7774.	The number is 243-00-7774.
_____ 44558 17.	_____ 44558 17.
_____ 7 8467 220 374.	_____ 7 8467 220 374.
No me acuerdo del[4] número.	I don't remember the number.

¿Tiene usted su tarjeta de medicare?	Do you have your Medicare card?
¿_____ seguro social?	_____ social security _____?
¿_____ identidad?	_____ identification _____?
¿_____ seguro de hospitalización?	_____ hospital insurance _____?

Sí, sí, aquí la tengo.	Yes, yes, I've got it right here.

¿Tiene usted seguro de hospitalización?	Do you have hospital insurance?

Sí, sí, tengo seguro.	Yes, yes, I've got insurance.
No, no _____.	No, I don't have insurance.

---

4. From **acordar (se)** (*to remember*) and followed by preposition **de** when used with an object.

¿Qué compañía de seguros tiene? — What insurance company do you have?

Aetna. — Aetna.
No tengo seguro. — I don't have insurance.

¿Quién va a pagar el hospital? — Who is going to pay the hospital?

Yo voy a pagar. — I'm going to pay.
Mi compañía de seguros va _____. — My insurance company ___.
Mi padre va _____. — My father ___.

¿A quién se notifica en caso de emergencia? — Who is to be notified in case of an emergency?

Se notifica al señor[5] Ramírez. — Mr. Ramírez is to be notified.
_____ a mi abuelo. — My grandfather _____.
_____ a mi tía. — My aunt _____.

¿Quién es su doctor? — Who is your doctor?
¿_____ encargado?[6] — _____ supervisor?

El Doctor Pérez. — Doctor Pérez.
Juan Sánchez. — Juan Sánchez.

¿Qué cuarto quiere? ¿Privado o doble? — What (kind of) room do you want? Private or semi-private (double)?

Quiero un cuarto privado. — I want a private room.
_____ doble. — _____ semi-private (double) _____.

5. Do not capitalize **señor, señora,** or **señorita** unless they are abbreviated.
6. **El supervisor, la supervisora** is the most frequent usage for *supervisor*.

NOTAS CULTURALES

1. The terms **madrina y padrino** generally refer to the godmother and godfather of the Hispanic child. The godparents, **los padrinos,** are usually married to each other, and very often they are close relatives or friends of the family. They are the guardians of the child's religion and education, and they can be the legal guardians in case of death of parents, serious accident, etc. In many areas of Latin America, the terms **comadre** and **compadre** are used to designate the godparents.

2. The terms for *wife* and *husband* (*spouse*) are **la esposa, el esposo** in Mexico, Central America, and many parts of Latin America. **El marido,** *husband,* and **la mujer,** *wife* (literally *woman*), are terms primarily used in Spain, among the upper classes in Cuba, and in some parts of Mexico and Latin America.

3. In the Hispanic community, several members of the family will often accompany a patient who is entering the hospital. Medical personnel must therefore remember to begin by asking who the patient is before proceeding with the admitting process, in order to prevent unnecessary confusion and delay. The phrase, **¿Quién es el (la) paciente?** should be used.

Ejercicios de conversación

A. *Complete cada oración con la forma correcta de un sustantivo. (Refiérase a la lista de sustantivos para "Familia y parientes" en el Vocabulario de esta lección.)*

Modelo: Los padres de mis padres son mis ___abuelos___.

1. Mis hijos son _____ de mis padres.
2. La hermana de mi madre es mi _____.
3. Los hijos de mis tíos son mis _____.
4. Mi cuñada es la _____ de mi hermano.
5. El marido de mi hija es mi _____.
6. Mi _____ es el hijo de mi tío.
7. La madre de mi esposa es mi _____.
8. Mis _____ son los padres de mis abuelos.
9. _____ son los hijos de los nietos.

B. *Preséntele a las personas indicadas a la Sra. García, una enfermera nueva.*

Modelo: Sr. Romero, un técnico
         Sra. García, quiero presentarle al Sr. Romero, un técnico.

1. Srta. Wilson, una paciente admitida
2. Dr. Martínez, un cirujano
3. Jeff Black, un interno
4. Srta. Roble, una residente

C. *Refiriéndose al "Formulario de Admisión" siguiente, escoja la letra del espacio en el formulario que corresponda con cada pregunta.*

Modelo: ___*j*___ ¿Quién es su doctor?

_____ **1.** ¿Cuál es el número de su teléfono?
_____ **2.** ¿Cómo se llama su pariente más cercano?
_____ **3.** ¿Dónde vive usted?
_____ **4.** ¿Dónde vive su pariente más cercano?
_____ **5.** ¿Cuál es su nombre? ¿Y su apellido?
_____ **6.** ¿Cuál es la ocupación de este paciente?
_____ **7.** ¿Qué parentesco tiene con usted?
_____ **8.** ¿Cuál es la fecha de nacimiento de esta paciente?
_____ **9.** ¿Es usted soltero o casado?

Hora/Time: _____
Llegada/Arrived: _____
Cuarto/Room: _____
Archivos médicos/M.R.: _____
Dependiente, Empleado/Clerk: _____

FORMULARIO DE ADMISIÓN

Favor de escribir en letra de imprenta

Nombre del paciente: _____*a*_____
           (Apellido)   (Nombre)   (Apellido de soltera)

Domicilio: _____*b*_____
      (Calle o Apartado) (Ciudad) (País)

Teléfono: _____*c*_____ Ocupación: _____*d*_____

Edad: _____ Fecha de Nacimiento: _____ Estado Civil ___*f*___
                  (Mes) (Día) (Año)

Pariente más cercano: (si es casado, esposa o esposo; etc.)

Nombre: _____*g*_____ Relación: _____*h*_____

Domicilio: _____*i*_____

Notificación de emergencia: (Se usa en caso de no poder comunicarse con el pariente más cercano. Favor de dar nombre del Hotel y el número de habitación si la persona está hospedada en Houston.)

Nombre: _____ Domicilio: _____ Teléfono: _____

El hospital requiere el pago de un depósito al ingresar: Depósito mínimo cardiología _____ Favor de pagar en estas oficinas.

Persona que garantiza el pago de esta cuenta:

Nombre: _____ Relación: _____

Médico de la familia: _____*j*_____ Médico de consulta: _____

Admisión previa: _____ Diagnóstico: _____

Compañía de Seguros: _____ Número de Póliza/Medicare: _____

Modo de pagar: _____ A plazos: _____ En efectivo: _____

D. *Conteste negativamente.*

    Modelo: ¿Desea usted algo?
                No, no deseo nada.

    1. ¿Necesita usted algo?
    2. Si quiere algo, dígame.
    3. ¿Puede servirle en algo?
    4. Si desea algo, llámeme.

E. *Conteste afirmativamente.*

    Modelo: ¿Puedo servirle en algo?
                Sí, quiero usar el teléfono.

    1. ¿Desea usted algo?
    2. Si quiere algo, dígame.
    3. ¿Necesita usted algo?
    4. Si desea algo, llámeme.

F. *Escoja la respuesta más correcta.*

    1. ¿Quién es?
        a. Es mi número.
        b. Es mi abuelo.

    2. ¿Cuál es su dirección?
        a. Vivo con mis padres.
        b. Vivo en la calle Crawford, 5702.

    3. ¿Cuándo nació usted?
        a. Nací el 22 de agosto de 1963.
        b. Nací en Acapulco.

    4. ¿Qué parentesco tiene con usted?
        a. Es mi hermano.
        b. Es abogado.

    5. ¿Cómo se llama usted?
        a. Su nombre es Juan.
        b. Mi nombre es María.

    6. ¿Tiene usted familia aquí?
        a. Sí, es mi pariente más cercano.
        b. Sí, mi familia vive en mi casa.

    7. ¿Qué número tiene su casa?
        a. El número de mi casa es 4255.
        b. El número de mi teléfono es 678-2596.

    8. ¿Dónde está el baño?
        a. El servicio público está en el primer piso.
        b. El servicio social está en el primer piso.

G. *Conteste según el modelo con las formas correctas de los siguientes verbos que terminan en -AR.*

Modelo: regresar

Yo _____ *regreso* _____ .
Usted _____ *regresa* _____ .
¿ _____ *Regresa* _____ usted?
_____ *Regrese* _____ (mandato).

1. descansar

Yo _____ .
Usted _____ .
¿ _____ usted?
_____ (mandato).

2. trabajar

Yo _____ .
Usted _____ .
¿ _____ usted?
_____ (mandato).

3. llamar

Yo _____ .
Usted _____ .
¿ _____ usted?
_____ (mandato).

4. terminar

Yo _____ .
Usted _____ .
¿ _____ usted?
_____ (mandato).

5. hablar

Yo _____ .
Usted _____ .
¿ _____ usted?
_____ (mandato).

6. preparar

Yo _____ .
Usted _____ .
¿ _____ usted?
_____ (mandato).

7. cambiar

Yo _____ .
Usted _____ .
¿ _____ usted?
_____ (mandato).

8. examinar

Yo _____ .
Usted _____ .
¿ _____ usted?
_____ (mandato).

9. ayudar

Yo _____ .
Usted _____ .
¿ _____ usted?
_____ (mandato).

10. completar

Yo _____ .
Usted _____ .
¿ _____ usted?
_____ (mandato).

Situación y simulación

You are an assistant in the hospital Admissions Office. Your supervisor has asked you to help Mrs. Ortega, who speaks almost no English, to fill out a "Pre-Admission Information" form (shown on the following page). Fill in the blanks of the suggested questions which appear below using the vocabulary words in the right column or in the *Vocabulario* at the back of the book.

Modelo:

Last Name: ¿Cuál es su apellido?
First: ¿Cuál es su nombre?
Street: ¿En qué calle vive usted? y ¿Cuál es el número de su casa?

Suggested questions:

1. ¿Cuál es su número de seguro _____ ?
2. ¿Cuál es su condado y _____?
3. ¿Cuál es su zona _____?
4. ¿Cuál es su número de _____?
5. ¿Qué _____ tiene con usted?
6. ¿Cuál es su _____?
7. ¿Cómo se llama su _____?
8. ¿ _____ es su religión?
9. ¿Tiene usted admisión _____?
10. ¿Tiene usted otra admisión en cualquier _____?
11. ¿Fuma usted?
12. ¿Cuál es la _____?
13. ¿ _____ tiempo hace que usted trabaja para la compañía?
14. ¿Tiene usted una tarjeta de _____?
15. ¿Tiene usted una _____ de seguro?

a. enseñar
b. duración
c. cuánto
d. tarjeta
e. cuál
f. social
g. estado
h. postal
i. teléfono
j. parentesco
k. medicare
l. hospital
m. ocupación
n. jefe
o. previa

THE METHODIST HOSPITAL		PRE-ADMISSION INFORMATION		HOUSTON, TEXAS

PATIENT

LAST NAME	FIRST	MIDDLE	WORK INJURY ☐ YES ☐ NO	CASE NO. — — — —
STREET			SOC. SEC. NO.	ADM. TIME	ADM. DATE
CITY	STATE	ZIP CODE	HOME PHONE	ROOM NO.	ROOM CODE	ROOM RATE

NEAREST RELATIVE

LAST NAME	FIRST	MIDDLE	RELATIONSHIP	AGE	BIRTH DATE
STREET			PHONE NUMBER	SEX	MS	R
CITY	STATE	ZIP CODE	INSURANCE TYPE	SERVICE	NURSING UNIT

NOTIFY EMERGENCY

LAST NAME	FIRST	MIDDLE	RELATIONSHIP	ADMITTING PHYSICIAN
STREET			PHONE NO.	PHYSICIAN CODE
CITY	STATE	ZIP CODE	INS. CLASS	PHYSICIAN

RESPONSIBLE PERSON

LAST NAME	FIRST	MIDDLE	RELATIONSHIP	PHYSICIAN CODE
STREET			OCCUPATION	RELIGION
CITY	STATE	ZIP CODE	PHONE NO.	CHURCH
EMPLOYER			HOW LONG EMPLOYED?	DEPOSIT AMOUNT
ADDRESS			PHONE NO.	PRIOR ADMISSION ☐ YES ☐ NO	DATE
CITY	STATE	ZIP CODE	SMOKER ☐ YES ☐ NO	OTHER NAME

| DIAGNOSIS | | ADMITTED BY |
| OTHER EMPLOYER | EMPLOYER NAME | CITY | STATE | PATIENT'S OCCUPATION |

HAVE YOU BEEN IN ANY HOSPITAL OR NURSING HOME IN PAST 60 DAYS? IF YES, GIVE NAME AND ADDRESS OF INSTITUTION AND DATE OF DISCHARGE

INSTITUTION NAME	ADDRESS	CITY	STATE	DATE OF DISCHARGE

MEDICARE

ALL INFORMATION SHOULD BE TAKEN FROM PATIENT'S RED-WHITE-BLUE CARD

| MEDICARE NO. | EFFECTIVE DATE | CHECK APPLICABLE BOX ▷ | ☐ PART A (HOSPITAL) ☐ PART B (MEDICAL) |

MEDICAID

ALL INFORMATION SHOULD BE TAKEN FROM PATIENTS/RECIPIENTS CURRENT ID CARD

| PATIENTS CASE NO. (MUST BE 9 DIGITS) | EFFECTIVE DATE | RECIPIENT'S NAME | STATE ENROLLED |

BLUE CROSS

CERTIFICATE HOLDER'S NAME	RELATIONSHIP TO PATIENT	CERTIFICATE OR R.O. NO.
ADDRESS	HOME CITY OF PLAN	GROUP NO.
CITY	STATE	ZIP	HOME STATE OF PLAN	COVERAGE NO.

| IF GROUP, CERTIFICATE HOLDERS PLACE OF EMPLOYMENT AND ADDRESS OF EMPLOYER | EFFECTIVE DATE OF COVERAGE |

GROUP INSURANCE THROUGH EMPLOYER OR UNION

EMPLOYER OR UNION

NAME	POLICY NO	NAME OF POLICY HOLDER
ADDRESS	POLICY HOLDER'S SOC. SEC. NO.	RELATIONSHIP TO PATIENT
CITY	STATE	ZIP	EMP. OR UNION LOCAL PHONE NO	NAME OF INSURANCE COMPANY

INDIVIDUAL OR FAMILY INSURANCE

NAME OF INSURANCE COMPANY	POLICY NUMBER
ADDRESS WHERE PREMIUMS ARE PAID	POLICY HOLDER'S NAME
CITY	STATE	ZIP	INS. CO. PHONE NO	RELATIONSHIP TO PATIENT

WORKMEN'S COMPENSATION   PLEASE SEND WRITTEN AUTHORIZATION FROM INSURANCE COMPANY

EMPLOYER

EMPLOYER'S NAME (WHERE INJURED)	DATE OF INJURY	INSURANCE COMPANY NAME
ADDRESS	EMPLOYER'S PHONE NO	ADDRESS
CITY	STATE	ZIP	INS. CLAIM NO	CITY	STATE

MEDICAL

NAME OF MILITARY MEMBER	PATIENT'S ID CARD NO	RANK
BRANCH AND ORGANIZATION	PATIENT'S BEGINNING ELIGIBILITY DATE	SERVICE NO
CITY	STATE	ZIP		

Juegos

A. Bring a photograph of someone in your family and describe his or her relationship to you and to each of the members of your immediate family. For example:

Éste es mi hermano Jorge.
Es el hijo de mis padres.
Es el nieto de mis abuelos.
Es el tío de mi hija Elena.
Es el padre de mi sobrino Roberto.
Y es el esposo de mi cuñada María.

B. This game is called *Cadena* ("Chain"). One person starts the game by saying a vocabulary word aloud. Class members respond to this and all subsequent words by saying a word that *begins with the ending letter of the word that has just been named.*

Modelo:
médic*o*
. . . operació*n*
. . . niet*a*
. . . all*í*
. . . izquierd*a*, etc.

Each person who contributes a (correct!) word for the chain gets two points if the word given is from the vocabulary for Lecciones 1 and 2 and one point for any other Spanish word.

PALABRAS COGNADAS

Read through the following admission form showing the typical information requests for admission to a hospital and note the cognate words. The words that have no English cognates are listed below and in the *Vocabulario* at the back of the book. This form is authentic and used in hospitals in Mexico and Central America.

HOJA[1] DE INGRESO[2] DEL ENFERMO

_____ ASEG.[3] _____ BENEF.[4] _____

Nombre _____ Cédula[5] _____ Clín. Ads.[6] _____

Fecha _____ Hora _____ Dom.[7] Enf. _____

Col. _____ Empresa:[8] _____

Dom. Empresa: _____ Tel. _____

En caso necesario comunicarse con: _____

Domicilio _____ Col.[10] _____

Tel. _____ Ingresa[9] al Servicio de: _____

Diagnóstico: _____

Médico de Admisión: _____ Cama No. _____

_____ Orden de hospitalización No. _____

Para ser llamado por el Archivo Clínico ☐ _____ Registro; _____ Céd. Patronal: _____

_____ Informó: _____

---

1. **la hoja** *page*
2. **el ingreso** *admission*
3. **aseg. = asegurado**
4. **benef. = beneficio**
5. **la cédula** *identification card*
6. **clín. ads. = clínica (admisión)**
7. **dom. = domicilio**
8. **la empresa** *firm, business*
9. **ingresa** *enters*
10. **col. = colonia**

Read through the following chart showing the types of medical facilities that typically serve populations of various sizes and note the cognate words, which are numerous. The words which have no English cognates are listed in the *Vocabulario* at the back of the book.

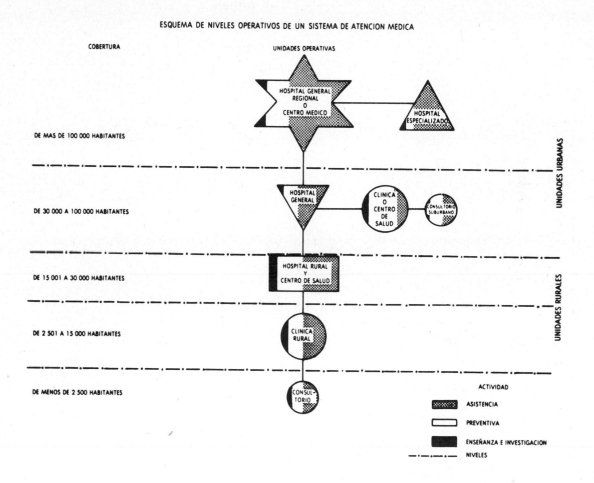

ESQUEMA DE NIVELES OPERATIVOS DE UN SISTEMA DE ATENCION MEDICA

COBERTURA

UNIDADES OPERATIVAS

HOSPITAL GENERAL REGIONAL O CENTRO MEDICO

HOSPITAL ESPECIALIZADO

DE MAS DE 100 000 HABITANTES

UNIDADES URBANAS

HOSPITAL GENERAL

CLINICA O CENTRO DE SALUD

CONSULTORIO SUBURBANO

DE 30 000 A 100 000 HABITANTES

HOSPITAL RURAL Y CENTRO DE SALUD

DE 15 001 A 30 000 HABITANTES

UNIDADES RURALES

CLINICA RURAL

DE 2 501 A 15 000 HABITANTES

CONSUL-TORIO

DE MENOS DE 2 500 HABITANTES

ACTIVIDAD

ASISTENCIA

PREVENTIVA

ENSEÑANZA E INVESTIGACION

NIVELES

Read through the following discharge form and note the cognate words, which are numerous. The words which have no English cognates are listed in the *Vocabulario* at the back of the book.

AVISO DE SALIDA

Del servicio de: _____ Cama No. _____

Diagnóstico de salida: _____

Operación: _____

Alta por: _____ Fecha _____ Hora _____

Nombre de la persona que recibe al enfermo: _____

Firma: _____ Fecha: _____

MEDICO TRATANTE   JEFE DEL SERVICIO

_____   _____
        (firma y clave)   (firma y clave)

Forma de ingreso y alta del paciente hospitalizado

VOCABULARIO

LA FAMILIA Y LOS PARIENTES	FAMILY AND RELATIVES
el abuelo	*grandfather*
la abuela	*grandmother*
los abuelos	*grandparents*
el ahijado	*godson*
la ahijada	*goddaughter*
el cuñado	*brother-in-law*
la cuñada	*sister-in-law*

LA FAMILIA Y LOS PARIENTES   FAMILY AND RELATIVES

el esposo	*husband (can be a literary term)*
la esposa	*wife*
el hermano	*brother*
la hermana	*sister*
los hermanos	*siblings*
el hijastro	*stepson*
la hijastra	*stepdaughter*
el hijo	*son*
la hija	*daughter*
los hijos	*children*
la madre	*mother*
la madrina	*godmother*
la mamá	*mother, mom*
el marido	*husband*
la mujer	*wife, woman (common-law wife in some areas)*
el nieto	*grandson*
la nieta	*granddaughter*
los nietos	*grandchildren*
el niño	*boy*
la niña	*girl*
los niños	*children*
la nuera	*daughter-in-law*
el padrino	*godfather*
el papá	*father*
el primo	*cousin*
la prima	*cousin*
el sobrino	*nephew*
la sobrina	*niece*
el suegro	*father-in-law*
la suegra	*mother-in-law*
el tío	*uncle*
la tía	*aunt*
los tíos	*aunt and uncle*
el yerno	*son-in-law*

LOS MESES   MONTHS

enero	julio	*January*	*July*
febrero	agosto	*February*	*August*
marzo	septiembre	*March*	*September*
abril	octubre	*April*	*October*
mayo	noviembre	*May*	*November*
junio	diciembre	*June*	*December*

LAS OCUPACIONES	OCCUPATIONS
el abogado; la abogada	lawyer
el/la agente	agent
el ama de casa	housewife
el/la atendiente; el/la ayudante	helper
el carpintero	carpenter
el cirujano; la cirujana	surgeon
el/la comerciante	merchant
el/la dependiente	clerk
el doctor, la doctora	doctor
el encargado	man in charge
la encargada	woman in charge
el enfermero; la enfermera	nurse
el/la estudiante	student
el/la gerente	manager
el hombre de negocios	businessman
el interno; la interna	intern
el maestro; la maestra	teacher
el mecánico	mechanic
el médico; la médica	doctor
la mujer de negocios	businesswoman
el policía	policeman
la policía	policewoman
el/la residente	resident

SUSTANTIVOS

NOUNS

la admisión	admission
el amigo; la amiga	friend
el año	year
el apartamento	apartment
el apellido	last name
la ayuda	help, assistance
el barrio	district, neighborhood, slum
el brazo	arm
la cabeza	head
la casa	house
el caso	case
la cédula	identification card
la ciudad	city
el ciudadano	citizen
la clave[1]	area code, key (of a test)
la colonia	colony, district
el compañero; la compañera	companion

1. *Zip code* can be expressed by **la clave, el código postal,** or **la zona postal.**

la compañía	company
el condado	county
el cuarto	room
la cuenta	bill
el depósito	deposit
el diagnóstico	diagnosis
los días	days
la dirección	address, direction
el dolor	pain
el domicilio	domicile, home
la edad	age
la emergencia	emergency
el empleo	job, occupation
el español	Spanish
la fábrica	factory
la fecha	date
el formulario; —de admisión	form; admission form
el gusto	pleasure
la hospitalización	hospitalization
el inglés	English
la identidad	identity
la licencia	license
la licencia de manejar	driver's license
el lugar	place
el nacimiento	birth
el nombre	first name
el número	number
la oficina	office
el país	country
el parentesco	relationship
el pariente	relative
la pena	pain
la pierna	leg
la póliza; —de seguro	policy; insurance policy
la pregunta	question
el registro	registry
la religión	religion
la respuesta	reply, response, answer
el seguro	insurance, safety pin
el seguro de hospitalización	hospitalization insurance
_____ social	social security
el/la solicitante	applicant
la tarjeta	card
el tiempo	time, weather
el trabajo	work
la zona	zone
la zona postal[2]	zip code

2. See **la clave** (footnote 1, page 34).

VERBOS

acordar(se)	to remember
ayudar	to help, assist
conocer[3]	to know
desear	to want, desire
examinar	to examine
hablar	to speak, talk
hacer	to do, make
llamar	to call
llamar(se)	to call (oneself)
llenar	to fill, fill out
necesitar	to need
notificar	to notify
operar	to operate
pagar	to pay
pasar	to pass, happen
preguntar	to ask
preparar	to prepare
presentar	to present
referirse	to refer to
regresar	to return
saber	to know
ser	to be
terminar	to finish, complete
tomar	to take; drink
usar	to use
vivir	to live

VERBS

ADJETIVOS

admitido	admitted
casado	married
católico	Catholic

ADJECTIVES

3. **Conocer** means "to be acquainted with" (a person, place, etc.).
Conozco al doctor Ramírez.
   I know doctor Ramírez. I am acquainted with doctor Ramírez.
Yo sé el número.
   I know the number. I know (in depth, by heart, I understand intellectually).
Note the irregularities in the present tense conjugations of **saber** and **conocer** in the first person singular **yo** form:

Yo sé	Nosotros sabemos
Tú sabes	
Él, ella sabe	Ellos, ellas saben
Yo conozco	Nosotros conocemos
Tú conoces	
Él, ella conoce	Ellos, ellas conocen

cercano	*near, close*
cuál	*which*
cuánto	*how much*
doble	*double*
encantado	*delighted*
fallecido	*deceased, expired*
hebreo, -a	*Hebrew*
mi	*my*
mucho	*much*
nuevo	*new*
poco	*little, few*
privado	*private*
protestante	*Protestant*
soltero	*single (unmarried)*
suyo	*his, hers, yours (formal)*
tanto	*so much*

ADVERBIOS

ADVERBS

cómo	*how*
cuándo	*when*
hoy	*today*
inmediatamente	*immediately*
más	*more, most*
muy	*very*
por qué	*why*
pues	*then, well*

CONJUNCIÓN

CONJUNCTION

donde	*where*

PRONOMBRES

PRONOUNS

algo	*something*
cuál, cuales	*which, which ones*
él	*he*
ella	*she*
le	*to him, her, it, you (formal); him, her, you (formal)*
me	*me, to me*
nada	*nothing*
que	*that*
quién	*who, whom*
yo	*I*

PREPOSICIONES

al (a + el)
del (de + el)
desde

PREPOSITIONS

to (the)
of (the), from (the)
from

FRASES ÚTILES

al contado
dar de alta
de alta
de nada
estar de alta
pagar al contado
por lo tanto
querer decir
tener
tener que (+ infinitive)

EXPRESSIONS

cash
to discharge
discharged
you're welcome, don't mention it
be discharged
pay in cash
therefore
mean, signify
to have
to have to (do something, fulfill an
    obligation)

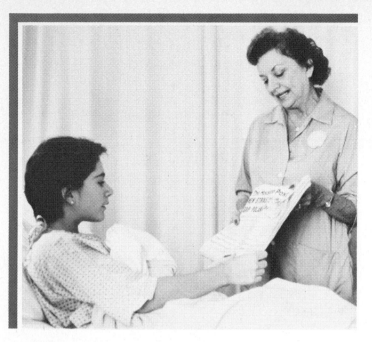

CUIDADO DEL PACIENTE

DIÁLOGO

Cumpliendo con los requisitos del paciente

La Srta. Kent, una ayudante, cuida al Sr. Miranda, un paciente enfermo.

Repita:

Srta. Kent	**Sr. Miranda**
(*Llama a la puerta*)	¡Adelante!
Buenos días. ¿En qué puedo servirle?	Buenos días, señorita. ¿Cómo se dice «televisor»[1] en inglés?

1. Both **el televisor** and **la televisión** are used for *television*. In addition to **el televisor,** which is the preferred use, one hears **la televisora** in some urban areas.

Se dice «*television*,» señor. ¿Por qué?

Sí, señor, en seguida. ¿Necesita usted algo más?

¿Tiene frío? ¡Pobrecito! Se la traigo inmediatamente.

Sí, claro. Si quiere algo más, llámeme. El zumbador[4] está aquí.

¡Ay de mí! No funciona[2] el televisor aquí. ¿Quiere usted llamar al departamento de mantenimiento?

Sí, necesito una manta[3] porque tengo frío.

Muchas gracias. Y, señorita, ¿puede usted apagar la luz, también?

Responding to the Patient's Requests

Miss Kent, an aide, is taking care of Mr. Miranda, a sick patient.

Repeat:

Miss Kent	**Mr. Miranda**
	Come in!
(*Knocks on the door*)	
Good morning. What can I do for you?	Good morning, miss. How does one say *televisor* in English?
One says "television," sir. Why?	Oh, my! The television here isn't working. Will you (do you want to) call the maintenance department?
Yes, sir, right away. Do you need anything else?	
You're cold? Poor thing! I'll bring it to you immediately.	Yes, I need a blanket because I'm cold.
Yes, of course. If you need anything else (more), call me. The buzzer is (right) here.	Thanks a lot. And, miss, can you turn off the light, too?

FRASES ÚTILES

Sustituya:

¿Qué necesita usted, Sra. Gómez?   *What do you need, Mrs. Gómez?*

2. **Funcionar** and **servir** are used to indicate that a machine functions or works (literally, serves its purpose). To indicate that a **person** works, however, the verb **trabajar** is used.

3. The words **la manta, la cobija, la frazada,** and **la frisa** are used with some variations throughout the Spanish-speaking world to indicate *blanket*.

4. Another word for **el zumbador** is **el timbre.**

Necesito una manta.   I need a blanket.
_____ una frazada.   _____ a blanket.
_____ una cobija   _____ a blanket.
_____ una almohada.   _____ a pillow.
_____ una toalla.   _____ a towel.
_____ un peine.   _____ a comb.
_____ un cepillo para el cabello.   _____ a hairbrush.
_____ un cepillo de dientes.   _____ a toothbrush.

¿Necesita ir al baño?   Do you need to go to the bathroom?
¿_____ ir a la sala de espera?   _____ waiting room?
¿_____ ir al lavabo?   _____ washbasin?
¿_____ caminar al lavabo?   _____ walk _____?
¿_____ caminar por el pasillo?   _____ down the hall?
¿_____ bajar de la cama?   _____ get off the bed?
¿_____ sentarse?   _____ sit down?

Sí, necesito ir al baño.   Yes, I need to go to the bathroom.
_____.   _____.
_____.   _____.
_____.   _____.
_____.   _____.
Sí, Necesito sentarme.   Yes. I need to sit down.

Favor de cerrar la puerta.   Please close the door
_____ el ropero[1].   _____ the closet.
_____ las cortinas.   _____ the curtains
_____ el cortinaje[2].   _____ the curtains (around bed)
Sí, señorita, en seguida.   Yes, Miss, right away.

1. **El ropero** and **el armario** both are used for closet. **El cabinete** is a southwest localism for closet.
2. Drapery around hospital bed; **las cortinas** refers to draw curtains in the patient's room.

¿Tiene usted frío?[3]	Are you cold?
¿_____ calor?	_____ hot?
¿_____ fiebre?	_____ feverish?
¿_____ sueño?	_____ sleepy?
¿_____ hambre?	_____ hungry?
¿_____ sed?	_____ thirsty?

Sí, tengo mucho frío.	Yes, I'm very cold.
_____ mucho calor.	_____ very hot.
_____ mucha fiebre.	_____ very feverish.
_____ mucho sueño.	_____ very sleepy.
_____ mucha hambre.	_____ very hungry.
_____ mucha sed.	_____ very thirsty.

¿En qué puedo servirle, Sr. Fernández?	What can I do for you, Mr. Fernández?

¿Quiere usted[4] traerme el desodorante?	Will you bring me the deodorant?
¿_____ la pasta de dientes?	_____ the toothpaste?
¿_____ el jabón?	_____ the soap?
¿_____ la máquina de afeitar?	_____ the (electric) shaver?
¿_____ hielo?	_____ (some) ice?

¿Quiere usted algo?	Do you want anything?

Sí, quiero un vaso de agua.	Yes, I want a glass of water.
_____ una revista.	_____ a magazine.
_____ un periódico.	_____ a newspaper.
_____ el orinal.[5]	_____ the urinal.

3. Whereas speakers of English use the verb *to be* followed by an adjective to indicate physical sensations (e.g., "I am cold," "I am sleepy"), the **hispanoparlante** (*Spanish-speaking person*) uses the verb **tener** (*to have*) followed by the noun which names the sensation. Hence, **tengo frío** literally means "I have cold," **tengo sueño** "I have sleep," **tengo hambre** "I have hunger," etc.

4. The word **quiere** (*will you*) is commonly used to express politeness and respect in making a request.

5. **El pato** is sometimes used in South America to indicate *the bedpan* or *the urinal*.

——————— el bacín.[6]
——————— un tazón para vómito.[7]

——————— *the bedpan.*
——————— *an emesis basin.*

¿Puedo traerle algo?

Can I bring you anything?

Sí, necesito una toallita.[8]
——————— una bata.
——————— mis cosméticos.
——————— un espejo.
——————— un florero.

Yes, I need a washcloth.
——————— *a robe.*
——————— *my cosmetics.*
——————— *a mirror.*
——————— *a vase.*

¿Puedo traerle algo?

Can I bring you anything?

Sí, ¿quiere usted traerme unos tampones?[9]

——————— unas servilletas sanitarias?

——————— unos pañuelos de papel?

——————— papel para el baño?[10]

——————— unas zapatillas?

Yes, will you bring me some tampons?

——————— *some sanitary napkins?*

——————— *some tissues?*

——————— *some toilet paper?*

——————— *some slippers?*

¿Qué necesita usted, Sra. Belmonte?
¿Me permite usar el teléfono?

¿——————— poner el televisor?
¿——————— apagar la luz?
¿——————— encender la luz?

What do you need, Mrs. Belmonte?

May I (will you permit me to) use the telephone?
——— *turn on the television?*
——— *turn off the light?*
——— *turn on the light?*

6. Other words for **el bacín** (*bedpan*) are **el bidet, la cuna, la taza, la silleta,** and **la paleta.** (Be careful in using **la paleta,** as this may mean "popsicle" to a Mexican!) **El bidet** may also mean a tub for a sitz bath.

7. An emesis basin is a plastic dish used as a receptacle for vomit and given to a patient who feels nauseated or must vomit.

8. **La toallita** can also be expressed as **toalla de mano.**

9. Another expression for *sanitary napkins* is **(unos) paños higiénicos** or **Kotex.**

10. or **(el) papel higiénico.**

¿Hay un buzón cerca?   *Is there a mailbox nearby?*
¿___ un teléfono ___?   _____ *a phone* ___?
¿___ una enfermera ___?   _____ *a nurse* ___?
¿___ una peluquería ___?   _____ *a hairdresser's* ___?

Señor, necesito cambiar la cama.   *Sir, I need to change the bed.*
_____ cerrar la puerta.   _____ *to close the door.*
_____ abrir la ventana.   _____ *to open the window.*
_____ levantar la   _____ *to raise the head of the*
cabecera de la cama.   *bed.*
_____ bajar los pies de la   _____ *to lower the foot of the*
cama.   *bed.*

¿Con quién va usted a hablar,   *With whom are you going to talk,*
Sr. Romero?   *Mr. Romero?*

Voy a hablar con la paciente   *I'm going to talk with the (admitted)*
admitida.   *patient.*
_____ el paciente dado   _____ *the*
de alta.   *discharged patient.*
_____ el director   _____ *the social*
personal de trabajo social.   *work director.*
_____ el dietista.   _____ *the dietician.*
                                           _____ *the*
_____ el personal de   *maintenance personnel.*
mantenimiento.   _____ *the supervisor*
_____ el supervisor de   *of laundry.*
lavandería.

¿Puedo ayudarle en algo, señorita?   *Can I help you with something,*
                                           miss?
Sí, ¿sabe usted dónde están mis   *Yes, do you know where my ball-*
bolígrafos?[11]   *point pens are?*
_____ los   _____ *the stamps*
sellos?[12]   ___?
_____ mis   _____ *my letters*
cartas?   ___?
_____ los   _____ *the papers*
papeles y sobres?   *and envelopes* ___?

11. **El bolígrafo** (*ball-point pen*) is also called **la lapicera** or **el lapicero**.

12. **Las estampillas** (*postage stamps*) are also called **los sellos** and **los timbres. Las estampillas** is mostly used in Mexico, Central America, Ecuador, Peru, and Bolivia.

¿Tiene usted una pregunta, señor? Sí, ¿quiere usted decirme cuándo llega el correo?	*Do you have a question, sir?* *Yes, will you (could you) tell me* *when the mail arrives?*
voy a mejorarme?	*I'm going to get better?*
debo levantarme?	*I ought to get up?*
puedo darme vuelta?[13]	*I can turn over?*
me van a dar de alta?	*I'll be discharged?*

Ejercicios de conversación

A. *Escriba oraciones usando las siguientes palabras, según el modelo.*

Modelo: querer / hambre / porque / tener / comer / el paciente
    El paciente quiere comer porque tiene hambre.

1. querer / Srta. Quevedo / inmediatamente / frazada
2. carta / para / lapicera / escribir / necesitar
3. florero / querer / rosas / para
4. apagar / luz / favor / de / y / puerta / cerrar
5. servir / en / que / le / puedo
6. paciente / caminar / pasillo / por / necesitar
7. tener / sed / agua / querer / vaso
8. teléfono / funcionar / querer / usar / otro

B. *Traduzca al español.*

1. I need a pillow. Will you bring me a glass of water also?
2. Will you permit me to turn on the television?
3. I'm looking for my letters. Do you know where they are?
4. Mrs. López, do you need to go to the bathroom?
5. Mr. Martínez, do you need the bedpan?
6. Mr. Beltrán, you need to walk down the hallway.
7. Mr. García, your wife is in the waiting room.
8. Mrs. Martínez, your sister needs a vase for the roses.
9. Please call the doctor, and turn off the light.
10. Please close the curtains and the door.

---

13. *To turn* = **doblar, volver;** *to turn over* = **voltearse, darse una vuelta;** *to bend over* = **doblarse, inclinarse.**

C.   *Escoja la respuesta correcta.*

1. Tengo mucho frío.
   a. Le traigo la lapicera.
   b. Le traigo una frazada.

2. Quiero dormir ahora.
   a. Apago la luz.
   b. Abro la ventana.

3. Necesito mandar estas cartas.
   a. El buzón está enfrente del ascensor.
   b. Las revistas están enfrente de la escalera.

4. Necesito ir al baño.
   a. Le traigo el orinal.
   b. Le traigo el tazón de vómito.

5. Quiero consultar con el médico.
   a. Llamo al doctor inmediatamente.
   b. Me llamo Juan Ramírez.

6. El acondicionador de aire no funciona.
   a. Usted tiene calor.
   b. Usted tiene sueño.

7. ¿Puedo traerle algo?
   a. Si desea algo, llámeme.
   b. Sí, hielo.

8. ¿Tiene usted una pregunta?
   a. Sí, tengo miedo.
   b. Sí, ¿cuándo viene el doctor?

9. Las sábanas están mojadas.
   a. Necesito bajar la cama.
   b. Necesito cambiar la cama.

10. ¿Con quién va usted a hablar?
    a. con el ayudante.
    b. con los médicos.

D.   *Describa un típico cuarto de hospital, usando el verbo impersonal* **hay** *(there is, there are).*

Modelo: *Hay dos camas en un cuarto doble.*
Hay un paciente en el cuarto.
Hay una revista en una de las camas.

E.   *Conteste según el modelo con las formas correctas de los siguientes verbos reflexivos.*

Modelo: levantar(se)   Yo ___*me levanto*___ .
(*to get up*)   Usted ___*se levanta*___ .
¿ ___*Se levanta*___ usted?
___*Levántese*___ (mandato).

1. despertarse   Yo _____ .
(*to wake up*)   Usted _____.
¿ _____ usted?
_____ (mandato).

2. doblarse
(*to bend over*)

Yo _____ .
Usted _____ .
¿ _____ usted?
_____ (mandato).

3. mejorarse
(*to get well*)

Yo _____ .
Usted _____ .
¿ _____ usted?
_____ (mandato).

4. lavarse
(*to wash oneself*)

Yo _____ .
Usted _____ .
¿ _____ usted?
_____ (mandato).

5. voltearse
(*to turn over to the
other side*)

Yo _____ .
Usted _____ .
¿ _____ usted?
_____ (mandato).

6. acostarse
(*to go to bed*)

Yo _____ .
Usted _____ .
¿ _____ usted?
_____ (mandato).

7. quedarse
(*to stay, to remain*)

Yo _____ .
Usted _____ .
¿ _____ usted?
_____ (mandato).

8. peinarse
(*to comb one's hair*)

Yo _____ .
Usted _____ .
¿ _____ usted?
_____ (mandato).

9. apurarse
(*to hurry up*)

Yo _____ .
Usted _____ .
¿ _____ usted?
_____ (mandato).

F.   Escoja la frase que mejor describe cada artículo.

1. la toallita
2. el buzón
3. el desodorante
4. la cama
5. la cafetería
6. la camilla
7. la medicina
8. la máquina de afeitar
9. el florero
10. el ascensor

a. Se usa para acostarse.
b. Se usa para afeitarse.
c. Se usa para subir al tercer piso.
d. Se usa para lavarse la cara.
e. Se usa para curar al enfermo.
f. Se usa para las rosas.
g. Se usa para poner las cartas.
h. Se puede comer aquí.
i. Se usa después de bañarse.
j. Se usa para mover al paciente.

Situación y simulación

You are a nurse on a busy surgical floor. Mrs. Vayar, a patient who speaks very little English, is just recovering from surgery. She is eager to be as active as she can, but because of her condition, she must often ask for your help in doing things. Write out the replies you would make to each of the following requests from Mrs. Vayar.

> **Modelo:** Sra. Roberts, ¿puede ayudarme? Tengo calor.
> Sí, claro. Hace mucho calor aquí. Abro la ventana en seguida, Sra. Vayar.

1. Voy a escribir unas cartas, Sra. Wilson. ¿Quiere traerme el papel, la lapicera, y los sobres? Están en esa silla. ¿Y puede decirme si se venden sellos aquí?
2. Siento molestarle otra vez, Sra. Wilson. Necesito llamarle a mi esposo. ¿Me permite usar el teléfono? ¿Dónde está? Pues, ¿tengo que usar la silla de ruedas?
3. Srita. Kennedy, estoy incómoda así. ¿Quiere usted bajarme los pies de la cama? Y también, ¿hay otra manta aquí?
4. Tengo mucho sueño, Sra. Jackson. ¿Puedo tomar la medicina ahora y entonces dormir un rato? ¿Quiere usted apagar la luz?

Juegos

A. Put the vocabulary words for Lessons 1-3 on large flash cards, with Spanish on one side and English on the other. (Concentrate primarily on the new vocabulary words you have learned for areas, directions, locations, admissions, relatives, and patient requests.)

The person leading the game holds up each card in front of the class, varying the game by showing the Spanish side of the card for some words and the English side for others.

Each person who gives the correct translation (Spanish or English) for the word shown receives one point and gets a chance to try using the word in a Spanish sentence. If the sentence is correct, the person receives two more points.

B. Bring to class a large bag of articles frequently requested or used by hospitalized patients. With the mouth of the bag held nearly closed, each person reaches into the bag (without peeking!) and selects an article. After trying to identify the article by touching it, the person names the article in Spanish and withdraws it from the bag.

Each person receives three points for correctly identifying and naming an article. Whenever a person incorrectly names an article removed from the bag, the article will be held in front of the class, and the first person to correctly name it in Spanish will receive one point.

PALABRAS COGNADAS

Read through the following chart showing the various avenues of access to medical attention and note the cognate words, which are numerous. The words which have no English cognates are listed in the *Vocabulario* at the back of the book.

ENTRADAS AL SISTEMA DE ATENCION MEDICA

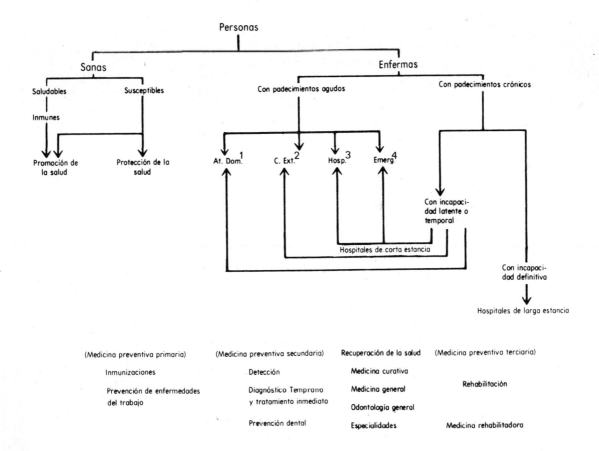

Read through the following chart showing an overview of the medical attention and evaluation process and note the cognate words, which are numerous. The words which have no English cognates are listed in the *Vocabulario* at the back of the book.

EL SISTEMA DE ATENCION MEDICA Y LA EVALUACION

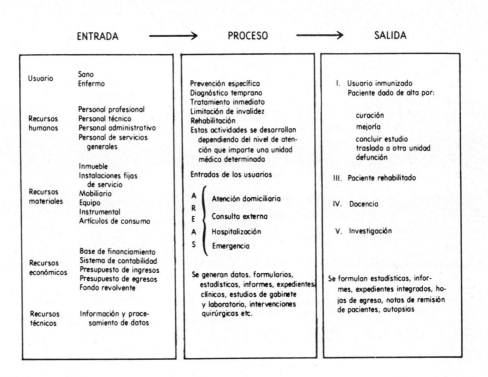

ENTRADA	PROCESO	SALIDA
Usuario Sano / Enfermo	Prevención específica / Diagnóstico temprano / Tratamiento inmediato / Limitación de invalidez / Rehabilitación / Estas actividades se desarrollan dependiendo del nivel de atención que imparte una unidad médica determinada	I. Usuario inmunizado / Paciente dado de alta por: / curación / mejoría / concluir estudio / traslado a otra unidad / defunción
Recursos humanos Personal profesional / Personal técnico / Personal administrativo / Personal de servicios generales	Entradas de los usuarios	III. Paciente rehabilitado
Recursos materiales Inmueble / Instalaciones fijas de servicio / Mobiliario / Equipo / Instrumental / Artículos de consumo	A R E A S Atención domiciliaria / Consulta externa / Hospitalización / Emergencia	IV. Docencia / V. Investigación
Recursos económicos Base de financiamiento / Sistema de contabilidad / Presupuesto de ingresos / Presupuesto de egresos / Fondo revolvente	Se generan datos, formularios, estadísticas, informes, expedientes clínicos, estudios de gabinete y laboratorio, intervenciones quirúrgicas etc.	Se formulan estadísticas, informes, expedientes integrados, hojas de egreso, notas de remisión de pacientes, autopsias
Recursos técnicos Información y procesamiento de datos		

VOCABULARIO

ARTÍCULOS DE USO PERSONAL	ARTICLES OF PERSONAL USE
la almohada	*pillow*
el bacín	*bedpan (most frequently used)*
la bata	*robe*
el bidet, bidé	*bidet, tub for sitz bath, bedpan*
el bolígrafo	*ballpoint pen*
la carta	*letter*
el cepillo para el cabello	*hairbrush*
_____dientes	*toothbrush*
la cobija	*blanket*
los cosméticos	*cosmetics*
la cuna	*bedpan (slang)*
el desodorante	*deodorant*

el espejo	mirror
la estampilla, el sello	stamp
el florero	vase
la frazada	blanket
el hielo	ice
el jabón	soap
la lapicera	ballpoint pen
la manta	blanket
la máquina de afeitar	(electric) shaver
el orinal	urinal
la paleta	bedpan
el pañuelo de papel	tissue
el papel	paper
el papel higiénico	toilet paper
la pasta de dientes	toothpaste
el pato	urinal
el peine	comb
el periódico	newspaper
la revista	magazine
el sello	stamp
la servilleta sanitaria; el paño higiénico	sanitary napkin
la silleta	bedpan
el sobre	envelope
el tampón	tampon
la taza	bedpan
el tazón para vómito[1]	emesis basin[1]
el timbre	stamp
la toalla	towel
la toalla de mano; la toallita[2]	washcloth
las zapatillas	slippers

PARTES DEL CUARTO DEL HOSPITAL	PARTS OF THE HOSPITAL ROOM
la cabecera	head (of a bed)
la cama	bed
la luz	light
la puerta	door
la silla	chair
la televisión; el televisor; la televisora	television
el zumbador	buzzer
el botón	button (bell) on chord

1. Note to nonmedical personnel: An emesis basin is a receptacle for vomit, expectoration, etc. that is provided for the patient's convenience.

2. The diminutive form—ito(s), ita(s) con be added to nouns to express endearment or smallness of size: e.g., muchachito, little boy, amorcito, sweetheart.

SUSTANTIVOS

el agua
el buzón
el calor
el cambio
la cara
el correo
el departamento de alimentación
_____ lavandería
_____ mantenimiento
_____ trabajo social
la fecha
la fiebre
el frío
el hambre
el hispanoparlante
la medicina
la peluquería
los pies
un rato
la respuesta
la sed
la silla de ruedas
el sueño
el vaso

NOUNS

water
mailbox
heat
change
face
mail
dietary services department
laundry _____
maintenance _____
social work _____
date
fever
cold
hunger
Spanish-speaking person
medicine
hairdresser's
feet
a (little) while
reply, answer
thirst
wheelchair
sleep
glass

VERBOS

abrir
acostarse
adjuntar
apagar
apurarse
arreglar
atender
bañar(se)
bañarse
cambiar
cerrar
cumplir (con)
darse vuelta
dejar
descansar
despertar(se)
doblar
doblarse
encender
escribir

VERBS

to open
to lie down, go to bed
to attach
to turn off
to be in a hurry
to fix, arrange
to look after
to bathe
to bathe oneself
to change
to close
to comply, carry out
to turn over
to cease, to stop doing something
to rest
to wake up
to bend
to turn oneself over
to turn on
to write

esperar	*to wait*
funcionar	*to function, work*
lavar	*to wash*
lavarse	*to wash oneself*
levantar	*to raise*
levantarse	*to get up*
mandar	*to send*
mejorar(se)	*to get better, to improve*
molestar	*to bother*
peinar	*to comb*
peinarse	*to comb oneself*
permitir	*to permit*
poner	*to put, turn on*
quedar(se)	*to remain, stay*
quitar(se)	*to remove, take off from oneself*
sacar	*to take, remove, extract*
traer	*to bring*
vender	*to sell*
ver	*to see*
voltear(se)	*to turn oneself over*

ADJETIVOS

ADJECTIVES

enfermo	*sick*
estimado	*esteemed*
incómodo	*uncomfortable*
otro	*other, another*
pobrecito	*poor thing*
su	*his, hers, yours (formal)*

ADVERBIOS

ADVERBS

además	*moreover, also*
ahora	*now*
así	*so, thus*
atentamente	*attentively*
bien	*well*
después	*after*
en seguida	*right away*
entonces	*then*
también	*also*

CONJUNCIÓN

CONJUNCTION

o (u before words beginning with o- or ho-)	*or*

FRASES ÚTILES

¡Adelante!
¡Ay de mí!
dejar de
en espera
en seguida
llamar a la puerta
otra vez

USEFUL EXPRESSIONS

Come in!
Woe is me! Oh, my!
to stop (doing something)
awaiting
right away
knock on the door
again (another time)

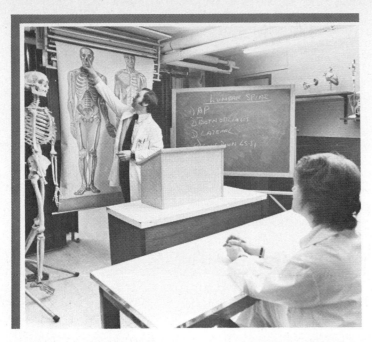

HISTORIA MÉDICA GENERAL

DIÁLOGO

Tomando la historia médica general

El Dr. Roberts, un médico, y la Sra. Cueva, una enfermera, entran en el cuarto del Sr. Menéndez, un paciente enfermo que está en su cama.

Repita:

Dr. Roberts:	**Sr. Menéndez:**
Buenos días, Sr. Menéndez. Me llamo Dr. Roberts, y le presento a mi enfermera, la Sra. Cueva.	Mucho gusto en conocerlos.

Sra. Cueva

Encantada, señor.   El gusto es mío.
¿Cómo se siente hoy?   Me siento muy mal.

Dr. Roberts

¿Qué le pasa?[1]   Tengo tos y me duele la garganta.
¿Cuándo le pasó esto?   Hace una semana.
¿Cuánto tiempo hace que tiene esa
    hinchazón en la garganta?   Hace tres o cuatro días.
Pues, sin ser indiscreto, quiero ha-
    cerle algunas preguntas acerca de
    su salud e historia médica.   Muy bien.
¿Es usted alérgico a alguna
    medicina?   No, ninguna.
Entonces, ¿no es alérgico a la
    penicilina?   No.
¿Ha tenido tendencia a sangrar?   Sí.
¿Y cuándo le pasó eso?   Hace dos años, cuando tuve un cho-
                                                que de coche.

¿Cuáles enfermedades de la infan-
    cia ha tenido?   Umm. Me es difícil recordar. Creo
                                                que he tenido la tos ferina, las
                                                paperas y la rubéola.

Taking General Medical History

Dr. Roberts, a physician, and Mrs. Cueva, a nurse, enter the room of Mr. Menéndez,
a sick patient who is in bed.

Repeat:

Dr. Roberts	Mr. Menéndez
Good morning, Mr. Menéndez. My name is Dr. Roberts, and this is (I introduce to you) my nurse, Mrs. Cueva.	A great pleasure to know you.

Mrs. Cueva

Pleased to meet you.   The pleasure is mine.
How do you feel today?   I feel very bad.

---

1. **¿Qué le pasa?** (*What's wrong with you?* or *What's happening to you?*) is an expression used to gain information about the physical or mental condition of a *person*. In contrast, the expression **¿Qué pasa?** (*What's happening?* or *What's going on?*) is used to gain information about *events*.

Dr. Roberts

What's wrong with you?

When did this happen?

And how long have you had that swelling in your throat?

Without being indiscreet I am going to ask you some questions about your health and medical history.

Mr. Menéndez, are you allergic to any medicines?

Then you're not allergic to penicillin?

Do you have a tendency to bleed?

When did that happen?

Which childhood diseases have you had?

I have a cough and my throat hurts.

A week ago.

For three or four days.

All right, doctor.

No, none.

No.

Yes.

Two years ago when I had an auto accident.

Hmm. It's difficult for me to remember. I believe I've had whooping cough, mumps, and German measles.

FRASES ÚTILES

Sustituya.

¿Dónde tiene el dolor? Indíqueme.[1]

Tengo un dolor aquí.

——————— a la derecha.

——————— a la izquierda.

Where do you have the pain? Show me.

I have a pain here.

——————— *on the right (side).*

——————— *on the left (side).*

Muestre la región.

Tengo un dolor arriba.[2]

——————— abajo.

Show (me) the area.

I have a pain up (here).

——————— *down (here).*

1. *Show me* is translated **Indíqueme, Muéstreme,** or **Enséñeme. Indíqueme** indicates a simple pointing action while **Enséñeme** is more involved (removing clothing, etc.).

2. **Arriba** (up, above) is generally followed by the preposition **de** when describing location of a place. The medical examiner would normally expect to hear:
Tengo un dolor arriba del abdomen. *I have a pain above my abdomen.*
The same idea applies to **debajo de** down (*from*) and **abajo** (*down, below*) therefore:
Tengo un dolor debajo de la cintura. I have a pain below my waist.
Unfortunately, as all medical personnel know, most sick people often don't speak grammatically correct language when they are in pain and can accidently mislead the examiner. N.B. Please note the use of the contraction form in the masculine singular noun:
arriba de el abdomen = del

¿Tiene usted hinchazón en el cuello?[3]

Do you have swelling in (your) neck?

¿————————— el codo?

————————————
elbow?

¿————————— la muñeca?

————————————
wrist?

¿————————— las articulaciones?[4]

————————————
joints?

Sí, tengo hinchazón y dolor, también.

Yes, I have swelling, and pain, too.

¿Ha tenido usted vértigo?

Have you had dizziness?

¿————————— gases?

————————— gas?

¿————————— mareo?

————————— seasickness?

¿————————— náusea?

————————— nausea?

¿————————— diarrea?

————————— diarrhea?

¿————————— estreñimento?[5]

————————— constipation?

Sí, muy frecuentemente.
No, muy raramente.

Yes, very often.
No, very seldom.

¿Tiene usted tendencia a sangrar?

Do you have a tendency to bleed?

¿————————— vomitar?

————————————— vomit?

¿—————————
desmayarse?

————————————— faint?

¿—————————
marearse?

————————————— get
seasick?

Sí, con frecuencia.

Yes, frequently.

¿Qué enfermedades ha tenido usted?

Which diseases have you had?

He tenido tuberculosis.

I've had tuberculosis.

————— úlceras.

————— ulcers.

————— sífilis.

————— syphilis.

————— trastornos en la vista.

————— problems with (my) eyesight.

3. In describing the parts of their bodies, Spanish-speaking persons do not use the possessive adjective *my*. For example, **Tengo hinchazón en el codo** literally means *I have a swelling in* **the** *elbow*; **Me duelen los brazos** means **The** *arms are painful to me*; **Tengo dolor en el abdomen** means *I have a pain in* **the** *abdomen*.

4. **La articulación** (joint) is also called **la coyuntura.**

5. **El estreñimiento** refers to constipation of the bowel while the adjectival form, **constipado, -a,** refers only to nasal congestion.

¿Cuánto tiempo hace que usted
tiene cáncer?
Hace un año que tengo cáncer.
_____ seis meses _____.
_____ tres semanas _____.

How long have you had cancer?

I've had cancer for a year.
_____ *six months.*
_____ *three weeks.*

¿Ha tenido usted enfermedades del
corazón?
¿_____ de
los ojos?
¿_____ de
los riñones?
¿_____ de
los oídos?
No, nunca.

Have you had (any) heart diseases?

_____ *eye* _____?

_____ *kidney*
_____?
_____ *ear* _____?

No, never.

¿Desde cuándo tiene usted tos?

Desde anoche.
_____ la semana pasada.
_____ ayer.
_____ anteayer.
_____ esta mañana.
_____ ayer por la tarde.

*How long (since when) have you
had a cough?*
Since last night.
_____ *last week.*
_____ *yesterday.*
_____ *the day before yesterday.*
_____ *this morning.*
_____ *yesterday afternoon.*

¿Ha tenido usted las enfermedades
de la infancia?
Sí, he tenido tos ferina.
_____ diftheria.
_____ sarampión.[6]
_____ escarlatina.
_____ fiebre reumática.
_____ varicela.
_____ paperas.

*Have you had the childhood
diseases?*
Yes, I've had whooping cough.
_____ *diphtheria.*
_____ *measles.*
_____ *scarlet fever.*
_____ *rheumatic fever.*
_____ *chicken pox.*
_____ *mumps.*

¿Tiene usted alergias?
¿_____ alta presión arterial?
¿_____ fiebre?[7]

Do you have allergies?
_____ *high blood pressure?*
_____ *a fever?*

---

6. **Sarampión** means regular *measles*. Although **rubéola** is a technical term, it is coming into
more frequent usage as it is used on international health cards to mean regular measles. In
English rubeola refers to the three-day rash type measles. Three-day measles in Spanish may
be referred to as **fiebre de tres días** and **sarampión (bastardo)** as well as other street names.

7. **La fiebre** (*fever*) is also called **la calentura.**

Sí, me molestan mucho.	*Yes, they bother me a lot.*
_____ molesta _____.	___ *it bothers* _____.
_____ molesta _____.	___ *it bothers* _____.

¿Es usted alérgica(-o) a la penicilina?	*Are you allergic to penicillin?*
No sé.	*I don't know.*
___, no soy alérgica(-o).	*No, I'm not allergic.*

¿Ha tomado usted penicilina antes?	*Have you taken penicillin before?*
¿_____ aspirina _____?	_____ *aspirin* _____?
¿_____ esta medicina _____?	_____ *this medicine* _____?
Sí, la he tomado.	*Yes, I've taken it.*

Usted tiene que quedarse en el hospital.	*You have to stay in the hospital.*
_____ quedarse aquí.	_____ *stay here.*
_____ guardar cama.	_____ *stay in bed.*
¡Qué lástima!	*What a pity!*

NOTA CULTURAL

1. When assisting with or conducting a physical examination or taking medical history, medical personnel are cautioned to ask for permission to touch the person or to ask personal questions. This courtesy will relieve fear and promote a feeling of trust.

   The phrases:
   Con su permiso . . .   *With your permission* . . .
   Sin querer ser indiscreto(a), necesito saber . . .
     Without wanting to be indiscreet, I need to know . . .

   are easy to use and will aid the professional in eliciting the best possible response.

Ejercicios de conversación

A. *Conteste en español.*

1. ¿Tiene usted alergias?
2. ¿Ha tenido usted las enfermedades de la infancia? ¿Cuáles?
3. ¿Qué le pasa?
4. ¿Qué pasa?
5. ¿Ha tomado usted penicilina antes?
6. ¿Qué tiene usted?
7. ¿Dónde tiene usted la hinchazón?
8. ¿Dónde tiene usted dolor? Indíqueme.
9. ¿Cuánto tiempo hace que usted tiene mareos?
10. ¿Ha tenido usted trastornos en la vista?

B. *Escoja las traducciones correctas.*

1. los pies	a. chest
2. el cuello	b. joints
3. los brazos	c. buttocks
4. el codo	d. neck
5. las nalgas	e. back
6. las articulaciones	f. elbow
7. la espalda	g. feet
8. el hombro	h. abdomen
9. el abdomen	i. arms
10. el pecho	j. shoulder

C. *Escoja la respuesta correcta.*

1. ¿Qué le pasa?
   a. Hace color aquí.
   b. Tengo dolor de estómago.
2. ¿Desde cuándo tiene esa hinchazón?
   a. Hace dos meses.
   b. Desde la semana pasada.
3. ¿Tiene usted alergias?
   a. No, ninguno.
   b. No, ninguna.
4. ¿Qué enfermedades de la infancia ha tenido?
   a. He tenido la sífilis.
   b. He tenido la rubéola.
5. ¿Dónde tiene el dolor?
   a. Tengo el dolor arriba del codo.
   b. Soy alérgico a la penicilina.
6. ¿Le duelen los brazos?
   a. Sí, me duele mucho.
   b. Sí, me duelen mucho.
7. ¿Ha tenido usted vértigo?
   a. Sí, me duele mucho.
   b. Sí, muy frecuentemente.

8. ¿Qué enfermedades ha tenido usted?
   a. He tenido sarampión y tuberculosis.
   b. He tenido muchos problemas.

9. ¿Ha tomado usted penicilina antes?
   a. Sí, la he tomado.
   b. Sí, lo he tomado.

10. Muestre la región.
    a. Tengo un dolor aquí.
    b. Tengo alta presión arterial.

D. *Traduzca al español.*

Modelo: I have a pain in my back.
   Tengo dolor en la espalda.

1. I have a pain in my abdomen.
2. I have a pain in my chest.
3. I have a headache (pain in my head).
4. I have a pain in my hand.

Modelo: My arms hurt me.
   Me duelen los brazos.

5. My leg hurts me.
6. My eyes hurt me.
7. My foot hurts me.
8. My stomach hurts me.

E. *Conteste en español, usando la palabra o frase sugerida.*

Modelo: ¿Cuánto tiempo hace que usted tiene fiebre? (*una semana*)
   Hace una semana que tengo fiebre.

1. ¿Cuánto tiempo hace que usted tiene hinchazón? (*un mes*)
2. ¿Cuánto tiempo hace que tiene enfermedad del corazón? (*un año y medio*)
3. ¿Cuánto tiempo hace que usted tiene tos? (*tres días*)
4. ¿Cuánto tiempo hace que usted tiene dolor en las manos? (mucho tiempo)

Modelo: ¿Desde cuándo tiene usted vértigo? (*la semana pasada*)
   Tengo vértigo desde la semana pasada.

5. ¿Desde cuándo tiene usted este problema? (*anteayer*)
6. ¿Desde cuándo le duelen las manos? (*ayer por la tarde*)
7. ¿Desde cuándo tiene usted náuseas? (*febrero*)
8. ¿Desde cuándo tiene usted la tendencia a vomitar? (*esta mañana*)

Situación y simulación

You are the doctor on the fourth floor. Visit with two male patients and take their medical history. (Use **consultar con** in Spanish.[1]) Be sure to use phrases from the preceding exercises. Tell one of the patients that:

he is discharged:	**Usted está dado de alta.**
he is cured:	**Usted está curado.**
he must stay here:	**Usted tiene que quedarse aquí.**
he must stay here in the hospital:	**Usted tiene que quedarse aquí en el hospital.**
he has to stay in bed:	**Usted tiene que guardar cama.**

Juego

Scavenger hunt.

Check in your area of the hospital to see if admitting, medical history, and discharge forms have been translated into Spanish. Collect the ones that have been designated for class use. If your hospital doesn't have any forms then check with the Department of Public Health. If you are unable to find translations, begin your own project by collecting the forms and putting them in a notebook and translate the phrases with sentences from this text. As your Spanish progresses, practice using the forms with Hispanic patients.

PALABRAS COGNADAS

Read through the following clinical history form on page 64 and the organization chart for a nursing staff on page 65 and note the cognate words, which are numerous. The words that have no English cognates are listed in the *Vocabulario* in the back of the book.

1. *To see the doctor* (*to consult with*) = **consultar con.**

HISTORIA CLINICA GENERAL

APELLIDOS PATERNO MATERNO (O CONYUGAL) NOMBRE _____ NUMERO DE REGISTRO _____ CALIDAD _____

SEXO _____ EDAD _____ MEDICO _____ CLAVE _____

SERVICIO _____ UNIDAD _____ FECHA _____

INTERROGATORIO

1). ANTECEDENTES FAMILIARES:

2). ANTECEDENTES: PERSONALES PATOLOGICOS NO PATOLOGICOS

3). ESTADO ACTUAL PADECIMIENTO ACTUAL:

4). APARATOS Y SISTEMAS:

5). SINTOMAS GENERALES:

6). TERAPEUTICA EMPLEADA Y EXAMENES PREVIOS:

EXPLORACION FISICA

Peso _____ Estatura _____ Temperatura _____

8). Inspección General

9). Cabeza y cuello

10). Torax

11) Abdomen

12). Extremidades Superiores

13). Extremidades Inferiores

Pulso _____ Tensión Arterial Máxima _____ Mínima _____

DIAGNOSTICOS

Firma del Médico _____ Clave _____

Anverso de la forma de la historia clínica.

Reverso de la forma de la historia clínica.

64

SERVICIO O CUERPO DE ENFERMERIA

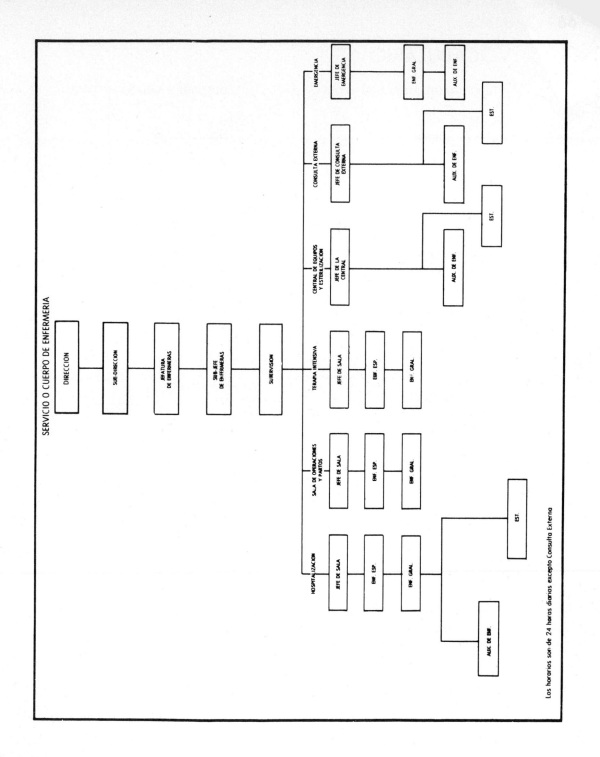

Los horarios son de 24 horas diarios excepto Consulta Externa

65

VOCABULARIO

ENFERMEDADES Y SÍNTOMAS	DISEASES AND SYMPTOMS
la alergia	allergy
la alta presión arterial[1]	high blood pressure
la calentura	fever
el cáncer	cancer
la diarrea	diarrhea
la difteria	diphtheria
la enfermedad	illness, disease
las enfermedades de la infancia	childhood diseases
la escarlatina	scarlet fever
la fiebre reumática	rheumatic fever
el gas	gas
la gripe	flu
la herida	injury, wound
la hinchazón	swelling
el mareo	seasickness
la náusea	nausea
la papera	goiter
las paperas	mumps
la rubéola	German measles
el sarampión	measles
la sífilis	syphilis
el síntoma	symptom
la tos	cough
la tos ferina	whooping cough
el trastorno	disturbance, problem
la tuberculosis	tuberculosis
la varicela	chicken pox

SUSTANTIVOS / NOUNS

SUSTANTIVOS	NOUNS
el accidente	accident
la articulación	joint
la aspirina	aspirin
el corazón	heart
la coyuntura	joint
el cuarto	room
el estómago	stomach
la historia	history
la mañana	morning

1. An alternate expression for high blood pressure is **la presión arterial alta.**

la medicina	medicine
la orina	urine
la penicilina	penicillin
la presión	pressure
el problema	problem
la región	region, area
los riñones	kidneys
la salud	health
la semana	week
la tarde	afternoon
la tendencia	tendency
la tos	cough
la vista	sight, vision

VERBOS

VERBS

creer	to believe
desmayar(se)	to faint
doler	to hurt
entrar	to enter
guardar cama	to be confined to bed
indicar	to indicate (show)
marear(se)	to get seasick
molestar	to bother
mostrar	to show
presentar	to introduce
quedarse	to stay, to remain
sangrar	to bleed
vomitar	to vomit

ADJETIVOS

ADJECTIVES

alérgico	allergic
alguno	some
alto	high, tall
arterial	arterial
concentrado	concentrated
general	general
médico	medical
mejor	better
ninguno	no (not any), none
pasado	past
poco	little, few

ADVERBIOS

abajo
acerca de
anoche
antes
anteayer
arriba
ayer
bastante
frecuentemente
mal
nunca
raramente

ADVERBS

down, below
about, with regard to
last night
before
day before yesterday
up, above
yesterday
fairly (pretty)
often, frequently
badly
never
seldom, rarely

FRASES ÚTILES

dar de alta
guardar cama
quedarse aquí
quedarse en el hospital
hasta luego
¡Qué lástima!

EXPRESSIONS

to be discharged
to stay in bed
to stay here
to stay in the hospital
so long, good-bye
What a pity! What a shame!

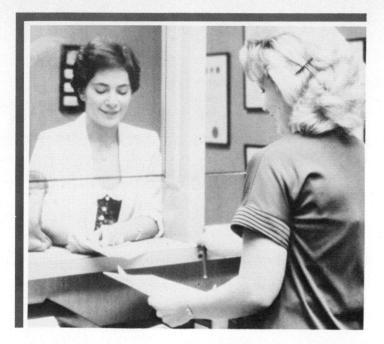

PRIMERA PRUEBA

Preguntas acerca de la lección primera

A. *Conteste en español.*

Modelo: ¿Dónde está el departamento de cardiología?
Está en el segundo piso enfrente del ascensor.

1. Busco la sala de operaciones. ¿Dónde está?
2. ¿Sabe usted dónde está la tienda de regalos?
3. ¿Está el banco de sangre en este piso?
4. ¿Dónde está la escalera?
5. ¿Puede usted decirme dónde está la clínica paciente-ambulante?

B. *Traduzca al español.*

Modelo: Go through this hallway and turn right.
Pase por este pasillo y doble a la derecha.

1. Sir, do you know where the cafeteria is?
2. Continue straight ahead, and the waiting room is there.
3. The nursery is on the sixth floor in front of the elevator.
4. The medical records department is in back of the Wilson Building.
5. The gift shop is on this floor. Follow me, please.
6. Go down the stairs to the first floor.
7. Yes, of course. It's in the basement.
8. I'm looking for the delivery room.
9. Where's the personnel department?
10. The bathroom is here on the left.

C. *Escriba una oración usando las siguientes palabras, recordando las reglas de concordancia.*

Modelo: estar / caja / segundo / departamento / piso
El departamento de caja está en el segundo piso.

1. estar / derecha / usted / allí / doblar / y
2. dónde / estar / usted / laboratorio / saber
3. emergencia / buscar (yo) / sala
4. planta baja / ascensor / farmacia / delante de / estar
5. usted / escalera / segundo / bajar / piso

D. *Complete cada oración con la forma correcta de un sustantivo.*

Modelo: Quiero llamar a mi esposo. ¿Puedo usar <u>el teléfono</u>?

1. Quiero comprar un regalo. Tengo que ir a _____ .
2. El médico tiene que examinar a mi hijo. Busco el departamento de
_____ .
3. Quiero subir al tercer piso. Tengo que usar _____ .
4. Me van a operar. Voy al departamento de _____ .
5. Necesito comer. Tengo que ir a _____ .

Preguntas acerca de la lección segunda

A. *Escoja la frase que mejor describe cada persona.*

1. La enfermera _____.   a. trabaja en la oficina.
2. El técnico _____.   b. cuida a los pacientes.
3. El dependiente _____.   c. opera a los enfermos.
4. La secretaria _____.   d. trabaja en una tienda.
5. La cirujana _____.   e. trabaja en el laboratorio.

B. *Traduzca al español.*

Modelo: I need to fill out an admissions form. Can you help me?
Necesito llenar un formulario de admisión. ¿Puede usted ayudarme?

1. I want a semiprivate room.
2. My sister Carmen is the patient.
3. What is the address of your house?
4. I was born on April 3, 1941.
5. What is your insurance policy number?

C. *Complete cada oración con la palabra correcta.*

Modelo: La esposa de mi hijo es mi *nuera*.

1. Los padres de mi madre son mis _____.
2. La madre de mi hermano es mi _____.
3. Los hijos de mis nietos son mis _____.
4. La esposa de mi hermano es mi _____.
5. La hermana de mi padre es mi _____.

D. *Conteste en español, usando la palabra o frase sugerida.*

Modelo: ¿Qué compañía de seguros tiene usted? (*Aetna*)
Mi compañía de seguros es Aetna.

1. ¿A quién se notifica en caso de emergencia? (*mi padre*)
2. ¿Qué trabajo hace su esposa? (*gerente*)
3. ¿Qué edad tiene usted? (*47 años*)
4. ¿Cuál es la dirección de su casa? (*1473 Oak Street*)
5. ¿Qué parentesco tiene la paciente con usted? (*hija*)

E. *Escoja la respuesta correcta.*

1. ¿Puedo llamar a mi esposo?
   a. Sí, el ascensor está allí.
   b. Sí, puede usar mi teléfono.
   c. Sí, mi esposo se llama Roberto.

2. ¿Cómo se llama el paciente?
   a. El paciente es mi padre.
   b. Me llamo Raúl Quintero.
   c. Se llama Ramón Bermúdez.

3. ¿Qué le pasa a su hijo?
   a. Le van a operar.
   b. Siento un dolor de cabeza.
   c. Pase por este pasillo.

4. ¿Dónde nació usted?
   a. Mi hija nació aquí.
   b. Nací en México, D. F.
   c. Nací el 6 de julio de 1949.

5. ¿Tiene usted tarjeta de identidad?
   a. No, no tengo seguro.
   b. Sí, claro. Aquí la tengo.
   c. Sí, el número de mi póliza es 42-007019-61.

Preguntas acerca de la lección tercera

A. *Complete la oración con la forma correcta de un sustantivo.*

Modelo: Siento frío. ¿Puede usted traerme <u>una manta</u>?

1. Quiero lavarme la cara. ¿Quiere usted traerme _____?
2. Tengo mucha sed. ¿Puede usted traerme _____?
3. Voy a dormir. ¿Me permite apagar _____?
4. Quiero mandar una carta. ¿Hay _____ en este piso?
5. Hace mucho calor aquí. ¿Quiere usted abrir _____?

B. *Escriba oraciones usando las siguientes palabras según el modelo.*

Modelo: necesitar / cama / señora / cambiar
Necesito cambiar la cama, señora.

1. pies / usted / bajar / cama / querer
2. con / ir / lavandería / personal / hablar
3. cerca / hay / peluquería
4. encender / me / luz / permitir
5. baño / necesitar / para / papel

C. *Traduzca al español.*

Modelo: Will you bring me some slippers?
¿Quiere usted traerme unas zapatillas?

1. Mr. Jackson, I need a toothbrush.
2. I'm very sleepy.
3. Will you bring me the towel? It's in the bathroom.
4. I want a glass of water with ice.
5. May I turn on the television?
6. Can I help you with something, sir?
7. Where is the discharged patient?
8. I want to write a letter. Do you know where my pen is?
9. Will you tell me when I'm going to get better?
10. Can I bring you anything?

D. *Escoja las traducciones correctas.*

1. _____ el zumbador   a. comb
2. _____ la cobija   b. blanket
3. _____ el peine   c. buzzer
4. _____ la almohada   d. paper
5. _____ el papel   e. pillow

Prueba final

I. A. *Choose a picture from any lesson of the text (1-4) and describe the action taking place.*

B. *Make up a dialogue based on one of the topics (1-4) while using the picture as a model for the class. Give your dialogue in Spanish and play all parts.*

II. *Complete the following sentences with phrases from the text.*

1. Me duele la garganta y _____.
2. ¿En qué puedo servirle? Sí,_____
3. ¿Ha tenido usted _____?
4. ¿Sabe usted dónde está _____?
5. Siga derecho y _____.
6. Le presento a _____.
7. ¿Cuál es su _____?
8. ¿Tiene usted tarjeta de _____?
9. ¿Qué parte del cuerpo le _____?
10. ¿Qué le pasa _____?

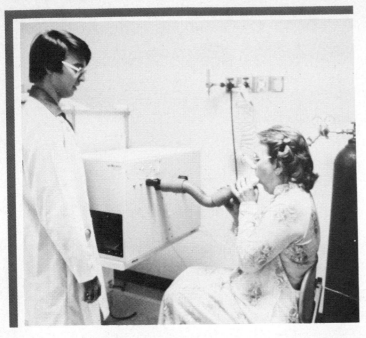

HISTORIA MÉDICA ESPECIALIZADA

DIÁLOGO

Tomando la historia médica
de un paciente con problemas respiratorios

La Dra. García está examinando al Sr. Torres, un paciente que tiene dificultad al respirar y otros problemas semejantes.

Repita:

Dra. García	Sr. Torres
Buenas tardes, Sr. Torres. ¿Cómo se siente hoy?	Muy buenas tardes, Dra. García. Me siento muy mal.
¿Qué tiene usted?	Tengo problemas al respirar.

¿Tiene la respiración corta?[1]
¿Tiene usted dolor en el pecho?

¿Tiene tos?

¿Y cuántas veces durante el día tiene tos?
¿Tiene usted expectoración,[2] también?

¿Tiene sangre en la expectoración?
¿Hay mucha sangre?
¿Cuántos catarros tiene usted al año?

Pues, usted tiene que quedarse en el hospital por varios días.

Sí, cuando camino rápidamente.
No, pero tengo dolores de cabeza bastante frecuentemente.
Sí, casi siempre la tengo al levantarme por la mañana.

Seis o siete veces.

Sí, cuando toso, siempre tengo expectoración.
Sí, a veces.
No, no mucha.
No sé exactamente. Quince o veinte, quizás.

Muy bien. ¡Ojalá que me mejore pronto!

Taking Medical History
from a Patient with Respiratory Problems

Dr. García is examining Mr. Torres, a patient who has difficulty in breathing and other related problems.

Repeat:

Dr. García

Good afternoon, Mr. Torres. How do you feel today?

What's wrong with you?
Do you have shortness of breath?
Do you have pain in your chest?
Do you have a cough?

And how many times during the day do you have a cough?
Do you have expectoration, too?

Do you have blood in your expectoration?
Is there much blood?
How many colds do you have per year?

Well, you (will) have to stay in the hospital for a few days.

Mr. Torres

Good afternoon, Dr. García. I feel very bad.
I'm having breathing problems.
Yes, when I walk fast.
No, but I have headaches pretty often.
Yes, I almost always have one when I get up in the morning.

Six or seven times.
Yes, when I cough, I always have expectoration.

Yes, sometimes (at times).
No, not much.
I don't know exactly. Fifteen or twenty, maybe.

Very well. I hope (God grant) that I get better (improve) soon.

1. Also, **ahoguío.**

2. Another term for **la expectoración** is **la flema.**

FRASES ÚTILES

Under this section of *Frases útiles* you will notice that the same questions can be used in different areas. For example: *Are you dizzy?* **¿Se marea usted?:** respiratory history, circulatory history, gastro-intestinal history, prematernity history, etc.

The phrases that can be used in several areas are marked with an asterisk. Perhaps you can find others.

Historia médica: el sistema circulatorio

Buenos días, señor.
¿Cómo se siente usted hoy?

Buenos días, doctor.
Mejor, gracias.

*¿Tiene la respiración corta?
*¿Tiene la presión alta de sangre?
¿Tiene hinchazón en los tobillos?
*¿Tiene dolor en el pecho?
¿Tiene dolor sobre el corazón?

Sí, la tengo.
Sí, la tengo.
No, no la tengo.
Sí, tengo mucho dolor.
Sí, lo tengo.

*¿Puede usted describir el dolor?
*¿Es quemante?
*¿Es frecuente?
*¿Es agudo?

Sí, es muy quemante.
Sí, es muy a menudo.
Sí, es un poco agudo.

Medical history: the circulatory system

Good morning, sir.
How do you feel today?

Good morning, doctor.
Better, thank you.

Do you have shortness of breath?
Do you have high blood pressure?
Do you have swelling in the
ankles?
Do you have pain in the chest?
Do you have pain over the heart?

Yes, I have it.
Yes, I have it.

No, I don't have it.
Yes, I have a lot.
Yes, I have it.

Can you describe the pain?
Is it burning?
Is it frequent?
Is it sharp?

Yes, it is very burning.
Yes, it is very frequent.
Yes, it is a little sharp.

Historia médica: el sistema respiratorio

¿Tiene usted la respiración corta?   Sí, cuando camino rápidamente.
¿Tiene dolor en el pecho?   No, tengo dolor de cabeza.
¿Tiene tos?   Sí, al levantarme por la mañana.
¿Cuántas veces al día tiene tos?   Muchas veces, pocas, varias, seis. . . .

¿Tiene expectoración?   Sí, cuando toso, tengo expectoración.

¿Tiene sangre en la expectoración?   Sí, no mucha.
¿Tiene dificultad al respirar?   De vez en cuando.
¿Cuántos catarros tiene usted al año?

Quince, dieciséis, cincuenta. . . .

Medical history: the respiratory system

Do you have shortness of breath?   Yes, when I walk fast.
Do you have pain in the chest?   No, I have a headache.
Do you have a cough?   Yes, on getting up in the morning.
How many times a day do you cough (have coughing)?   Many times, few, various, six. . . .
Do you have expectoration?   Yes, when I cough, I have expectoration.

Do you have blood in the expectoration?   Yes, not much.
Do you have difficulty in breathing?   From time to time.
How many colds do you have per year?   Fifteen, sixteen, fifty. . . .

Historia médica: el sistema nervioso

*¿Cómo se siente usted?   Me siento irritable y nervioso(-a).
*¿Tiene usted dolor de cabeza?   No, tengo dolor de espalda.
*¿Tiene usted vértigo?   Sí, me mareo también.
*¿Ha perdido usted el conocimiento?   No, nunca.
*¿Es ésta la primera vez que tiene usted esta condición?   No, ésta es la tercera vez.

Medical history: the nervous system

How do you feel?   I feel irritable and nervous.
Do you have a headache?   No, I have a backache.
Do you have vertigo?   Yes, I get seasick, too.
Have you lost consciousness?   No, never.
Is this the first time that you have this condition?   No, this is the third time.

Historia médica: el sistema gastro-intestinal

*¿Tiene náusea?   Sí, tengo náusea durante mi regla.
¿Tiene buen apetito?   No, no tengo buen apetito.
¿Tiene eructos?   Sí, tengo eructos después de
                                         comer.
*¿Tiene dolor en el estómago?   Sí, tengo mucho dolor.
¿Tiene diarrea?   Sí, cuando como lechuga.
*¿Tiene sangre en el excremento?   Sí, tengo sangre en el excremento.

Medical history: the gastro-intestinal system

Do you have nausea?   Yes, I have nausea during my
                                         period.
Do you have a good appetite?   No, I don't have a good appetite.
Do you have belching?   Yes, I have belching after eating.
Do you have pain in the stomach?   Yes, I have a lot of pain.
Do you have diarrhea?   Yes, when I eat lettuce.
Do you have blood in the
excrement?   Yes, I have blood in the
                                         excrement.

Sustituya:

¿Tiene la respiración corta?   *Do you have shortness of breath?*
¿_____ la presión alta de sangre?   _____ *high blood pressure?*
¿_____ hinchazón en los tobillos?   _____ *swelling in your*
                                         ankles?

Sí, la tengo.   *Yes, I have it.*
__ la _____ .   _____ *it.*
__ lo _____ .   _____ *it.*

¿Tiene dolor en el pecho?   *Do you have pain in your chest?*
¿_____ sobre el corazón?   _____ *over your heart?*

Sí, tengo mucho dolor.   *Yes, I have a lot of pain.*
No, no tengo dolor sobre el   *No, I don't have pain over my heart.*
corazón.

¿Puede usted describir el dolor?
¿Es quemante?
¿———————————————
—— frecuente?
¿———————————————
—— agudo?

Can you describe the pain? Is it
burning?
———————————————
frequent?
———————————————
sharp?

Sí, es muy quemante.
——————— frecuente.
——————— agudo.

Yes, it's very burning.
——————— frequent.
——————— sharp.

¿Cuántas veces al día tiene el
dolor?
Tengo el dolor de vez en cuando.
——————— pocas veces.
——————— varias veces.
——————— al menos quince
veces.

How many times a day do you have
the pain?
I have the pain from time to time.
——————— a few times.
——————— several times.
——————— at least fifteen times.

¿Cómo se siente usted?

How do you feel?

Me siento nervioso.
——————— un poco mejor.
——————— peor.

I feel nervous.
——————— a little better.
——————— worse.

¿Tiene usted vértigo?
¿——————— dolor de cabeza?
¿——————— dificultad al andar?

Do you have dizziness?
——————— a headache?
——————— difficulty walking?

Sí, y me siento irritable, también.
——————— cansado, ———.

Yes, and I feel irritable, too.
——————— tired, ——.

¿Ha perdido usted el
conocimiento?

Have you lost consciousness?

Sí, varias veces.
—— tres ———.
—— muchas ———.

Yes, several times.
—— three ———.
—— many ———.

¿Es ésta la primera vez que tiene usted esta condición?

Is this the first time you've had this condition?

No, ésta es la tercera vez.
No, _____ quinta ___.
Sí, _____ primera ___.

No, this is the third time.
No, _____ fifth ___.
Yes, _____ first ___.

¿Tiene usted náuseas?

Do you have nausea?

Sí, tengo náuseas durante mi regla.
_____ después de comer.
_____ al levantarme por la mañana.

Yes, I have nausea during my period.
_____ after eating.
_____ when I get up in the morning.

¿Tiene buen apetito?
¿_____ eructos después de comer?
¿_____ dolor de estómago?

Do you have a good appetite?
_____ belching after eating?
_____ pain in your stomach (stomachache)?

No, no tengo buen apetito.
_____ eructos después de comer.
_____ dolor de estómago.

No, I don't have a good appetite.
_____ belching after eating.
_____ pain in my stomach (stomachache).

¿Tiene diarrea?

Do you have diarrhea?

Sí, cuando como lechuga.
_____ tomo la penicilina.
_____ como demasiado.

Yes, when I eat lettuce.
_____ take penicillin.
_____ eat too much.

¿Tiene sangre en el excremento?

¿_____ dolor en el abdomen?

Do you have blood in your excrement?
_____ pain in your abdomen?

Sí, la tengo.
___ lo ___.

Yes, I have it.
_____ it.

NOTA CULTURAL

1. For the Hispanics from Mexico, Central America, and the Caribbean area—who still hold to their witchcraft or folk-healing beliefs—the **aires** represent the spirits who help the witch cast evil spells. Supposedly, germs are transmitted through the "air" at night, bringing about the initial cause for colds; also, ice water could make the throat cold thereby causing throat infection. People refuse to sleep at night with the windows open, or in the light of the moon, since this would make them—according to their superstitions—go crazy.

Ejercicios de conversación

A. *Conteste en español.*

Modelo: ¿Tiene la respiración corta?
Sí, cuando camino mucho.

1. ¿Cuántos catarros tiene usted al año?
2. ¿Ha perdido alguna vez el conocimiento?
3. ¿Es ésta la primera vez que tiene usted esta condición?
4. ¿Tiene usted dolor de cabeza?
5. ¿Puede usted describir el dolor?
6. ¿Dónde tiene usted el dolor? Indíqueme.
7. ¿Cómo se siente usted?
8. ¿Qué le paso?
9. ¿Por qué viene al hospital?
10. ¿Ha tenido las enfermedades de la infancia? ¿Cuáles?

B. *Complete con la forma correcta de una palabra interrogativa de la lista de la página siguiente. (Algunas de las palabras interrogativas se pueden usar más de una vez.)*

Modelo: ¿ *Cuántas* veces tiene tos, Sr. Ramírez?

1. ¿———— se siente usted hoy?
2. ¿———— tiene el dolor? Muéstreme.
3. ¿———— catarros tiene usted al año?
4. ¿———— tiene náuseas? ¿Al levantarse por la mañana?
5. ¿———— le pasa?
6. ¿———— sangre tiene en la orina?
7. ¿———— está la hinchazón? ¿En los tobillos?

8. ¿_____ está usted? ¿Un poco mejor?
9. ¿_____ es el nombre de su médico?
10. ¿ _____ es su pariente más cercano?

Palabras Interrogativas

Cuánto	Qué	Dónde
Cuánta	Cuál	Cuándo
Cuántos	Cómo	Quién
Cuántas		

C. *Forme oraciones usando las siguientes palabras, según el modelo.*

Modelo: muy / tos / frecuentemente / tener (yo)
          Tengo tos muy frecuentemente.

1. sangre / su / hay / excremento / mucho / en
2. año / tener / catarro / cuánto / usted
3. dificultad / respirar / mucho / tener / el paciente
4. ir / el / domingo / operar / paciente / la / los médicos / a / a
5. náuseas / tener / usted / cuando / respirar / profundo
6. eructos / el / doctor / querer / tener / cuando / saber / paciente
7. tener / vértigo / marearse / y / frecuentamente
8. querer / enfermera / tomarle / vitales / signos / usted
9. tener / cuando / lechuga / comer / yo / diarrea
10. donde / indicar / dolor / tener / el / paciente

D. *Llene el espacio con la letra que corresponda con la respuesta más correcta.*

1. ¿Tiene la respiración corta?
   _____

2. ¿Cuántos catarros tiene usted al año? _____

3. ¿Tiene dolor del pecho?
   _____

4. ¿Puede usted describir el dolor? _____

5. ¿Cuándo tiene usted eructos?
   _____

6. ¿Tiene usted tos?
   _____

7. ¿Tiene usted vértigo?
   _____

8. ¿Ha perdido usted el conocimiento? _____

9. ¿Tiene dificultad al respirar?
   _____

10. ¿Tiene la presión alta de sangre? _____

a. Sí, y me mareo también.
b. No, tengo dolor de cabeza.
c. Sí, al levantarme por la mañana.
d. Es quemante.
e. después de comer.
f. de vez en cuando.
g. Sí, cuando camino mucho.
h. Sí, la tengo.
i. No, nunca.
j. Cinco o seis.

E.   *Conteste negativamente, dando una alternativa.*

Modelo: ¿Tiene usted la respiración corta?
No, no tengo la respiración corta, pero tengo dolor en el pecho.

1. ¿Tiene usted sangre en su expectoración?
2. ¿Tiene usted náusea al levantarse?
3. ¿Tiene usted vértigo al subir la escalera?
4. ¿Tiene eructos después de comer?
5. ¿Tiene usted dificultad en respirar al andar?
6. ¿Tiene tos al acostarse?
7. ¿Tiene mucho dolor de pecho?
8. ¿Tiene muchos catarros al año?
9. ¿Tiene usted trastornos en la vista?
10. ¿Tiene usted fiebre y escalofríos?

Situación y simulación

You are taking medical history from Mrs. Valdez, an elderly Spanish-speaking lady who seems to be having gastro-intestinal problems. Write, in dialogue format, the conversation that takes place between yourself and Mrs. Valdez. Include in your conversation at least ten questions or statements from you and at least ten responses or questions from Mrs. Valdez. Use complete sentences for all questions and responses. Your conversation should cover several of Mrs. Valdez's symptoms, how long she has had them, how frequently, and how severe they are. Aside from those limitations, the precise details of her illness can be anything you invent, as long as the conversation makes logical sense and is grammatically correct.

Juego

Write out in English on separate slips of paper a number of fairly detailed descriptions of illnesses or syndromes. (Have enough for everyone in the class.) One such description, for example, might read

I have high blood pressure, frequent headaches, and pain in my ears. I often take aspirin for the headaches. I've fainted twice in the past month and sometimes feel very dizzy. I have had this problem for nearly two months and have a poor appetite when I feel dizzy.

Fold the slips and mix them in a container. Each class member takes a turn as the "patient." He or she picks a slip, silently reads the description of his or her "symptoms," and chooses another class member to be his or her "doctor." The "doctor" takes the "patient's" medical history, asking as many questions as is necessary to get a clear picture of the "patient's" "symptoms." ("Patients" may feel free to add appropriate details to their "symptoms," while keeping within the broad outlines of the descriptions on the slips of paper.) For the foregoing example, the conversation might begin like this:

Médico	Paciente
Buenos días. ¿Cómo se siente usted?	Me siento muy mal.
¿Qué tiene usted?	Tengo dolor de cabeza.
¿Lo tiene muy frecuentemente?	Sí, tengo dolores de cabeza bastante frecuentemente.

PALABRAS COGNADAS

Read through the following medical history form and note the cognate words, which are numerous. The words that have no English cognates are listed in the *Vocabulario* in the back of the book.

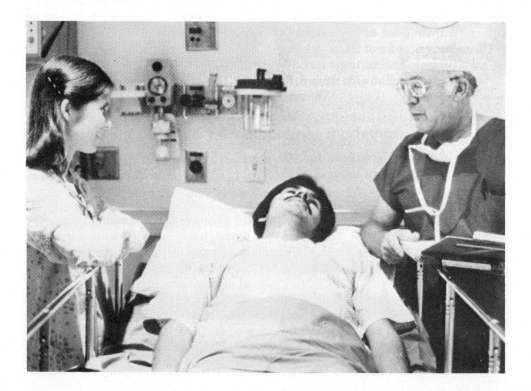

FORMULARIO DE HISTORIA MEDICA

Instrucciones: Ponga una "X" en el columno apropiado si HA TENIDO o TIENE ahora el problema indicado. Encierre en un círculo el problema que tiene o ha tenido si es posible elegir.

Ejemplo: ☐ ☒ Tiene catarro a menudo O tose diariamente.

HA TENIDO	TIENE	
		—malestar general O sudores excesivos por la noche O falta de energía.
		—enfermedad seria O le han recetado que tome medicinas diariamente.
		—problemas con el corazón O ataques al corazón O falta de aire al caminar.
		—presión alta U opresión en el pecho.
		—asma O bronquitis O tos diaria O frecuentes resfríos.
		—dificultad en respirar O tose sangre O tuberculosis (TB).
		—dolores de estómago O vómitos de sangre.
		—dolores de estómago después de comer algun tipo de comida (algunas veces comidas grasosas pueden causar ésto).
		—hernia ("rotura") U operación de hernia.
		—secreción purulenta del pene O enfermedades venerias O gonorrea.
		—dolores de menstruación que no permitan ninguna actividad.
		—dolores en la región baja de la espalda que se dan problemas en alzar o empujar.
		—heridas u operación de la espalda o piernas O heridas en los brazos o manos.
		—dolores o rigidez en las coyunturas O infección de la piel de las manos.
		—hepatitis O fiebre amarilla U orina de color amarillo.
		—desmayos O mareos O convulsiones/arrebatamientos pasajeros.
		—dificultad en oir O en ver aun con lentes.
		—otras enfermedades serias (como diabetes sacarina, úlcera, enfisema, tumor).
		—heridas serias estando en el trabajo a cualquier hora.

Tengo un médico con quien consulto regularmente, por un problema particular. Sí ☐ No ☐

La fecha aproximada de mi última visita médica es:

La fecha aproximada de mi última vacuna de tétano ("trismo") es:

Read through the following clinical history form and note the cognate words, which are numerous. The words that have no English cognates are listed in the *Vocabulario* in the back of the book.

HOJA ANALITICA DEL EXPEDIENTE CLINICO EN EVALUACION MEDICA	NO NECESARIO	CALIFICACION	OMITIDO	TARDIO	INSUFICIENTE	EXCESIVO	NO VALORADO	INADECUADO
I. HISTORIA CLINICA								
A. INTERROGATORIO								
1. Antecedentes familiares								
2. Antecedentes personales no patológicos								
3. Antecedentes personales patológicos								
4. Mención del contenido de la forma de envio								
5. Cronología del padecimiento actual								
6. Semiología del padecimiento actual								
7. Aparatos y sistemas								
8. Terapéutica y exámenes previos								
B. EXPLORACION								
9. Inspección general								
10. Estatura								
11. Peso actual								
12. Peso ideal								
13. Temperatura								
14. Pulso								
15. Respiración								
16. Tensión arterial								
17. Tegumentos y faneras								
18. Cabeza								
19. Oftalmología								
20. Fondo de ojo								
21. Otorrinolaringología								
22. Bucodental								
23. Cuello								
24. Glándulas mamarias								
25. Tórax								
26. Area precordial								
27. Abdominal								
28. Genital								
29. Rectal								
30. Músculo-esquelético								
31. Neurología								
32. Vascular periférica								
II. NOTAS CLINICAS								
INICIAL								
33. Resumen de los datos diagnósticos								
34. Programa de estudio								

HOJA ANALITICA DEL EXPEDIENTE CLINICO EN EVALUACION MEDICA								
DE REVISION O ACTUALIZACION	NO NECESARIO	CALIFICACION	OMITIDO	TARDIO	INSUFICIENTE	EXCESIVO	NO VALORADO	INADECUADO
35. Programa terapéutico								
36. Consideraciones pronósticas								
37. Del diagnóstico y evolución								
38. Del programa de estudio								
39. Interpretación de resultados de laboratorio								
40. Interpretación de resultados de gabinete								
41. Utilización de interconsultas								
42. Del programa terapéutico								
43. De las consideraciones pronósticas								
DE CIRUGIA								
44. Preoperatoria								
45. Técnica quirúrgica								
46. Hallazgos quirúrgicos								
47. Accidentes transoperatorios								
48. Posoperatorio								
DE ANESTESIA								
49. Preanestesia								
50. Posanestesia								
DE EVOLUCION								
51. Evolución								
52. Obstétrica								
53. Del consultante dentro de la unidad								
54. Del consultado dentro de la unidad								
55. Del consultante fuera de la unidad								
56. Del consultado fuera de la unidad								
57. Urgencias								
58. Consulta a domicilio								
59. Citas								
MEDICINA PREVENTIVA								
60. Antecedentes de inmunizaciones								
61. Búsqueda de enfermedades neoplásicas								
62. Medidas profilácticas para evitar infecciones e infestaciones								
63. Inmunizaciones								
64. Campañas de Medicina Preventiva								
MEDICINA DEL TRABAJO								
65. Medicina del trabajo								
DE ALTA O DEFUNCION								
66. Diagnósticos								
67. Resumen de evolución								
68. Resumen terapéutico								
69. Pronóstico								
70. Terapéutica posterior								

VOCABULARIO

LOS HUESOS DEL ESQUELETO

EL SISTEMA CIRCULATORIO

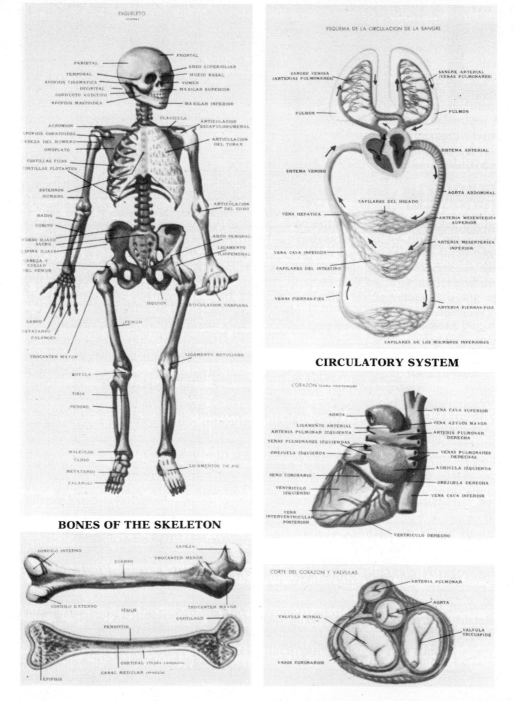

CIRCULATORY SYSTEM

BONES OF THE SKELETON

EL SISTEMA DIGESTIVO

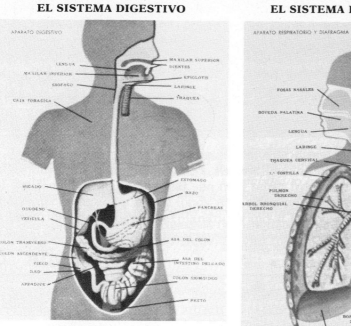

DIGESTIVE SYSTEM

EL SISTEMA RESPIRATORIO

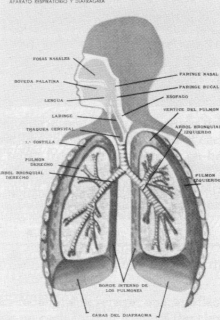

RESPIRATORY SYSTEM

EL SISTEMA URINARIO

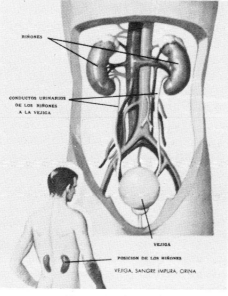

URINARY SYSTEM

LOS ÓRGANOS MÁS IMPORTANTES   THE MOST IMPORTANT ORGANS

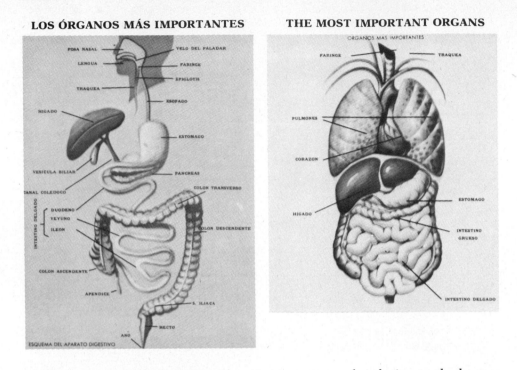

The following is a list of the most important words relating to the human body. Medical personnel will be delighted to see how close the Spanish words correspond with the English words, as the roots are either Latin or Greek. The vocabulary has been kept to an intermediate level.

EL ESQUELETO	THE SKELETON
el hueso	bone
el periósteo	periosteum
la médula	medulla
el cartílago	cartilage
el tendón; los tendones	tendon
las costillas	ribs
el craneo	cranium

EL SISTEMA CIRCULATORIO	THE CIRCULATORY SYSTEM
el corazón	heart
la sangre	blood
la vena	vein
la arteria	artery
el vaso capilar	capillary
el capilar	capillary

el vaso sanguíneo	*blood vessel*
la válvula	*valve*
la aorta	*aorta*
el sistema venoso	*venous system*

EL SISTEMA (APARATO[1]) DIGESTIVO   THE DIGESTIVE SYSTEM

la boca	*mouth*
el esófago	*esophagus*
la caja torácica	*thorax cavity*
el estómago	*stomach*
el hígado	*liver*
la vesícula	*gall bladder*
el páncreas	*pancreas*
el colon	*colon*
el intestino grueso	*large intestine*
el intestino delgado	*small intestine*
el recto	*rectum*
el ano	*anus*

EL SISTEMA RESPIRATORIO   THE RESPIRATORY SYSTEM

la lengua	*tongue*
la tráquea	*trachea*
el esófago	*esophagus*
el pulmón	*lung*
el diafragma	*diaphragm*
los bronquios	*bronchials*

EL SISTEMA URINARIO   THE URINARY SYSTEM

los riñónes	*kidneys*
la vejiga	*bladder*
la orina	*urine*
la uretra	*urethra*

SUSTANTIVOS   NOUNS

el apetito	*appetite*
el armazón	*framework*
la articulación	*joint*
el catarro	*cold*
la condición	*condition*

1. **Aparato** also means **sistema,** or *system.*

el conocimiento	consciousness, knowledge
el cuadrado	square
la dificultad	difficulty
el eructo	belch
el excremento	excrement
la expectoración	expectoration
la falta	lack, need
la lechuga	lettuce
el malestar	discomfort
la médula	medulla
la onda	wave
el pene	penis
la presión (alta) de sangre	(high) blood pressure
la regla	menstrual period
la respiración	breathing, respiration
el sudor	sweat
la vacuna	vaccination
la vez	time

VERBOS

VERBS

alzar	to lift
andar	to walk
caminar	to walk
deber	to owe; must, ought
describir	to describe
elegir	to choose
empujar	to push
encerrar	to encircle
luchar	to fight, struggle
perder	to lose
resolver	to solve
respirar	to breathe
sanar	to heal, recover
toser	to cough

ADJETIVOS

ADJECTIVES

agudo	sharp
alguna	some, any
corto	short
cualquier	whatever, whichever
especializado	specialized
frecuente	frequent
irritable	irritable
nervioso	nervous

ninguna	*no other*
peor	*worse*
pronto	*soon*
quemante	*burning*
semejante	*similar*
varios	*various, several*

ADVERBIOS

ADVERBS

aun	*even*
casi	*almost*
demasiado	*too much*
diariamente	*daily*
durante	*during*
exactamente	*exactly*
quizás	*perhaps, maybe*
rápidamente	*rapidly*
siempre	*always*

CONJUNCIÓN

CONJUNCTION

pero	*but*

PREPOSICIÓN

PREPOSITION

sobre	*over*

FRASES ÚTILES

EXPRESSIONS

a menudo	*often*
a veces	*sometimes, at times*
al año	*per year*
al menos	*at least*
de vez en cuando	*from time to time*
¡Ojalá que . . . !	*I hope that . . . !, Would that . . . !, God grant that . . . !*

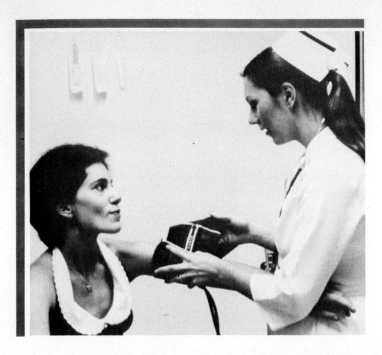

TRATAMIENTO, DOSIS Y TERAPIA

DIÁLOGO

Administrando las medicinas y la terapia física[1]

La Sra. Smith-MacKay, una enfermera, le habla a la Srta. Belmonte, una paciente nueva, acerca de las medicinas que ella debe tomar. Después la paciente, que acaba de tener una operación, va para la terapia física, administrada por la terapeuta, Srta. Goodwin.

Repita:

Sra. Smith-MacKay	**Srta. Belmonte**
Buenos días, Srta. Belmonte. ¿Me permite tomarle los signos vitales?	Buenos días. Sí, claro que me puede tomar los signos vitales.

1. Also, **fisioterapia.**

94

Antes de darle la medicina, tengo que hacerle algunas preguntas.

¿Toma usted ahora cualquier medicina?

¿Tiene usted alergias?

¿Ni a las medicinas?

Bueno, ahora usted debe tomar estas dos cápsulas.

Después de que regrese de la terapia física. Usted va allí a las dos en punto.

Más tarde . . .

Srta. Goodwin

Buenas tardes, Srta. Belmonte. ¿Cómo está usted hoy?

Estoy aquí para ayudarle y enseñarle a hacer ejercicios físicos. Si se siente incómoda, dígame. Vamos a empezar . . .

Muy bien.

No, no tomo ninguna medicina.

No, no las tengo.

Tampoco.

¿Y cuándo puedo tomar un tranquilizante?

Gracias.

Srta. Belmonte

Muy buenas tardes, señorita. Creo que me siento un poco mejor.

Muy bien.

Administering Medicines and Physical Therapy

Mrs. Smith-MacKay, a nurse, speaks with Miss Belmonte, a new patient, about the medicines that she should take. Afterward, the patient, who has just had an operation, goes for physical therapy, administered by the therapist, Miss Goodwin.

Repeat:

Mrs. Smith-MacKay

Good morning, Miss Belmonte. May I (will you permit me to) take your vital signs?

Before giving you the (your) medicine, I have to ask you some questions.

Do you now take any medication?

Do you have (any) allergies?

Not to medicines, either?

All right, now you should take these two capsules.

After you return from physical therapy. You're going there at precisely two o'clock (on the dot).

Miss Belmonte

Good morning. Yes, of course you may take my vital signs.

OK.

No, I don't take any medication.

No, I don't have any allergy.

Neither.

And when can I take a tranquilizer?

Thanks.

Later . . .

Miss Goodwin	**Miss Belmonte**
Good afternoon, Miss Belmonte. How are you today?	A very good afternoon, miss. I believe I feel a little better.
I am here to help you and to teach you how to do physical exercises. If you feel uncomfortable, tell me. Let's start. . . .	Very well.

FRASES ÚTILES

Sustituya:

¿Toma usted medicina para alergias?	*Do you take medicine for allergies?*
Sí, tomo medicina porque soy alérgico al polvo. _____ polen. _____ pelo de los perros y gatos.	*Yes, I take medicine because I'm allergic to dust.* *_____ pollen.* *_____ dog and cat fur.*
¿Que clase de medicina toma usted?	*What type of medicine do you take?*
Bueno, no sé exactamente. Aquí está la etiqueta. _____. Mi médico puede decírselo.	*Well, I don't know exactly. Here's the label.* *_____. My doctor can tell (it to) you.*
¿Ha tomado usted las dos píldoras blancas? ¿_____ el medicamento? ¿_____ la cápsula?	*Have you taken the two white pills?* *_____ the medicine?* *_____ the capsule?*
No, todavía no las he tomado. _____ lo _____. _____ la _____.	*No, I haven't taken them yet.* *_____ it ___.* *_____ it ___.*

Sr. Fernández, usted debe tomar
la leche de magnesia.
_____ un laxante.
_____ estas cápsulas.

Mr. Fernández, you should (ought
to) take milk of magnesia.
_____ a laxative.
_____ these capsules.

Muy bien, la tomo.
_____ lo _____.
_____ las _____.

Very well, I'll take it.
_____ it.
_____ them.

Tómelo ahora, por favor.
Tómelas _____.
Tómela _____.
Bueno.

Take it now, please.
Take them _____.
Take it _____.
All right.

Tome usted un tranquilizante y
descanse bien.
_____ este
líquido _____.
_____
estas píldoras _____.
Muchas gracias.

Take a tranquilizer and rest well.

_____ this liquid _____.

_____ these pills _____.

Thanks.

¿Tiene usted una pregunta,
señorita?
Sí, ¿cuándo debo tomar un
tranquilizante?
_____ la
medicina?
_____ un
laxante?

Do you have a question, miss?

Yes, when should I take a
tranquilizer?
_____ the
medicine?
_____ a laxative?

¿Ha tomado usted una cápsula
azul y amarilla?
¿_____
roja y gris?
¿_____
violeta y blanca?
No, nadie me la dio.

Have you taken a blue and yellow
capsule?
_____ red and grey
_____?
_____ violet and white
_____?
No, nobody gave it to me.

Usted debe tomarla dos veces al día. | You should take it twice a day.

_____ cada día. | _____ every day.

_____ cada cuatro horas. | _____ every four hours.

_____ según la etiqueta. | _____ according to the label.

_____ según la receta. | _____ according to the prescription.

_____ según el dolor que tiene. | _____ according to the pain you have.

¿Ha tomado usted el líquido color de rosa?[1] | Have you taken the rose-colored (pink) liquid?

¿_____ azul? | _____ blue _____?

¿_____ amarillo claro? | _____ light yellow _____?

¿_____ verde oscuro? | _____ dark green _____?

¿Quiere usted decirme cuándo debo tomarlo? | Will you tell me when I should take it?

¿_____ cuánto debo tomar? | _____ how much I should take?

¿_____ por qué debo tomarlo? | _____ why I should take it?

Tómelo a las cuatro en punto. | Take it at precisely four o'clock.

_____ a la una y media. | _____ at one-thirty

_____ a las ocho. | _____ at eight o'clock.

_____ después de comer. | _____ after eating.

_____ antes del desayuno. | _____ before breakfast.

_____ cuatro veces al día. | _____ four times a day.

Usted debe tomar dos cucharaditas. | You should take two teaspoonfuls.

_____ una cucharada. | _____ a tablespoonful.

_____ medio vaso. | _____ half a glass.

---

1. **Color de rosa,** meaning *pink,* is preferable to the grammatically correct **color rosado** because in street language **rosado (-a)** has a very bad connotation.

¿Quiere usted que las tome ahora?	Do you want me to take them now?
¿———————— la ————?	———————————— it ——?
¿———————— lo ————?	———————————— it ——?

Voy a introducirle² este tubo.	I am going to insert this tube in you.
———————————— esta intravenosa.	———————————— an IV.
———————————— esta sonda.	———————————— probe, foley catheter.

¡Ay, qué dolor!	Oh, how painful!
¡—— barbaridad!	—— awful!
¡—— horror!	—— horrible!

Voy a darle una inyección.	I am going to give you an injection.
———————— un purgante.	———————————— a laxative.
———————— una vacuna.	———————————— a vaccination.
———————— una inyección de tétanos.	———————————— a tetanus shot.
———————— una inyección de refuerzo.³	———————————— a booster shot.

¡No, no, usted está equivocada! No necesito una inyección.	No, you are wrong, I don't need an injection.
¡———————— un purgante.	———————————— a laxative.
¡———————— una vacuna.	———————————— a vaccination.
¡———————— una inyección de tétanos.	———————————— a tetanus shot.
¡———————— una inyección de refuerzo.	———————————— a booster shot.

Voy a sacarle⁴ sangre.	I am going to draw your blood.
———————— una radiografía.	———————— take an x-ray of you.

2. Also, **ponerle.**

3. Also, **estimulante** and **de nuevo.**

4. Note the differences in expressing actions in English and Spanish:

to draw (blood)	} **sacar**		
to take a picture		to introduce (social introduction)	**presentar**
to draw (picture)	**dibujar**	to take (vital signs)	**tomar**
to inject	**introducir, poner**	to eat, to take into the body	**tomar**

Sentado o parado . . .   Seated or standing . . .
Favor de sentarse.   Please sit down.
Favor de ponerse de pie.   Please stand up.
Favor de pararse.   Please stand up.
Favor de estirar.   Please stretch.
_____ moverse.   _____ move.
_____ rotar.   _____ rotate.
_____ aflojar.   _____ loosen, relax.
_____ levantarse.   _____ get up.
_____ acostarse.   _____ lie down.
_____ subir.   _____ go up.
_____ repetir.   _____ repeat.
_____ bajar.   _____ go down.
_____ doblarse.   _____ bend.
_____ tratar de hacerlo.   _____ try to do it.
Siéntese.   Sit down.
Póngase de pie.   Stand up.
Párese.   Stand up.
Estire.   Stretch.
Muévase.   Move.
Rote, gire.   Rotate.
Afloje.   Loosen, relax.
Levántese.   Get up.
Acuéstese.   Lie down.
Suba.   Go up.
Repita.   Repeat.
Baje.   Go down.
Dóblese.   Bend.
Trate de hacerlo.   Try to do it.

Favor de estirar las rodillas.   Please stretch your knees.
_____ mover _____.   _____ move _____.
_____ rotar _____.   _____ rotate _____.
_____ hacer circular[5]   _____ turn in a circle _____.
_____.

Estire las rodillas.   Stretch them.
Mueva _____.   Move _____.
Rote _____.   Rotate _____.
Haga circular _____.   Circle _____.

5. Also, **girar, gire.**

Favor de circular el pie a la
derecha.

Please circle (your) foot to the right.

_____ izquierda.

Please circle (your) foot to the left.

Circule a la derecha.
_____ izquierda.

Circle to the right.
Circle to the left.

Favor de mover la cabeza de lado
a lado.

_Please move (your) head from side
to side._

_____ de barba
al pecho.

_Please move (your) head from chin
to chest._

Mueva de lado a lado.
_____ de barba al pecho.

Move from side to side.
_____ _from chin to chest._

Acuéstese boca arriba.
Acuéstese boca abajo.

Lie down on your back (mouth up).
_Lie down on your stomach (mouth
down)._

Dóblese hacia el frente.
_____ la pared.
_____ la mesa.
_____ la cama.
_____ la silla.
_____ el armazón.

Bend forward.
_____ _to the wall._
_____ _to the table._
_____ _to the bed._
_____ _to the chair._
_____ _to the framework._

Sosténgase con las manos.
_____ los pies.
_____ los codos.
_____ las nalgas.

_____ las rodillas.

Sustain yourself with your hands.
_____ feet._
_____ elbows._
_____
buttocks._
_____ knees._

Estire la pierna hacia atrás.
_____ el pie _____.
_____ la mano _____.
_____ el brazo _____.

Stretch your leg backward.
_____ foot _____.
_____ hand _____.
_____ arm _____.

Estire la pierna hacia atrás.
_____ hacia afuera.
_____ hacia un lado.
_____ hacia el frente.

Stretch your leg backward.
_____ forward.
_____ to one side.
_____ to the front.

Levante la mano hacia arriba.
_____ hacia el frente.
_____ arriba hacia
abajo.
_____ hacia la pared.
_____ hacia los lados.

Raise your hand up.
_____ forward.
_____ up and down.

_____ to the wall.
_____ to the sides.

Ayuda a relajar los músculos del
cuello.
_____ del
brazo.
_____ del
pie.
_____ de la
espalda.
_____ del
hombro.

(It) helps to relax the neck muscles.
_____ arm _____.
_____ foot _____.
_____ back
_____.
_____ shoulder
_____.

Ayuda a aflojar los músculos de la
pierna.
_____ del
diafragma.
_____ del
antebrazo.
_____ del
pecho.
_____ del
muslo.

(It) helps to loosen the leg muscles.
_____ diaphragm
_____.
_____ forearm
_____.
_____ chest
_____.
_____ thigh
_____.

Ejercicios de conversación

A. *Conteste en español, usando la palabra o frase sugerida.*

> **Modelo:** ¿Cuándo debo tomar la medicina? (*cada seis horas*)
> *Usted debe tomar la medicina* **cada seis horas.**

1. ¿Cuál medicamento debo tomar? (*estas cápsulas*)
2. ¿Cuántas píldoras debo tomar? (*dos cada cuatro horas*)
3. ¿Cuándo debo tomar un laxante? (*antes de acostarse*)
4. ¿Debo tomarlo esta tarde? (*Sí, a la tres y media*)
5. ¿A qué hora debo tomar el líquido? (*a las once de la mañana*)
6. ¿Cuándo necesito tomar las tabletas? (*dos veces al día*)
7. ¿Debo tomar el purgante esta mañana? (*Sí, lo más pronto possible*)
8. ¿Cuándo debo tomar las pastillas? (*según la receta*)
9. ¿Cuántas aspirinas debo tomar? (*una cada quince minutos*)
10. ¿A qué hora debo tomar la píldora blanca? (*al mediodía, a media-noche*)

B. *Traduzca al español.*

> **Modelo:** Take a yellow and green capsule every day before breakfast.
> *Tome una cápsula amarilla y verde cada día antes del desayuno.*

1. You should take two teaspoonfuls now and two more after eating.
2. Do you have any allergies?
3. Take two teaspoonfuls of the pink liquid before breakfast.
4. Take the two brown capsules but don't chew them.[1]
5. Take four tablets every four hours but don't swallow them.[2]
6. Do you have the doctor's prescription?
7. Chew the medicine.[3]
8. Suck the tablets[4] but don't swallow them.[5]
9. Take one tablespoon this morning and one this afternoon.
10. Please drink water (**favor de beber**) with your medicine.

1. **No las mastique**
2. **No las trague**
3. **Mastique la medicina**
4. **Chupe las tabletas**
5. **No las traque**

C. *Escriba cada oración en el pretérito perfecto.*

Modelo: Tomo dos píldoras azules.
He tomado dos píldoras azules.

1. La Sra. Romero descansa mucho.
2. Ella toma la medicina.
3. La enfermera le trae el líquido.
4. Se lo pregunto al médico.
5. ¿Tiene usted alergias?

D. *Complete cada oración con un adverbio, formándolo del adjetivo dado en paréntesis.*

Modelo: *INMEDIATO (A) + MENTE*
El paciente debe tomar esta medicina <u>inmediatamente</u>
(inmediato).

1. Ella toma las cápsulas porque tiene alergias muy
_____ (frecuente).
2. El paciente que ha tenido la operación duerme _____
(tranquilo).
3. He tenido problemas al tomar medicinas muy
_____ (raro).
4. _____ (general) tomo el líquido verde claro antes de
acostarme.
5. Tengo mucho dolor. ¿Quiere usted traerme las cápsulas
_____ (rápido)?

E. *Traduzca al español.*

1. This is the physical therapy room.
2. I want to show you some physical exercises.
3. Stand up and stretch your legs.
4. Bend your knees forward.
5. Rotate your foot to the left and then to the right.
6. Sit down on the table, lie down on your back.
7. Raise your leg to the left and then to the right.
8. Raise your arms up and then down.
9. Relax and loosen your muscles.
10. If you feel any of the following symptoms, call me.

Situación y simulación

A. As a physical therapist write out a program for a stroke victim who is
partially paralyzed. Explain the exercises and ask the patient to do the
exercises twice daily. Remember to caution the patient to call you if he
or she feels badly. Also, remember to emphasize how you hope the pa-

tient will improve. Use the material found in the *Frases Útiles* as well as the translation exercise. This exercise is designed primarily for physical therapists but all health care personnel must give movement instructions and commands at one point or another.

B. You are Miss Whitney, a floor nurse. Shown below is a conversation between yourself and Mr. Quiñones, a Spanish-speaking patient to whom you are explaining dosage and medication schedules. During your discussions, Mr. Quiñones requests information about his medication and asks you to clarify a number of points. Blanks have been left in the conversation where your replies to his questions would appear. Write out the answers you would give to help Mr. Quiñones thoroughly understand his medication. The exact information you give to Mr. Quiñones can be anything that makes sense in the context of the conversation.

Srta. Whitney	Sr. Quiñones
Muy buenas tardes, Sr. Quiñones.	Buenas tardes. Usted se llama Srta. Whitney, ¿verdad?
Sí, señor. ¿Ha tomado usted la medicina?	No, no la he tomado. ¿Cuál medicina es?
	¿Cuántas veces al día debo tomarla?
_____	
_____	
Además, usted debe tomar estas cápsulas grises.	Bueno, ¿y para qué son las cápsulas?
	¿Cuántas cápsulas debo tomar?
_____	¿Las tomo antes o después de comer?
_____	Srta. Whitney, creo que necesito un laxante. ¿Quiere usted traérmelo?
_____	
Sr. Quiñones, dice aquí en este formulario que usted toma medicina para las alergias. ¿Cuál medicina es?	
	No recuerdo cómo se llama, pero la otra enfermera tiene la medicina. A propósito, ¿puedo tomar esa medicina para mis alergias esta noche?
_____	Y señorita, una pregunta más— ¿después que me den de alta, todavía debo tomar las medicinas

que usted me ha dado y por
cuánto tiempo?

Si tiene usted cualquier otra pregunta, llámeme, Sr. Quiñones.

Muchísimas gracias, Srta. Whitney.

Juego

Write out in English on separate slips of paper a number of descriptions
of imaginary dosages and medication schedules that might apply to various
patients. (Have enough for everyone in the class.) One such description, for
instance, might read

> The patient must take two blue pills three times a day, and should con-
> tinue taking the pills after being discharged from the hospital. The
> patient must also take some of the light green liquid before going to
> bed each night and may take a laxative if desired. One capsule may
> also be taken in response (according) to pain, but the capsules may not
> be taken more than four times a day.

Fold the slips and mix them in a container. Each class member takes a
turn as the "nurse." He or she picks a slip, silently reads the description of
dosage and medication schedules, and chooses another class member to be
the "patient." The "nurse" then explains the medication to the "patient,"
with the "patient" asking any questions that seem appropriate. (*Note:* to
make the game more fun, some essential details should be omitted from the
descriptions, as has been done in the foregoing example, where the "nurse"
doesn't say what color the pain capsule is, how much blue liquid is to be
taken, for how long the pink pills are to be continued, etc. This will give
"patients" a number of valid questions to ask.)

"Patients" should be alert for any details that "nurses" may fail to provide
or anything that is unclear and question the "nurses" about it. ("Patients"
should be certain, for instance, that they understand the form and color of
the medications they are to take, how often and at what times they are to
be taken, and for how long.) "Patients" are also encouraged to ask any other
questions about medication which they feel are appropriate. "Nurses" are
free to answer "patients'" questions with any dosage and medication details
that are appropriate within the broad context of what is written on the slip
of paper. For the foregoing example, the conversation might begin like this:

Enfermera	Paciente
Buenos días. ¿Se siente mejor hoy?	Buenos días. Sí, me siento un poco major.
Bueno, usted debe tomar estas píl-doras azules tres veces al día.	¿Las tomo antes o después de comer?

PALABRAS COGNADAS

Read through the following appointment cards and note the cognate words, which are numerous. The words that have no English cognates are listed in the *Vocabulario* in the back of the book.

INSTRUCCIONES

1. — *Acuda puntualmente a las citas de su médico, precisamente el día y la hora señalada en la tarjeta.*

2. — *Cumpla cuidadosamente todas las instrucciones de su médico.*

3. — *Procure no traer más de un acompañante a la Clínica.*

4. — *Haga sus llamadas telefónicamente sólo a las horas que tiene señaladas en esta tarjeta.*

5. — *En casos de verdadera urgencia, preséntese para recibir atención inmediata en el "Servicio de urgencia de esta Clínica".*

6. — *Cuide esta tarjeta y consérvela en las mejores condiciones para que en ella le anoten sus citas con el médico.*

TARJETA DE CITAS

CLINICA NUM. _____

Nombre _____

Número de registro _____

Médico familiar _____

Tarjeta para citar pacientes en la consulta externa (anverso)

Cuando no tenga cita debe acudir a consulta de

_____ Hs. a _____ Hs.

Cuando solicite atención domiciliaria hable a los teléfonos:

_____

____ de _____ Hs. a _____ Hs.

En casos de urgencia puede hablar a los teléfonos:

_____

FECHAS DE CONSULTA

FECHA	HORA	SERVICIO	RUBRICA

Tarjeta para citar pacientes en la consulta externa (reverso)

VOCABULARIO

SUSTANTIVOS

la cápsula
la cita
la dósis
la etiqueta
la hora
la inyección
el lado
el laxante
la leche
la píldora
el purgante
la receta
la rubrica
los signos vitales
la sonda
la tarjeta
el tranquilixante
el tratamiento
la vacuna

NOUNS

the capsule
the appointment
dosage
label
hour
injection
side
laxative
milk
pill
laxative
prescription
heading
vital signs
catheter, probe
card
tranquilizer
treatment
vaccination

VERBOS

deber
descansar
empezar
permitir
sacar
tener
tomar

VERBS

to ought to
to rest
to start
to permit
to draw
to have
to take

MANDATOS

acuéstese (acostarse)
circule (circular)
chupe (chupar)
dóblese (doblarse)
estire (estirar)
gire (girar)
levante (levantar)
mantenga (mantener)
mastique (masticar)
muévase (moverse)
párese (pararse)
siéntese (sentarse)
sosténgase (sostenerse)
trague (tragar)

COMMANDS

lie down
circulate, turn in a circle
suck
bend
stretch, straight
turn, rotate
raise
maintain
chew
move
stand up
sit down
sustain
swallow

ADJETIVOS

alguna
cada
claro-a
cualquier
equivocado-a
incómodo-a
ninguna
nuevo-a
obscuro-a
otro-a
señalado-a
verdadero-a

COLORES

amarillo-a
azul (es)
café
color de rosa, rosado-a
dorado-a
gris (es)
lavandulo-a, lavando-a
morado-a
naranjado-a
negro-a
pardo-a
rojo-a
verde
violeta, púrpuro-a

ADVERBIOS

ahora
afuera
al frente
atrás
arriba (de)
abajo (de)
bien
boca abajo
boca arriba
claro
despacio
hacia
muy
mejor
nunca
todavía
tampoco

ADJECTIVES

some, any
each
clear, light
which
wrong, incorrect
uncomfortable
none, no other
new
dark
other
indicated
true

COLORS

yellow
blue
brown
pink
golden
grey
lavender
purple
orange
black
brown
red
green
purple

ADVERBS

now
away, outside
forward
behind
up
down
well
head down (on stomach)
head up (mouth up, on back)
sure
slowly
toward
very
better
never
still, yet
neither, nor

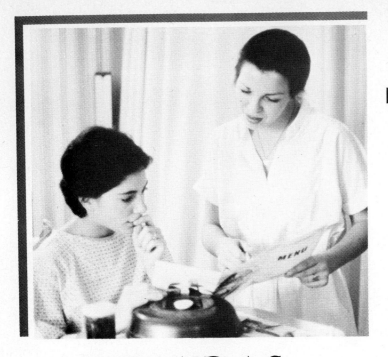

COMIDAS Y DIETAS

DIÁLOGO

Explicando las restricciones dietéticas

La Sra. O'Brien, dietista, habla con la Sra. Ríos, una paciente gorda a quién se le acaban de operar. Ella le explica a la Sra. Ríos las restricciones dietéticas que debe observar.

Repita:

Sra. O'Brien

Buenos días, Sra. Ríos. Me llamo Julia O'Brien y soy dietista. ¿Cómo está usted?

Sra. Ríos

Buenos días. Estoy bastante bien, pero tengo mucha sed. Quiero un vaso de agua fría, por favor.

No, señora. No le permite.

La enferma.

El tubo digestivo no puede aguantar el agua fría después de la operación. Usted puede tomar sólo pedacitos de hielo o chupar una toallita mojada.

Bueno, estoy aquí para explicarle la dieta que debe[1] seguir.

Sí, para bajar el nivel de colesterol en la dieta.

No, no lo permite.

Usted no debe comer dulces. Debe perder mucho peso.

Debe perder dos kilos y medio a la semana.

Usted necesita marcar[2] el plato ahora. ¿Quiere ver el menú?

¿Le gusta la fruta?

No le permite.

No, señora. Sólo le permite una papa pequeña, hervida y sin mantequilla.

¡No me permite! ¿Por qué?

¡Me enferma! ¿Por qué?

¡Qué barbaridad!

¿Debo seguir una dieta especial?

Pues, ¿me permite tomar postre? Me encanta postre.

¡No lo permite! ¿Por qué?

¡Ay de mí! ¿Cuánto peso debo perder?

¡Imposible! Tengo mucha hambre.

Sí, sí, por favor.

Prefiero la torta de chocolate.

Muy bien. Tráigame fruta, entonces. Dice aquí que hay papas fritas. ¿Me permite . . .?

¡Me muero de hambre!

Explaining Dietary Restrictions

Mrs. O'Brien, a dietitian, talks with Mrs. Ríos, a rather overweight patient who has just had an operation. She explains to Mrs. Ríos the dietary restrictions she should observe.

Repeat:

Mrs. O'Brien	Mrs. Ríos
Good morning, Mrs. Ríos. My name is Julia O'Brien, and I'm a dietitian. How are you?	
	Good morning. I'm pretty good, but I'm very thirsty. I'd like a glass of cold water, please.

1. While **deber** (*should, ought, must*) and **tener que** (*have to, must*) both convey the sense of obligation, **deber** is less forceful and more courteous than **tener que** in making polite requests. Try, therefore, to avoid using **tener que** unless a patient is unmanageable.

2. Also, **elegir** = *to choose.*

No, ma'am. It's not allowed (permitted to you).

It makes you sick.

The (your) digestive tract isn't able to stand cold water after the operation. You can only have small pieces of ice or suck on a wet towel.

All right, I'm here to explain the diet you should follow.

Yes, in order to lower the level of cholesterol in the (your) diet.

No, it's not allowed.

You shouldn't eat sweets. You ought to lose a lot of weight.

You ought to lose two and one-half kilos a week.

You need to mark your selection now. Do you want to see the menu?

Do you like fruit?

It's not permitted.

No ma'am. You're only allowed one small potato, boiled and without butter.

It's not allowed (permitted to me)! Why?

It makes me sick! Why?

How horrible!

Should I follow a special diet?

Well, am I allowed to eat dessert? I love dessert.

It's not allowed. Why?

Oh, my! How much weight should I lose?

Impossible! I'm very hungry.

Yes, yes, please.

I prefer chocolate cake.

Very well. Bring me fruit, then. It says here that there are french fries. Am I allowed . . .?

I'm dying of hunger!

FRASES ÚTILES

Sustituya:

¿Le gusta[1] a usted la fruta?
¿——————— el jugo?
¿——————— el pescado?

Do you like fruit?
——————— *juice?*
——————— *fish?*

Sí, me gusta la fruta.
——————— el jugo.
——————— el pescado.

Yes, I like fruit.
——————— *juice.*
——————— *fish.*

1. English conveys the idea of "liking" with a grammatical construction in which the person who does the liking is the subject, and that which is liked is the direct object (e.g., I like fruit; he likes potatoes). Spanish conveys the same idea of "liking" with a grammatical construction in which that which is liked is the subject and the person who does the liking is the indirect object. Hence, **Me gusta la fruta** (*I like fruit*) literally means "The fruit is pleasing me," and **Le gustan las papas** (*He likes the potatoes*) literally means "The potatoes are pleasing him."

¿Le gustan a usted los huevos revueltos?

¿_____ las legumbres?

¿_____ las papas fritas?

Do you like scrambled eggs?

_____ *vegetables?*

_____ *french fries?*

No, no me gustan los huevos revueltos.

_____ las legumbres.

_____ las papas fritas.

No, I don't like scrambled eggs.

_____ *vegetables.*

_____ *french fries.*

¿Le gusta a usted el tocino?

¿__ gustan _____ los dulces?

¿__ gusta _____ el helado?

¿__ gustan _____ las uvas?

Do you like bacon?

_____ *like sweets?*

_____ *like ice cream?*

_____ *like grapes?*

No, totalmente no.

No, absolutely not.

Usted debe comer los vegetales secos.

_____ mucho arroz.

_____ las ensaladas.

You should eat dried vegetables.

_____ *lots of rice.*

_____ *salads.*

No me gustan. ¡Qué barbaridad!

_____ gusta. ¡_____!

_____ gustan. ¡_____!

I don't like them. How horrible!

_____ *it.* _____!

_____ *them.* _____!

Usted no debe comer la carne asada.

_____ la mantequilla.

_____ la torta.

You shouldn't eat broiled meat.

_____ *butter.*

_____ *cake.*

¡No debo comerla! ¿Por qué?

I shouldn't eat it! Why?

Usted no debe tomar cerveza.
_____ crema con el café.
_____ limonada.

You shouldn't drink beer.
_____ cream with the (your) coffee.
_____ lemonade.

¿Por qué? Es muy deliciosa.

Why? It's very delicious.

Usted debe perder mucho peso.
_____ perder al menos veinte kilos.
_____ ganar[2] mucho peso.
_____ ganar al menos cinco kilos.

You should lose a lot of weight.
_____ lose at least twenty kilos.
_____ gain a lot of weight.
_____ gain at least five kilos.

¡Ay de mí!

Oh, my!

Usted debe comer comidas sin especias.
_____ con menos sal.
_____ con menos grasa y más fibras.

You should eat foods without spices.
_____ with less salt.
_____ with less fat and more roughage.

¡Ay! ¡Las comidas con especias me gustan tanto!
_____ sal ___
_____!
_____ grasa ___
_____!

Oh! I like foods with spices so much!
_____ salt
_____!
_____ fat
_____!

Sí, señorita. ¿Tiene usted una pregunta?

Yes, miss. Do you have a question?

Sí, quiero hablar con el personal dietético.
_____ el dietista.

_____ el jefe de dietética.

Yes, I'd like to talk with the dietary personnel.
_____ the dietitian.
_____ the head dietitian.

---

2. **Aumentar de peso** is also frequently used. **Perder libras, kilos, peso** = *to lose weight;* also, **adelgazar, bajar de peso.**

Usted debe seguir una dieta balanceada.

_____ con pocos carbohidratos.

_____ con poco sodio.

_____ con mucha proteína.

You should follow a balanced diet.

_____ *with few carbohydrates (low carbohydrate).*

_____ *with little sodium (low sodium).*

_____ *with lots of protein (high protein).*

¿Quiere usted explicarme cómo es?

Will you explain to me what it's like?

¿Tiene usted alergia a los camarones?

¿_____ los tomates?

¿_____ los melones?

Are you allergic (do you have an allergy) to shrimp?

_____
_____ *tomatoes?*

_____
_____ *melons?*

¿Es usted alérgica a las ciruelas?

¿ _____ a los espárragos?

¿ _____ al jugo de naranja?

Are you allergic to plums?

_____ *to asparagus?*

_____ *to orange juice?*

Sí, soy alérgica.

Yes, I'm allergic.

¿Necesita un tenedor?

_____ un cuchillo?

_____ una cuchara?

_____ una servilleta?

_____ un vaso de agua?

_____ una bandeja?

_____ una taza?

_____ un plato?

_____ un platillo?

_____ algo más?

Do you need a fork?

_____ *a knife?*

_____ *a spoon?*

_____ *a napkin?*

_____ *a glass of water?*

_____ *a tray?*

_____ *a cup?*

_____ *a plate?*

_____ *a saucer?*

_____ *anything else?*

NOTAS CULTURALES

1. Throughout the Hispanic world the terms for breakfast, lunch, and dinner are:

el desayuno	*breakfast*
el almuerzo	*lunch*
la cena	*dinner*

The general term for meal is **la comida** and will mainly refer to lunch as most Hispanic families eat their main meal at lunchtime.

Notice the verbs that accompany the nouns:

el desayuno	desayunarse
el almuerzo	almorzar
la cena	cenar

2. Since most Latin Americans are accustomed to the metric system, in conversing with them, it will be helpful to express weights in terms of **kilos** (*kilograms*) rather than **libras** (*pounds*).

¿Quiere ver un menú?	*Do you want to see a menu?*
¿Quiere seleccionar la comida?	*Do you want to choose your meal?*
¿———— marcar el plato con esta lapicera?	*Do you want to mark (select) the dish with this ballpoint pen (pencil)?*
¿———— desayunarse?	*Do you want to eat breakfast?*
¿———— almorzar?	*Do you want to eat lunch?*
¿———— cenar?	*Do you want to eat dinner?*
¿Qué quiere para el desayuno?	*What do you want to eat for breakfast?*
¿———————— el almuerzo?	*What do you want to eat for lunch?*
¿———————— la cena?	*What do you want to eat for dinner?*
¿Quiere escoger cereal o pan?	*Do you want to choose cereal or bread?*
¿———————— verduras o legumbres?	*Do you want to choose greens or legumes?*
¿———————— papas o fideo?	*Do you want to choose potatoes or noodles?*

¿Qué quiere tomar para la ensalada?

What do you want for salad?

¿_____ la sopa?

What do you want for soup?

¿_____ la carne?

What do you want for meat?

¿_____ el postre?

What do you want for dessert?

¿Quiere elegir un aderezo o mayonesa?

Do you want to choose dressing or mayonnaise?

¿_____ un consommé o gazpacho?

Do you want to choose consommé or gazpacho?

¿_____ una carne de res o jamón?

Do you want to choose beef or ham?

¿_____ un helado o flan?

Do you want to choose ice cream or caramel custard?

¿Quiere ud. darme una lista de los alimentos prohibidos?

Do you want to give me a list of the prohibited foods?

_____

que se deben evitar?

foods that one should avoid?

_____

necesarios?

necessary foods?

_____

incluídos en mi dieta?

included in my diet?

_____

más baratos?

cheaper foods?

_____

sustituidos?

substituted foods?

¿Quiere ud. darme más informaciones sobre esta dieta especial?

Will you give me more information on this special diet?

_____ nueva?

_____ new diet?

_____ estricta?

_____ strict diet?

¿Hay otros elementos nutritivos que se pueden sustituir en esta dieta?

Are there other nutritious elements that can be substituted in this diet?

_____ cereales

_____ cereals

_____
_____?

_____?

_____ productos lácteos

_____ dairy products

_____
_____?

_____?

¿Por cuánto tiempo debo seguir
esta dieta?
¿___ especial?
¿___ estricta?
¿___ nutritiva?

(For) how long do I need to follow
this diet?
___ special diet?
___ strict diet?
___ nutritious diet?

Por dos semanas.
Por dos meses.
Por toda su vida.
Hasta que hable con el médico.
_____ se mejore.
_____ adelgace, baje de peso.
_____ me den de alta.

For two weeks.
For two months.
For your whole life.
Until you can talk with the doctor.
Until you get better.
Until you lose weight.
Until you're discharged.

Estos alimentos son demasiado
caros, ¿hay otros más baratos?
_____ platos _____?
_____ productos lácteos
_____?

These foods are too expensive. Are
there others that are cheaper?
___ dishes _____?
___ dairy products
_____?

¿Me quiere decir cómo preparar
estos alimentos nutritivos?
¿___ platos dietéticos?
¿___ productos lácteos?

Will you tell me how to prepare
these nutritious foods?
___ dietetic dishes?
___ dairy products?

No sé cocinar.[3]
___ preparar la comida.

___ hervir el agua.
___ elegir el plato.

I don't know how to cook.
_____ prepare the
meal.
_____ boil water.
_____ to choose the
dish.

3. **No sé** is translated *I don't know how.*

Ejercicios de conversación

A. *Escoja la mejor descripción de cada elemento nutritivo.*

1. _____ la lechuga
2. _____ el queso
3. _____ la sal
4. _____ el biftec
5. _____ la leche
6. _____ el helado
7. _____ la mantequilla
8. _____ la espinaca
9. _____ la naranja
10. _____ el azúcar

a. un condimento dulce que se debe evitar para bajar de peso
b. una fruta con mucha vitamina C
c. un producto lácteo que aumenta la grasa en la dieta
d. un vegetal que se usa en las ensaladas
e. un producto lácteo que se come en los sandwichs
f. un condimento que se sirve con la pimienta
g. un producto lácteo que se bebe
h. una carne que tiene mucha proteína
i. un producto lácteo que se come como postre
j. un vegetal que contiene mucho hierro

B. *Conteste en español, usando la palabra o frase sugerida.*

Modelo: ¿Qué clase de postre le gusta? (*la torta*)
   Me gusta la torta.

1. ¿Cuántos kilos debo perder? (*cinco kilos al mes*)
2. ¿Qué clase de dieta debo seguir? (*sin carbohidratos*)
3. ¿Quién prepara las dietas? (*la dietista*)
4. ¿Cuáles son los productos lácteos que contienen mucha proteína? (*queso, leche y requesón*)
5. ¿Cuáles son las frutas que tienen carbohidratos? (*manzana, melón, fresas y plátanos*)

C. *Complete según el modelo.*

Modelo: No quiero torta, porque no me gusta(n) *los postres*.

1. No me traiga salmón, porque no me gusta(n) _____.
2. No quiero leche, porque no puedo comer _____.

3. No me traiga pan, porque no me gusta(n) _____.

4. Tengo alergia al queso y no me gusta(n) _____.

5. No me prepare jamón frito, porque no me gusta(n)

_____.

D. *Traduzca al español.*

Modelo: No, I don't like vegetables. I prefer fried eggs.
 No, no me gustan los vegetales. Prefiero los huevos fritos.

1. You ought to eat salads and lots of vegetables.
2. You shouldn't eat eggs, because you're following a low-cholesterol diet.
3. Sir, you must lose twenty pounds (kilograms), please follow this diet.
4. Which do you like the most, cottage cheese or beef?
5. You must not eat salt because you are on (following) a low-sodium diet.

E. *Llene el espacio con el nombre apropiado de una dieta.*

Modelo: Usted debe comer mucha carne, porque sigue una dieta
 con mucha proteína

1. Usted no debe comer papas, porque sigue una dieta

_____.

2. No le permite comer postres, porque sigue una dieta

_____.

3. No debe comer huevos, porque sigue una dieta

_____.

4. No le permite sal, porque sigue una dieta _____.
5. Usted debe comer muchos carbohidratos, porque sigue una dieta

_____.

6. Usted no debe sustituir los alimentos nutritivos, porque sigue una dieta _____.
7. Usted no puede comer ahora, porque sigue una dieta

_____ y todavía no llega de la cocina el plato especial.

8. Usted debe comer proteínas, carbohidratos, minerales, vitaminas y grasa, porque sigue una dieta _____.
9. Usted no debe comer ni mantequilla, ni mayonesa, porque sigue una dieta sin _____.
10. Usted debe comer mucha espinaca, porque sigue una dieta

_____.

Situación y simulación

You are a nurse who is helping Mrs. Ribera, a patient, to select the foods she will have for supper from the "Daily Menu" on the following page. Mrs. Ribera is on a _____ diet and can pick from selections number _____, _____, and _____. In addition, she is not allowed to drink _____ or eat _____ or _____. Since Mrs. Ribera speaks almost no English, you will have to explain her dietary options and restrictions and respond to her questions.

Using complete sentences, write, in dialogue format, the conversation that takes place between you and Mrs. Ribera. Include your explanation of each of the foods on the menu that she may select from, the restrictions on her diet, and the specific listed foods that she may not eat. Also include Mrs. Ribera's responses to your explanations and at least five questions from Mrs. Ribera about her diet and its restrictions. (Also provide your answers to her questions, of course.)

Juego

Write the Spanish vocabulary words for foods and beverages on large flash cards. The person leading the game holds up each card in front of the class and calls on students to give each word in a complete Spanish sentence, using one of the following three patterns:

1. No puedo comer (vocabulary word), porque sigo una dieta (type of diet).

   Modelo: No puedo comer *papas*, porque sigo una dieta *sin carbohidratos*.

2. No me gusta(n) (vocabulary word).
   Prefiero (alternative food or beverage).

   Modelo: No me gusta *pescado*.
   Prefiero *carne*.

3. No quiero (vocabulary word), porque no me gusta(a) (type of food).

   Modelo: No quiero *queso*, porque no me gustan *los productos lácteos*.

The game will go more smoothly if each of the patterns is dealt with separately. This can be done by posting in front of the class or writing on the board only one of the three patterns at a time during the game.

MENÚ

LISTA I   **Productos Lácteos**   Porción del día _____

leche 1 taza
yogurt 1 taza

una porción contiene:	
carbohidratos	12 gramos
proteínas	8 gramos
grasas	10 gramos
calorías	170

LISTA II   **Vegetales**   Porción del día _____

lechuga   coliflor   brócoli[1]
tomate   espárragos
habichuelas espinacas
zanahoria   cebolla
frijoles   apio

LISTA III   **Frutas**   Porción del día _____

manzana
plátano
melón

una porción contiene	
carbohidratos	10 gramos
calorías	40

dátiles   papaya   sandía
toronja   durazno   uvas
mango   pera
             naranja

LISTA IV   **Pan/Céréal/Carbohidrato**   Porción del día _____

pan
tortillas   (3)
galletas   (4)
papa   (1)
camote   (1)

una porción contiene	
carbohidratos	15 gramos
proteínas	2 gramos
calorías	70

LISTA V   **Carnes**   Porción del día _____

una porción contiene	
proteínas	7 gramos
grasas	5 gramos
calorías	75

carne de res o pollo   1 onza
pescado (trucha)   1 onza
salmón   media taza
camarones   5
queso   1 onza
huevo   1

LISTA VI   **Grasa**   Porción del día _____

una porción contiene	
grasa	5 gramos
calorías	45

mayonesa   1 cucharadita
aceite   1 cucharadita
nueces   6
mantequilla 1 cucharadita
aderezo   1 cucharada

1. Also, **brécol.**

VOCABULARIO

| SUSTANTIVOS DE NUTRICIÓN | NOUNS RELATED TO NUTRITION |

GRUPOS ALIMENTICOS

los carbohidratos
las proteínas
las grasas
las fibras

NUTRITIONAL GROUPS

carbohydrates
proteins
fats
fibers, roughage

ELEMENTOS NUTRITIVOS

las vitaminas
los minerales
el hierro
los ácidos

NUTRITIONAL ELEMENTS

vitamins
minerals
iron
acids

DIETAS

una dieta especial
    estricta
    balanceada
    con vitaminas[1]
    con proteínas
    con minerales
    sin sal
    sin carbohidratos
    sin grasa
    sin colesterol
    con pocos carbohidratos
    con poco sodio
    con poca sal

DIETS

a special diet
    strict
    balanced
    high-vitamin
    high-protein
    high-mineral
    salt-free
    carbohydrate-free
    fat-free
    cholesterol-free
    low carbohydrate
    low sodium
    low salt

ESPECIAS Y CONDIMENTOS

el azúcar
la sacarina
la sal
la pimienta
el aceite
el vinagre
el aderezo
la salsa picante
el ajo

SPICES AND CONDIMENTS

sugar
saccharine
salt
pepper
oil
vinegar
seasoning, dressing
hot sauce
garlic

1. **Con vitaminas** means *high-potency;* **con muchas vitaminas** means *containing many (different) vitamins.*

VEGETALES
(LEGUMBRES, VERDURAS)   VEGETABLES

el ajo	garlic
el apio	celery
el arroz	rice
el brócoli, brécol	broccoli
la cebolla	onion
los chícharos	peas
los coles de Bruselas	Brussels sprouts
la coliflor	cauliflower
los espárragos	asparagus
la espinaca	spinach
los frijoles	beans
los guisantes	peas
las habichuelas	green beans
los hongos	mushrooms
la lechuga	lettuce
la papa, patata	potato
el pepino	cucumber
el rábano	radish
el repollo	cabbage
la zanahoria	carrot

POSTRES   DESSERTS

el arroz con leche	rice pudding
el chocolate	chocolate
el coctel de frutas	fruit cocktail
los dulces	sweets, candy
el flan	flan, custard with caramel sauce
las galletas dulces	cookies
la gelatina	jello, gelatin, jelly
el helado	ice cream
el pastek	pie
el pudín	pudding
la tapioca	tapioca pudding
la torta	cake

UTENSILIOS   UTENSILS

la bandeja	tray
la cuchara	spoon
el cuchillo	knife
el plato	plate
el platillo	saucer
la sopera	soup tureen
la taza	cup
el tenedor	fork
la servilleta	napkin

BEBIDAS   BEVERAGES

el agua (feminine gender)	*water*
la bebida gaseosa sin alcohólica	*soda water, Coca-Cola, Sprite, etc.*
el café	*coffee*
la cerveza	*beer*
la leche	*milk*
el licor	*liquor*
la limonada	*lemonade*
el jugo de naranja	*orange juice*
_____ de manzana	*apple*
_____ de piña (ananá)	*pineapple*
_____ de tomate	*tomato*
_____ de toronja (pomelo)	*grapefruit*
el refresco	*refreshment*
el vino	*wine*

FRUTAS   FRUITS

el albaricoque	*apricot*
la cereza	*cherry*
la ciruela	*plum*
la cirucla pasa	*prune*
el dátil	*date*
el durazno	*peach*
la fresa	*strawberry*
la lima	*lime*
el limón	*lemon*
el mango	*mango*
la manzana	*apple*
el melón	*melon*
la naranja	*orange*
la papaya	*papaya*
la pera	*pear*
el plátano	*banana*
la piña, ananá	*pineapple*
la toronja, pomelo	*grapefruit*

CARNES   MEATS

el biftec	*steak*
la carne de cordero	*lamb*
la carne de puerco, cerdo	*pork*
la carne de res	*beef*
la carne de ternera	*veal*
el hígado	*liver*
el jamón	*ham*
el rosbif	*roast beef*
la salchicha	*sausage*
el tocino, la tocineta	*bacon*

AVES	POULTRY
el pavo guajalote (México)	*turkey*
el pollo	*chicken*
el pollo frito	*fried chicken*
el pollo asado	*roast chicken*

PESCADOS Y MARISCOS	SEAFOOD (FISH AND SHELLFISH)
el atún	*tuna*
el pescado	*fish*
los camarones	*shrimp*
el salmón	*salmon*

HUEVOS	EGGS
los huevos fritos	*fried eggs*
revueltos	*scrambled*
duros	*hard-boiled*
pasados por agua	*soft-boiled*
escalfados	*poached*
la tortilla	*omelette*

COMIDAS	MEALS
el desayuno	*breakfast*
el almuerzo	*lunch*
la cena	*supper*
la merienda	*snack*

PLATOS	DISHES
el aperitivo	*appetizer*
el pan	*bread*
la sopa	*soup*
el caldo	*broth*
la cacerola	*casserole*
la pasta	*pasta*
el plato principal	*main dish*
la ensalada	*salad*
la bebida	*beverage*
el vegetal	*vegetable*
la fruta	*fruit*
el postre	*dessert*
el sandwich	*sandwich*

PRODUCTOS LÁCTEOS	DAIRY PRODUCTS
la crema	cream
el helado	ice cream
la leche	milk
la mantequilla	butter
la margarina	margarine
el queso	cheese
el requesón	cottage cheese
el yogur	yogurt

SUSTANTIVOS GENERALES / GENERAL NOUNS

la dieta, estar de dieta	diet, to be on a diet
la fecha	date (calendar)
el hambre; (feminine) tener hambre	hunger; to be hungry
el hierro	iron
el, la jefe	boss
la libra	pound
el nivel	level
el peso	weight
el tubo	system; tube

VERBOS / VERBS

adelgazar	to lose weight
aguantar	to stand, put up with
aumentar	to increase
bajar, —de peso	to go down, —lose weight
contestar	to answer
chupar	to suck
deber	ought to
encantar	to charm
enfermar	to fall ill
escoger, elegir	to choose
evitar	to avoid
gustar	to please
marcar	to mark (telephone)
perder	to lose
poder	can, be able
recomendar	to recommend
seleccionar, elegir	to choose
seguir	to follow
traer	to bring
ver	to see

ADJETIVOS

balanceado-a
hinchado-a
mojado-a
seco-a

ADJECTIVES

balanced
swollen
damp
dry

ADVERBIOS

cuidadosamente
fácilmente
lentamente

ADVERBS

carefully
easily
slowly

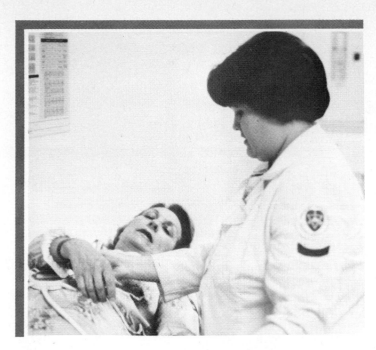

EN EL LABORATORIO

DIÁLOGO

Haciendo pruebas[1]

La técnica, Srta. Morales, está trabajando en el laboratorio. La Sra. Díaz llega para unos análisis.

Repita:

Srta. Morales	**Sra. Díaz**
	Buenas tardes, señorita.
Muy buenas tardes, señora. Josefina Morales, para servirle. ¿su nombre?	
	Me llamo Teresa Díaz.
Y su médico, ¿Cómo se llama él?	Mi médico se llama Dr. Evans.
¿Tiene usted la orden escrita del doctor?	
	Sí, aquí la tengo.

1. **Prueba** also is used to refer to a test in school.

Muy bien. Tenemos que examinar
la orina y la sangre. Vaya al cuarto
de baño y orine en este recipiente. Límpiese bien con la toallita de papel higiénico.

Muy bien.

Un poco más tarde . . .

Siéntese, por favor, y haga un puño.
Le voy a sacar sangre.

¿Duele mucho?

No se preocupe, Sra. Díaz. Apenas
duele. . . . Bueno, ya terminamos.
Abra la mano.

¡Qué alivio! Usted tiene razón: casi
no duele.

Pues, su médico obtendrá los resultados de los tests dentro de dos
días.

Muchas gracias, Srta. Morales.

Performing Tests

The technician, Miss Morales, is working in the laboratory. Mrs. Díaz arrives for some tests.

Repeat:

Miss Morales	Mrs. Díaz
	Good afternoon, miss.
A very good afternoon, ma'am. My name is Josefina Morales, at your service. What's your name?	My name is Teresa Díaz.
And your doctor, what's his name?	My doctor's name is Dr. Evans.
Do you have the written order from your doctor?	Yes, I have it here.
OK. We have to examine the (your) urine and blood. Go into the bathroom and urinate into this container. Clean yourself well with this antiseptic paper towelette.	Very well.

A little later . . .

Sit down, please, and make a fist. I'm going to draw blood.	Does this hurt much?
Don't worry, Mrs. Díaz. It hardly hurts. . . . All right, we're done already. Open your hand.	What a relief to finish that! You're right: it hardly hurts (almost doesn't hurt).
Well, your doctor will get the results of the tests within two days.	Thanks, Miss Morales.

FRASES ÚTILES

Sustituya:

Buenos días, señor. ¿Qué parte del cuerpo necesita ser examinada?	*Good day, sir. What part of your body needs examination?*
La pierna derecha.	*My right leg.*
La mano izquierda.	*My left hand.*
Vaya al cuarto de vestir.	*Go to the dressing room.*
_____ al otro lado del cuarto.	*___ to the other side of the room.*
_____ allí.	*___ (over) there.*
Muy bien.	*OK.*
Quítese la ropa y póngase esta bata.	*Take off your clothes and put on this gown.*
_____ este camisón.	*_____ this nightshirt.*
Bueno, ¿Dónde está el vestuario?	*OK. Where's the dressing room?*
Párese y pásese a esa mesa.	*Stand up and move over to that table.*
_____ la silla de ruedas.	*_____ the wheelchair.*
_____ la camilla.	*_____ the stretcher.*
¿Quiere usted ayudarme a andar?	*Will you help me walk?*
Espere hasta que le llame.[1]	*Wait until you're called.*
_____ llegue[1] el técnico.	*_____ the technician arrives.*
_____ le traigan[1] la silla de ruedas.	*_____ they bring you the wheelchair.*

1. The subjunctive form of the verb is used after **hasta que: llame (llamar); llegue (llegar); traigan (traer).**

Bueno, espero aquí.

OK, I'll wait here.

Siéntese sobre esta mesa.
Acuéstese _____.

Sit down on this table.
Lie down _____.

¿Debo quedarme aquí por mucho tiempo?

Do I have to stay here for long?

Levante la pierna.
_____ el brazo.
_____ el pie.

Raise your leg.
_____ your arm.
_____ your foot.

Bueno, pero me duele un poco.

OK, but it hurts me a bit.

Esté muy quieto.[2]
_____ tranquilo.

Be very still.
_____ quiet.

¿Por qué? ¿Duele esto?

Why? Does this hurt?

Respire hondo.
_____ profundamente.
_____ normalmente.
_____ rápidamente.

Breathe deeply.
_____ deeply.
_____ normally.
_____ rapidly.

¿Así?

Like this?

Mantenga[3] la respiración.

Hold your breath.

Es difícil hacerlo.
Me duele _____.

It's difficult to do it.
It hurts me _____.

Bájese de la mesa y siéntese aquí.

Get down from the table and sit here.

_____ la camilla
_____.

_____ the stretcher
_____.

---

2. **Esté muy quieto** (*Be very still*) is also expressed by **Cálmese.**

3. **Mantenga** (**mantener** = *to maintain*) or **contenga** (**contener** = *to contain*) can both be used.

Muy bien. ¿Quiere usted ayudarme?	*Very well. Will you help me?*
Acuéstese sin moverse.[4] Quédese allí _____.	*Lie down without moving. Stay here _____.*
¿Está usted casi terminado?	*Are you almost finished?*
Dóblese y quédese así. Voltéese[5] _____.	*Bend and stay that way. Turn _____.*
¿Quiere que me quede así?	*You want me to stay like this?*

El médico quiere una muestra de orina.

_____

sangre.

_____

excremento.

_____

glóbulos de sangre.

_____

expectoración.

_____

saliva.

The doctor wants a urine specimen.

_____ *blood*

_____.

_____ *fecal*

_____.

_____ *corpuscle*

_____.

_____ *sputum*

_____.

_____ *saliva*

_____.

Favor de poner la orina en este recipiente.

_____ el excremento

_____.

_____ la expectoración

_____.

_____ la saliva

_____.

Please put urine in this container.

_____ *excrement*

_____.

_____ *sputum*

_____.

_____ *saliva*

_____.

---

4. Or **y no se mueva** (*and don't move*).

5. **Dése vuelta** (**darse**) or **voltéese** (**voltearse**).

NOTA CULTURAL

1. The laboratory is one area where hospital personnel may be called on to carry through with extended conversations with the patient on subjects other than health care. Most of the subjects will revolve around social pleasantries, but medical personnel must keep in mind that the patient's interests can be mainly his family, friends, hobbies, politics, athletics (bullfight, soccer) and his concern for himself. The latter is what is known to sociologists as *personalismo*. Ask the patient questions about his town, his family or his country.

¿Qué opina usted de . . .? *(What is your opinion of . . .?)* will help start a conversation and put the patient at ease.

Ejercicios de conversación

A. *Sustituya el objeto directo por la palabra sugerida en paréntesis.*[1]

Modelo: Tenemos que examinar el estómago. (la paciente)
Tenemos que examinar a la paciente.

1. El técnico va a traer a la enfermera. (la silla de ruedas)
2. El médico necesita examinar los resultados. (el paciente operado)
3. La paciente tiene la muestra. (el recipiente)
4. Levante la pierna. (el brazo)
5. La paciente se baja de la cama. (la mesa)
6. La enfermera introduce[2] la sonda. (la jeringuilla)
7. El médico obtiene los resultados. (los archivos médicos)
8. La paciente va a seguir la dieta. (el dependiente)
9. Los pacientes hablan español. (el médico)
10. El paciente-ambulante llama mucha atención. (la enfermera)

1. Remember that in Spanish the preposition **a** is used when the object of the verb is a person. This grammatical process is called the *personal* **a.**

2. To introduce people socially in Spanish one must use the expression: **presentarle uno al otro. Introducir** means to introduce something (apparatus, etc.) into someone's body.

B. *Cambie los verbos al futuro, usando las formas de IR A y el infinitivo.*

   Modelo: El técnico le saca sangre al paciente.
   El técnico va a sacarle sangre al paciente.

   1. La paciente admitida se baja de la mesa.
   2. El señor enfermo se acuesta en la camilla.
   3. El paciente come los platos seleccionados.
   4. El médico viene al hospital por la mañana.
   5. El equipo de cirujanos le operan mañana temprano.
   6. La persona responsable paga la cuenta en la caja.
   7. El paciente del cuarto 405 se pone la bata limpia.
   8. La Señora Hurtado le toma los signos vitales a usted y le da los resultados.
   9. La cafetería para los clientes del hospital se abre a las once de la mañana.

C. *Traduzca al español.*

   Modelo: Mrs. García, go in the dressing room, please, remove your clothes, and put on this gown.
   Sra. García, vaya al vestuario, por favor, quítese la ropa, y póngase esta bata.

   1. I have to draw blood from you, sir. Sit here, please, and make a fist.
   2. The technician is bringing the written order from the doctor.
   3. The doctor needs a fecal specimen. Please use this container.
   4. Please go to the lab and wait in the waiting room.
   5. The nurse is going to bring the technician.

D. *Escoja la frase correcta.*

   1. Haga un puño, señorita.
      a. Vamos a examinar la pierna.
      b. Vamos a sacarle sangre.

   2. Acuéstese aquí en la mesa, por favor.
      a. Tenemos que examinar el estómago.
      b. Tenemos que examinar la orina.

   3. Usted no se preocupe porque no es nada grave.
      a. Es una prueba rutinaria.
      b. Es una prueba de 10 horas.

   4. La señora se sube la manga.
      a. Le va a tomar los signos vitales.
      b. Va a introducirle una sonda.

   5. Póngase esta bata y espere en la sala de espera.
      a. Tenemos que examinar el nivel de colesterol en la sangre.
      b. Tenemos que sacarle una radiografía.

E. *Escriba las frases siguientes en forma de mandatos.*

Modelo: La señorita se sienta sobre la camilla.
Siéntese sobre la camilla, señorita.

1. El señor va al cuarto de vestir.
2. La señora se queda allí.
3. El visitante dobla a la izquierda y se baja en el ascensor.
4. El paciente nuevo se acuesta a las ocho.
5. La señora cubana se calma y descansa.
6. El paciente respira profundamente.
7. La paciente joven se inclina hacia al médico.
8. Sé que usted tiene mucho dolor. ¿Me indica dónde tiene el dolor?
9. La señora se sube la manga porque le va a tomar los signos vitales.
10. La señora Díaz se voltea en la mesa boca arriba.

Situación y simulación

A. You are working in the laboratory when Mr. Cuevas, a Spanish-speaking patient comes in. His doctor's order says that he needs blood and urine specimens taken as well as _____ and _____. His doctor will receive the results of these tests in three days. After you take the required specimens, Mr. Cuevas is to go to X-ray.

Write out, in dialogue format, the conversation that takes place between you and Mr. Cuevas, including your instructions to him for obtaining each of the specimens, your explanation of when his doctor will have the test results, and your directions to help him find the X-ray department. Also include Mr. Cuevas's replies to you and several questions he asks you about his tests or their results.

B. You are a technician who must take X-rays of Miss Martínez, an outpatient who speaks very little English. Her doctor's order says her X-ray series must cover the following areas: chest, lower lumbar region, right kneecap, left forearm, and right heel.

Write out, in dialogue format, the conversation that takes place between you and Miss Martínez, including your request for her doctor's order, your request for her to remove her clothing and put on a gown, and your instructions to her for each of the X-rays you must take. Also include Miss Martínez's replies and several questions that she asks you about her X-rays or their results.

Juego

Write out in English on separate slips of paper a number of imaginary instructions from physicians for medical tests that need to be run on a patient. (Have enough instructions for everyone in the class.) One such instruction, for instance, might read:

> Blood and urine specimens must be obtained from the patient, and _____, _____, and _____ tests must be performed. After specimens have been taken and tests performed, the patient should be sent to _____.

Fold the slips and mix them in a container. Each class member takes a turn as the "patient." He or she picks a slip, chooses another student to be the "technician," and presents the "technician" with the slip containing instructions from the "patient's" physician for the tests that are to be run. The "technician" silently reads the instructions, then converses with the "patient," making the requests and giving the instructions that would be necessary to help the "patient" through the tests. "Patients" are to comply (insofar as possible) with "technician's" instructions and requests (e.g., by sitting where asked, making a fist, pretending to accept a specimen container, etc.). "Patients" are also encouraged to question "technicians" about instructions or requests that may be unclear, and to ask any other questions about the tests or their results that may seem appropriate.

PALABRAS COGNADAS

Read through the clinical analysis lab forms on pages 138–139 and note the cognate words, which are numerous. The words that have no English cognates are listed in the *Vocabulario* in the back of the book.

LABORATORIOS DE ANALISIS CLINICOS   ORDEN NUM

Médico solicitante:

(clave y firma)
Fecha de la solicitud

Diagnóstico de Presunción o datos clínicos

Unidad:

Servicio:

Externo ☐   Cama Núm.:

Fecha Próxima consulta

Cita: _____ Hora

Nombre:

Núm. de Registro

Calidad:

OTROS ESTUDIOS:

RESULTADOS:

OBSERVACIONES:

OTROS ESTUDIOS

Nombre y firma del responsable

Fecha

138

LABORATORIOS DE ANALISIS CLINICOS   ORDEN NUM.

Médico solicitante:	Unidad: _____	Cita: _____ Hora: _____
(Clave y firma)	Servicio _____	Nombre _____
	Externo ☐ Cama Núm _____	No. de Registro _____
Fecha de la solicitud: _____	Fecha Próxima consulta: _____	Calidad: _____

Diagnóstico de Presunción o datos clínicos _____

100.-GLUCOSA _____ mg.	109.-COLESTEROL TOTAL _____ mg.	120.-FOSFATASA ACIDA _____ Us.
101.-UREA _____ mg.	110.-ESTERIFICACION _____	121.-AMILASA _____ Us.
103.-CREATININA _____ mg.	111.-BILIRRUBINAS _____	152.-DEHIDROGENASA LACTICA _____
107.-TOLERANCIA A LA	_____ a) Directa _____	_____ Us.
GLUCOSA _____	_____ b) Indirecta _____	122.-FOSFORO _____ mg.
60′ _____ mg.		12.-CALCIO _____ mg.
120′ _____ mg.	112.-BROMOSULFALEINA _____	124.-CO2 _____ mEq/L
180′ _____ mg.	_____ T. Retención _____ por 100	125.-PH _____
132.-GENERAL DE ORINA _____	113.-CEFALINA _____	126.-CLORO _____ mEq/L
Volumen _____	114.-TIMOL _____	127.-POTASIO _____ mEq/L
Densidad _____	Turbiedad: _____ Us.	128.-SODIO _____ mEq/L
pH _____	Floculación _____ 18 hs.	102.-ACIDO URICO _____ mg.
Albúmina _____ g/1		
Glucosa _____ g/1	115.-PROTEINAS TOTALES _____ g.	Otros Estudios _____
Acetona _____	_____ Albúminas _____ g.	_____
Bilirrubina _____	_____ Globulinas _____ g.	_____
Hemoglobina _____	_____ Relación A/G _____	_____
Sedimento.-Objetivo seco Fuerte _____	117.-TRANSAMINASA OXALACETICA _____	_____
Leucocitos _____ Por campo _____	_____ Us.	_____
Eritrocitos _____ Por campo _____	118.-TRANSAMINASA PIRUVICA _____	_____
Cilindros _____ Por campo _____	_____ Us.	_____
	119.-FOSFATASA ALCALINA _____	_____
133.-CALCIO EN ORINA _____	_____ Us.	_____

QUIMICA CLINICA-1-

_____
(Nombre y firma del responsable)

_____
Fecha

VOCABULARIO

SUSTANTIVOS

NOUNS

la camilla	stretcher
el camisón	night shirt, gown
el equipo	equipment
el excremento	bowel movement, excrement
el fosfato	phosphate
el glóbulo	corpuscle
la jeringuilla	syringe
el lado	side
la muestra	specimen
el nivel	level
la orden	order
la prueba	test
el puño	fist
la radiografía	X-ray
la razón; tener razón	reason; to be right
la silla de ruedas	wheelchair
la sonda	catheter
el vestuario	dressing room

VERBOS

abrir	to open
abra	open
bajarse	to go down, to lower one's self
calmarse	to calm down
descansarse	to rest
doblarse	to bend, to turn
doler (duele)	to hurt, ache
esperar	to wait
hacer	to do, to make
bájese	go down
cálmese	calm down
déscanse	relax, rest
dóblese	turn, bend
hagar	to make
inclinarse	to bend forward
indicar	to show, to indicate
introducir	to introduce into the body, to interject
limpiarse	to clean one's self
mantener	to maintain
obtener	to obtain
pasarse	to move over
	to swallow
ponerse	to put on
preocuparse	to worry
quedarse	to stay
respirar	to breathe
sacar	to draw blood
	to photograph
sentarse	to sit down
subirse	to go up
traer	to bring
vestirse	to dress
voltearse	to turn over

ADJETIVOS

fuerte	strong
grave	serious
higiénico, -a	hygienic
limpio, -a	clean
rutinario, -a	routine
seco, -a	dry
sucio, -a	dirty
tranquillo, -a	quiet, still

ADVERBIOS

apenas
así
casi

ADVERBS

barely, scarcely
thus, this way
almost

PREPOSICIONES

dentro de

PREPOSITIONS

within

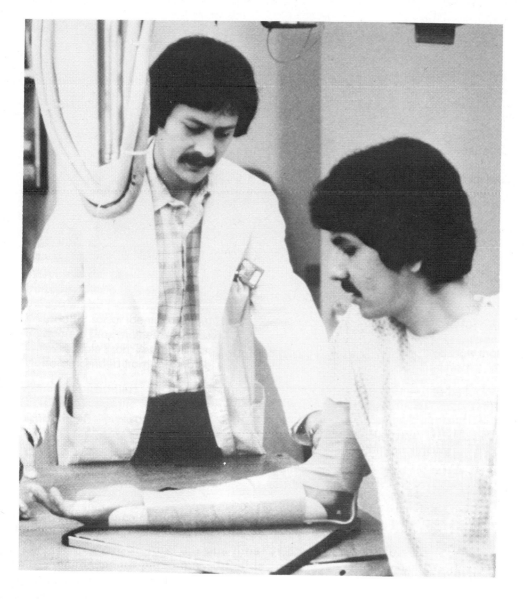

SEGUNDA PRUEBA

Preguntas acerca de la lección quinta

A. *Complete con la forma correcta de una palabra interrogativa.*

Modelo: ¿*Cómo* se siente usted esta tarde, Sr. Romero?

1. ¿_____ dolor tiene en el pecho? Si tiene mucho, voy a llamar al médico en seguida.
2. ¿_____ catarros tiene usted al mes?
3. ¡Adelante! ¡Pase! ¿_____ es?
4. ¿_____ es su motivo de venir al hospital?
5. Sabe usted ¿_____ abre la cafetería?

B. *Conteste en oraciones completas.*

Modelo: *Me duele aquí en el estómago.*
¿Dónde tiene el dolor? ¿Aquí arriba en el pecho o más bajo en el estómago?

1. Usted me dice que tiene vértigo. ¿Qué otros síntomas tiene?
2. ¿Cuándo tiene náuseas?
3. ¿Tiene usted la respiración corta después de subir la escalera?
4. ¿Cómo se siente hoy? ¿Le gusta la medicina nueva?
5. Según el médico, ¿cuántas tabletas tiene que tomar usted?

C. *Traduzca al español.*

Modelo: *Después de comer, ¿tiene dolor de estómago o eructos?*
   After you eat, do you have a stomachache or belching?

1. In the past month, how many times have you lost consciousness?
2. Do you have shortness of breath when you sit, too?
3. After walking a lot, do you cough a lot?
4. Show me where you have pain. Can you describe the pain?
5. You will have to stay in the hospital for several months.
6. I don't know how many colds I have a year.
7. How many times a day do you have a headache?
8. Are you dizzy? Do you need to sit down?
9. Do you often have pain in your chest, near your heart?
10. Do you have a good appetite? Are you hungry now?

D. *Escoja la respuesta correcta.*

1. ¿Tiene usted problemas al respirar?
   a. Sí, tengo problemas con la presión alta de la sangre.
   b. No, casi nunca tengo dolores de cabeza.
   c. Sí, tengo la respiración corta.

2. ¿Cuántos catarros tiene usted al año?
   a. Varias veces, según la receta.
   b. No sé exactamente.
   c. Frecuentemente, al primero del mes.

3. ¿Cuándo se siente peor?
   a. Después de bañarme.
   b. Después de bañar al paciente.
   c. Después del mes de junio.

4. ¿Es la primera vez que tiene usted esta condición?
   a. No, es la tercera vez.
   b. Sí, varias veces.
   c. Tengo eructos con esta condición.

5. ¿Cuándo tiene náuseas?
   a. Me mareo muchas veces.
   b. Al levantarme.
   c. A la enfermera.

Preguntas acerca de la lección sexta

A. *Escriba cada oración según el modelo.*

   Modelo: *Tengo problemas frecuentes con esta medicina.*
   He tenido problemas frecuentes con esta medicina.

   1. ¿Toma usted las dos píldoras azules?
   2. Hablo con la enfermera acerca de la alergia que tiene el paciente.
   3. ¿Duerme usted bien?
   4. La paciente come toda la ensalada y la carne.
   5. ¿Regresa la enfermera de la sala de operaciones?

B. *Conteste en español, usando la palabra o frase sugerida.*

   Modelo: *Usted va a la terapia física a la una.*
   ¿Cuándo voy a la terapia física? (*la una*)

   1. ¿Cuál de estas medicinas debo tomar ahora? (*el líquido verde*)
   2. ¿Cuándo debo tomar las cápsulas? (*cada cuatro horas*)
   3. ¿Qué clase de medicina me va a dar el médico ahora? (*un antibiótico*)
   4. ¿Cuándo puedo tomar un tranquilizante? (*más tarde*)
   5. ¿Quién me va a enseñar los ejercicios físicos? (*la terapista*)

C. *Traduzca al español.*

   Modelo: You should take half a teaspoonful now and one more teaspoonful at three-thirty.
   Usted debe tomar media cucharadita ahora y una cucharadita
   más a las tres y media.

   1. I don't know exactly what type of medicine it is. The nurse knows.
   2. Mr. Bermúdez, you shouldn't take a laxative with that medicine.
   3. Can you describe the pain? Is it sharp and burning?
   4. I am here to show you how to do physical exercises. First, please
      stretch your legs and arms. Rotate your head to the left and then to
      the right.
   5. Will you allow me to take your vital signs?

D. *Escoja la respuesta correcta.*

1. Usted debe tomar estas
   píldoras ahora.
      a. Muy bien, los tomo.
      b. Muy bien, las tomo.

2. ¿Ha tomado usted la cápsula
   azul?
      a. No, nadie me la dio.
      b. No, nadie me los dio.

3. La paciente habla a la
   enfermera.
      a. Sí, la habla frecuentemente.
      b. Sí, lo habla frecuentemente.

4. ¿Quiere usted hacer los
   ejercicios físicos?
      a. No los quiero hacer.
      b. No lo quiero hacer.

5. ¿Va a sacar sangre el técnico?
      a. Sí, la ha sacado.
      b. Sí, lo saca en seguida.

Preguntas acerca de la lección séptima

A. *Escoja las traducciones correctas.*

1. _____ el queso.
2. _____ el postre.
3. _____ el pescado.
4. _____ los vegetales
   secos.
5. _____ la lechuga.

   a. fish
   b. cheese
   c. lettuce
   d. dessert
   e. dry vegetables

B. *Conteste en oraciones completas.*

Modelo: En esta dieta especial, ¿me permite comer pescado?
    Sí, le permite comer pescado, pero no debe comer postres.

1. ¿Cuánto peso debo perder a la semana?
2. ¿Qué clase de huevos prefiere usted?
3. Para bajar el nivel de colesterol en la dieta, ¿qué clase de proteínas
   debo evitar?
4. Para bajar de peso, ¿qué dieta debo seguir?
5. Después de ser operado, ¿qué puedo beber?
6. Señor, no se le permite comer postre, ¿qué quiere como sustitución?
7. ¿Le gustan las comidas con especias?
8. ¿Qué le gusta comer en el desayuno, en el almuerzo y en la cena?
9. Usted no debe seguir una dieta con muchos carbohidratos porque
   debe adelgazar un poco. ¿Cuánto pesa usted ahora?
10. ¿Cuál le gusta más, el requesón o el yogur?

C. *Complete con el nombre de los alimentos correspondientes.*

Modelo: Porque usted sigue una dieta sin carbohidratos, *no* debe
comer *azúcar, postres, muchas papas, etc.*

1. Porque usted sigue una dieta sin proteínas, no debe comer
_____.

2. Porque usted sigue una dieta con proteínas, no debe comer
_____.

3. Porque usted sigue una dieta balanceada, debe comer
_____.

4. Porque usted sigue una dieta con poca sal, usted no debe comer
_____.

5. Porque usted sigue una dieta sin grasa, usted no debe comer
_____.

D. *Escoja el alimento correspondiente a cada grupo alimenticio.*

1. _____ un postre   **a.** el requesón
2. _____ un vegetal   **b.** el jamón
3. _____ una carne   **c.** el pan
4. _____ un producto   **d.** la zanahoria
     lácteo   **e.** el flan
5. _____ un cereal

Preguntas acerca de la lección octava

A. *Traduzca al español.*

Modelo: Your doctor will get the results of the tests tomorrow.
Su médico obtendrá los resultados de las pruebas mañana.

1. Sit down on the table, please, and raise your left leg.
2. Wait until the technician arrives with the doctor's written order.
3. Please sit down and make a fist.
4. Go to the dressing room, take off your clothes and put on this gown.
5. The doctor wants a urine specimen. Please clean yourself, and urinate
   in this container.

B. *Conteste las siguientes preguntas usando la frase en paréntesis usando la palabra o frase sugerida.*

Modelo: *Usted tiene que analizar la orina y la sangre.*
¿Qué tengo que analizar? (la orina y la sangre)

1. ¿Qué parte del cuerpo necesita examinar? (*el estómago*)
2. ¿Debo quedarme aquí por mucho tiempo? (*media hora más*)
3. ¿Qué va a ponerle la enfermera? (*una intravenosa*)
4. ¿Cuándo va a obtener los resultados de la prueba? (*una semana*)
5. ¿Cuál necesito levantar primero, el brazo o la pierna? (*el brazo*)

C. *Cambie los verbos usando las formas de IR A y el infinitivo.*

Modelo: La paciente abre la mano.
La paciente va a abrir la mano.

1. El paciente se pone esta bata.
2. La mano derecha necesita terapia física.
3. La enferma se baja de la camilla.
4. El señor cubano consulta ahora con el médico.
5. La terapista enseña los ejercicios físicos por la mañana.

D. *Escriba las frases siguientes en forma de mandatos.*

Modelo: La Sra. Morales se sienta en la silla de ruedas.
Sra. Morales, siéntese en la silla de ruedas.

1. El Sr. Ramírez va al otro lado del cuarto.
2. La señorita se pone de pie y pasa a la mesa.
3. El técnico llama a la enfermera.
4. El doctor Huerta se baja en el ascensor y dobla a la derecha.
5. La señorita Díaz me trae la cuenta correcta.

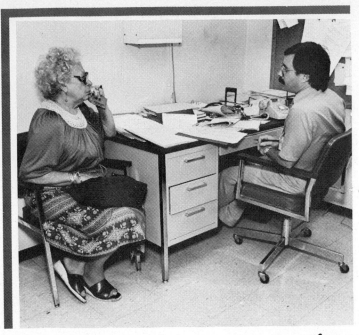

LA SALUD PÚBLICA

DIÁLOGO

La familia y los problemas modernos

La Sra. Valdéz, una viuda, es la paciente del Dr. Cortés, a quien consulta ahora sus problemas de familia.

Sra. Valdéz

Buenas tardes, doctor. Aquí tengo una copia del aviso a los padres de familia, para que nuestros niños reciban la vacuna contra la polio.

Bien, gracias.

Dr. Cortés

Muy buenas, señora. Siéntese aquí, por favor. ¿Cómo está la familia? ¿Sabe usted que la vacuna contra la polio es gratis? Le aconsejo que su niño la reciba lo más pronto posible.

¿Adónde debo dirigirme para conseguir la vacuna?

Usted debe dirigirse al Centro de Salud Pública, donde le ofrecen muchos servicios médicos gratuitos. Llame o visite el departamento de enfermedades comunicables.

¡Ay de mí! Creo que todo el mundo tiene problemas.
¿Qué se yo? Trato de aceptar lo que Dios me manda. (*Empieza a llorar*)

¿Pasa algo en su familia?

¡Pobrecita! Cálmese y cuénteme todo.

No comprendo, ¿por qué tengo que firmar este aviso?

Bueno, de acuerdo con la ley de inmunizaciones, usted debe llevar a sus hijos en edad preescolar al Centro y firmar la nota de autorización. No demore, señora, por favor.

Debe tener razón. En estos días estoy muy preocupada. Mi suegra tiene el cáncer y yo tengo miedo de contraerlo.

Señora, no se preocupe. Sabemos que el cáncer no es contagioso; sin embargo, es importante conocer las siete señales de aviso del cáncer. Si usted tiene cualquiera de estas señales de aviso, visíteme. Llame a la recepcionista y haga una cita.

Muy bien, gracias. Así lo haré.

Pasando a otro tema, ¿cómo está su sobrina Elisa?

Bastante bien. El viernes va a celebrar su quinceañera.

¡El viernes! ¿Ya tiene quince años? ¡Increíble!

Así, lo ve. La familia tiene problemas porque ella sale con su novio Jorge todo el tiempo. Están enamorados y . . . la tentación y la voluntad necesaria . . . Me preocupo mucho por ella.

Usted no está equivocada. El tener relaciones sexuales a esa edad no es raro. Es mejor ofrecerles informes sobre la contracepción. Tengo un folleto aquí que explica

Y mi hermano sigue tomando las drogas. Confieso que no va a mejorarse sin ayuda.

Muchas gracias, doctor. Adiós.

Más tarde . . .

la planificación de la familia. Vea la primera página. Si necesita más información, diríjase al Centro de Salud Pública.

Le aconsejo que aproveche los servicios del Centro, no sólo para los informes sobre la contracepción o control de nacimiento, sino también para las enfermedades venéreas, la ayuda al drogadicto y al alcohólico. Mi secretaria va a darle la dirección. ¡Que le vaya bien!

Sra. Valdéz	**La secretaria**
Señorita, ¿puede decirme dónde ofrecen ayuda a los alcohólicos?	¿Quiere usted los números de teléfonos?
Realmente, no sé qué hacer . . .	Primero, llame a los servicios informativos especializados que están en la guía telefónica (el directorio), en las páginas amarillas.
Ay, pero tengo dificultad con el inglés. Apenas lo leo.	Entonces, llame a la operadora o a su sacerdote. ¿Es usted católica?
Sí, y mi sacerdote es bilingüe.	¡Ay, qué suerte! También en el Centro de Salud Pública dan material impreso bilingüe. Hay una organización que se llama «Alcohólicos Anónimos» que ofrece ayuda a sus miembros y a sus parientes. Visite el Centro para saber dónde queda la más cercana a su casa. También puede llamar al departamento de Policía.[1]
Ah, bien. Me siento mejor. Voy a lla-	

1. **Los federales, los rurales la guardia** (**nacional, civil**) etc. are other types of police organizations.

mar al Centro de Salud Pública y después al Servicio Social a ver si puedo obtener el dinero para pagar los gastos. Mil gracias por todo.

De nada, señora.

Public Health:
The Family and Modern Problems

Mrs. Valdéz is a widow, and a patient of Dr. Cortés with whom she is consulting now the problems of her family.

Mrs. Valdéz	Dr. Cortés
Good afternoon, doctor. Here I have a copy of the note to the parents, so that our children can have the vaccine against poliomyelitis.	
	Good afternoon, Ma'am. Please, sit down here. How is the family?
Well, thanks.	Do you know that the vaccine against polio is free? I advise you to have your child vaccinated as soon as possible.
Where can I go to get the vaccine?	You must go to the Public Health Center where many medical services are offered free of charge. Call or visit the department of communicable diseases.
Oh, my! I think everybody has problems.	What else is going on in your family?
What do I know? I try to accept whatever God has in store for me. (*She starts crying.*)	Poor thing! Calm down and tell me everything.
I don't understand. Why do I have to sign this paper?	OK. According to the law that requires immunization, you must take your preschool-aged child to the Center and sign your authorization. Please, don't delay, Ma'am.
You must be right. These days I am very worried. My mother-in-law has cancer, and I am afraid (that I will) catch it.	Ma'am, don't worry. We know that cancer is not contagious. Nevertheless, it is important to be acquainted with the seven warning signs of cancer. If you have any of these warning signs, see me. Call the receptionist and make an appointment.
Very well, thanks. I'll do it.	By the way, how is your niece, Elisa?

Pretty well. She celebrates her fifteenth birthday on Friday.

So, you see! The family has problems because she goes out with her boy friend George all the time. They are in love and . . . the temptation and the necessary willpower. . . . I worry a lot about her.

And my brother continues taking drugs. I admit that he isn't going to improve without help.

Thanks a lot, doctor. Good-bye!

Later . . .

Mrs. Valdéz

Miss, can you tell me where it's possible to get help for alcoholics?
Really, I don't know what to do . . .

Ah, but I have problems with English. I can hardly read it.

Yes, and my priest is bilingual.

Oh, good. I feel better already. I am going to call the Public Health Center first, and then the Social Service to see if

On Friday! She is already fifteen years old? That is incredible!

You are not wrong. Having sex at that age is not rare. It's better to offer them information about contraception. I have a folder here that explains family planning. Look at page one. If you need more information, go to the Public Health Center.

I advise you to take advantage of the services offered by this Center not only on contraception or birth control, but also on venereal disease, the treatment of the drug addict and the alcoholic. My secretary is going to give you the address. I hope everything goes well!

The secretary

Do you want the telephone numbers?
First, call the specialized information service, which is in the telephone book (directory), in the yellow pages.

Then, call the operator or the priest. Are you a Catholic?
Oh, how lucky! Also, the Public Health Center offers bilingual printed materials. There is an organization called "Alcoholics Anonymous" that offers help to its members and their relatives. Visit the Center to find out where is the closest one to your home. You can also call the Police Department.

I can get enough money to pay the expenses. Many thanks for everything.

Don't mention it.

FRASES ÚTILES

¿Adónde debo dirigirme?
¿————————— ir?
¿————————— llamar?

Where should I go to?
————————— I go?
————————— I call?

Al Centro de Salud Pública.
— departamento de Policía.
— enfermedades comunicables.

To the Public Health Center.
————— Police Department.
————— department of communicable diseases.

¿Qué ofrece el Centro?
Ayuda a los niños.
————————— alcohólicos.
————————— drogadictos.

What does the Center offer?
It helps children.
————— alcoholics.
————— drug addicts.

¿Qué informes da el Centro?

What information does the Center give?

Sobre la planificación de la familia.
————— la contracepción.
————— el control de nacimiento.
————— las enfermedades venéreas.

About family planning.
————— contraception.
————— birth control.
————— venereal diseases.

¿Quién puede ayudarme?

Who can help me?

Puede ayudarle el médico.
————————— el sacerdote.
————————— la operadora.

The doctor can help you.
The priest —————————.
The operator —————————.

¿Cuánto cuesta el servicio médico?

How much does the medical service cost?

Es gratis.
— gratuito.

It is free.
———— free of charge.

NOTA CULTURAL

1. Teenage pregnancy is a difficult problem for all parents, and Hispanics are not an exception. In general, Hispanic culture strongly condemns premarital sex and the seeking of information to avoid pregnancy. However, once a girl has become pregnant and the family accepts the fact, everyone will pitch in and help the young mother. Studies show that when a girl becomes pregnant under the age of fifteen, she is likely to become pregnant again if she is not given adequate birth control instruction. In most cases, dissemination of this instruction will be hampered by:

   a) the language barrier
   b) the teachings of the Catholic Church—90 percent of Hispanics are Catholic
   c) the **macho** syndrome, which purports to emphasize manhood by fathering a child

Ejercicios de conversación

Conteste en español las siguientes preguntas.

   1. ¿Adónde se debe dirigir para obtener la vacuna contra la polio?
   2. ¿Cuánto cuesta la vacuna en el Centro de Salud Pública?
   3. ¿Dónde se puede conseguir impresos bilingües que traten de los problemas del drogadicto, alcohólico, etc.?
   4. ¿Cuál división del centro de Salud Pública tiene informes sobre la vacuna?
   5. ¿Cuáles son los términos para explicar la planificación de la familia?

Situación y simulación

You are a secretary in a doctor's office and one of his patients drops by without an appointment. The patient becomes very nervous and upset and needs to talk with someone about his/her family problems. You offer coffee and sympathy and try to give as much help and information as possible. Remember to ask the patient where he/she lives, who is in his/her family . . . all the personal information so that the patient can be readily identifiable to the doctor. Give the patient several ideas as to how he/she may help him/herself and as many sources of information concerning family problems as possible. Also, remember to ask about all of the relatives (the brother-in-law, the daughter-in-law, the niece and all the grandchildren).

PALABRAS COGNADAS

Read through the following form noting the cognate words. Words that don't have English cognates appear in the *Vocabulario*.

NO DEMORE . . .
INMUNICELOS HOY!

- **Sin Citas**
- **Sin Lineas**
- **Sin Esperas**
- **Sin Cobros**

Departamento de Salud Publica de la Cuidad de Houston
Centros de Salud

Muchos niños de edad escolar y pre-escolar no han recibido todas las inmunizaciones recomendadas. Compare las tarjetas de inmunizaciones de sus niños con el horario de inmunizaciones recomendadas:

Edad	Vacunaciones
2 Meses	• DPT (Difteria-Tos Ferina-Tétanos), Polio
4 Meses	• DPT, Polio
6 Meses	• DPT, Polio
6-12 Meses	• Prueba de Tuberculina
15 Meses	• Vacuna combinada de Sarampión, Rubéola y Paperas
12-24 Meses	• Refuerzo para DPT y Polio
4-5 Años	• Refuerzo para DPT y Polio
Mayores de 5 Años (Incluyendo Adultos)	• Refuerzo para DT (Difteria-Tétanos) cada 10 Años. Prueba de Tuberculina para entrar en los distritos escolares, si es un requisito.

(Este itinerario puede variar para diferentes personas — pregúntele a su médico)

Inmunizaciones y pruebas de tuberculina para niños se pueden obtener AHORA, en los siguientes centros de salud de la ciudad:

Canal	7228 Canal	921-2134
Casa de Amigos	1906 Cochran	224-3194
Fidelity	9525 Clinton	676-2171
Lyons	5602 Lyons Avenue	675-7531
Northside	8504 Schuller	697-4878
Ripley House	4401 Lovejoy	921-2117
Riverside	3315 Delano	526-4277
Sunnyside	9314 Cullen	734-6699
West End	190 Heights Blvd.	869-5951

Traiga las tarjetas de inmunizaciones de sus niños con Ud. NO DEMORE . . . INMUNICELOS HOY! Si usted no puede usar esta informacion, pásela a alguna persona que si puede. Gracias!

Inmunizaciones y pruebas de tuberculina también se pueden obtener en las unidades móviles en los siguientes sitios:

Efectivo a Septiembre 30, 1979			
LUNES	8:30 A.M. - 12:00 Noon	Bracewell Library	Weingartens
	1:00 P.M. - 3.30 P.M.	10115 Kleckley	239-W. 20th
MARTES	8:30 A.M. - 12:00 Noon	Vinson Library	Weingartens
	1:00 P.M. - 3:30 P.M.	3100 West Fuqua	7061 Lawndale
MIERCALES	8:30 A.M. - 12:00 Noon	Ring Library	Palm Center Shopping Center
	1:00 P.M. - 3:30 P.M.	8835 Long Point	5280 Griggs
JUEVES	8:30 A.M. - 12:00 Noon	Weingartens	Westwood Shopping Center
	1:00 P.M. - 3:30 P.M.	5815 Lockwood	Southwest Freeway & Bissonnet
VIERNES	8:30 A.M. - 12:00 Noon	Sage	Oak Forest Library
	1:00 P.M. - 3:30 P.M.	4645 Beechnut	1349 W. 43rd

City of Houston Health Department

VOCABULARIO

SUSTANTIVOS

la ansiedad	*anxiety*
el aviso	*notice*
la ayuda	*help*
la cita	*appointment, date*
el drogadicto	*drug addict*
la edad	*age*
el folleto	*folder*
la guía	*guide*
el horario	*schedule*
la hoja	*page (leaf)*
la inmunización	*immunization*
el impreso	*printed matter*
el jefe	*boss*
la ley	*law*
el mundo	*world*
el nacimiento	*birth*
el novio	*sweetheart, steady*
el sacerdote	*priest*
la señal	*sign*
el sitio	*place, site*
la tarjeta	*card*
el tratamiento	*treatment*
la vacuna	*vaccine*
la viuda	*widow*
la voluntad	*will, will power*

NOUNS

VERBOS

aconsejar	*to advise*
aprovecharse de	*to profit by*
ayudar	*to help*
creer	*to believe*
confesar	*to admit*
conseguir	*to get*
contar	*to tell, to count*
dejar	*to leave, to drop*
demorar	*to delay*
dirigirse	*to go to*
enterarse de	*to be informed of*
escuchar	*to listen to*
fijarse en	*to notice*
firmar	*to sign*
ingresar	*to enroll*

VERBS

leer	*to read*
llevar	*to carry*
querer	*to want*
requerir	*to require*
vacunar	*to vaccinate*
ver	*to see*

ADJETIVOS

ADJECTIVES

cercana	*near*
disponible	*available*
enamorado, -a	*enamored, in love*
gratis	*free*
gratuito	*free of charge*
ligero, -a	*light*
preescolar	*pre-school*

ADVERBIOS

ADVERBS

bastante	*quite, sufficiently*
ya	*already*

FRASES ÚTILES

EXPRESSIONS

¡Pobrecita!	*Poor thing!*
¡Qué le vaya bien!	*Hope everything goes well!*
Adiós	*Good-bye*
¡Qué suerte!	*How lucky!*
De nada.	*Don't mention it.*

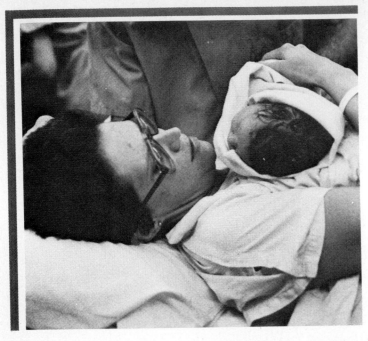

LA MATERNIDAD: I

DIÁLOGO

La historia del embarazo y la planificación de la familia

La señora López está encinta con su cuarto hijo y habla francamente con su médico en la sala de consulta.[1]

Repita:

Sra. López	**El Dr. Fernández**
Buenos días, doctor.	Buenos días, señora. Tengo que hacerle unas preguntas sobre la historia de su embarazo. ¿Esta criatura va a ser la cuarta, no?
Sí, si Dios quiere.	¿Cómo se siente hoy? No ha aumentado mucho de peso. Sólo 15 kilos.

1. Also, **el consultorio.**

Bastante bien, gracias.

Tengo dos.

Se me murió en el parto; un nacido muerto.[2]

No. Nunca he tenido un aborto, gracias a Dios.

Tampoco.

No, prefiero la anestesia local o quizás una raquídea según me dice.

Biberón. Doctor, ahora tengo dolores frecuentes. No me siento muy bien.

Veamos . . . cada cinco minutos creo yo.

¿Cuántos niños tiene usted?

¿Y el tercero?

Mi sentido pésame. ¿Ha tenido usted un aborto accidental o provocado?

¿Ni una operación cesárea tampoco?

¿Quiere usted un parto natural?

Señora, si usted no se siente muy mal, puede tener un parto muy fácil. Le aconsejo que escoja la anestesia local. ¿Quiere darle el pecho o el biberón al niño?

Mmm. (*Escribe en su cuaderno.*)

¿Con qué frecuencia?

Muy bien, acuéstese y descanse. Voy a llamar a la enfermera para que espere el parto con usted.

Más tarde la enfermera registrada entra en el cuarto de la señora López para atenderla antes del parto.

La Enfermera

Buenas tardes, señora, tengo que prepararla y afeitarla.

Sí, tener un niño, un angelito, es un milagro de la creación.

Muy bien. Aquí tiene un folleto. Léalo y si no lo entiende puede hacerle preguntas al médico. Bueno, por fin, termino. Ahora

Sra. López

¡Ay de mi¡ Es tan fastidioso pero vale la pena si uno quiere dar a luz[3] un niño.

Sí, lo sé, pero quiero saber más acerca del control de natalidad.

2. **Un nacido muerto** or **muerto alnacer** = *stillborn.*

3. **Dar a luz** = *to give light* (lit.), *to give birth;* also, **partir.**

tengo que tomarle los signos vitales.

Muy bien, inmediatamente. ¿Cómo se siente?

Entra el médico:

Me han dicho que usted quiere hablar conmigo acerca de los métodos de control de natalidad, o sea la planificación de familia y la contracepción.

Un método es el *Metodo de Ritmo.* Todo mujer tiene una regla segura cada mes cuando puede tener relaciones sexuales sin ponerse encinta. Un médico de salud pública puede ayudarle a calcular cuando es más probable que usted se ponga encinta.

No, no es tan seguro. Un método que es muy seguro es *La Pastilla.* Se toma por la boca. Primero un médico tiene que examinarla y luego decide cual pastilla le mejor conviene.

O, si quiere, puede usar el *Diafragma y Jalea.*

Es un pequeño dispositivo contraceptivo de goma.[4] Usted tiene que colocarlo adentro de la vagina antes de tener relaciones sexuales. Es necesario cubrir un lado del dispositivo con jalea antes de colocarlo.

No, no mucho. Pero si quiere, puede usar *Espuma para control de natalidad.*

Enfermera, por favor, dígale al médico que quiero hablar con él sobre estos métodos de control de natalidad.

Mejor, mucho mejor.

Yo sé que es una buena idea planificar mis tiempos de embarazo. ¿Cuáles son los métodos de control de natalidad?

¿Es muy seguro este método?

No me gusta tomar medicina.

¿Qué es el diafragma?

¿Es muy fastidioso?

Sí, la conozco. Antes de tener rela-

---

4. Also, **hule** (used mostly in Mexico).

El *I.U.D.*[5] *o lazo* es un objeto de plástico que el médico le coloca en la matriz hasta que usted quiera tener hijos.

Bueno, el médico hace una pequeña incisión en el abdomen para cortar y amarrar[6] los tubos que llevan el óvulo a la matriz.

ciones sexuales pongo esta espuma en la vagina y no la quito sino hasta seis horas después de tener relaciones sexuales. ¿Qué es un I.U.D.?

¿Y la esterilización para mujeres?

Eso es lo que yo quiero. Deseo la ligazón[7] de los tubos. De esta manera nunca puedo ponerme encinta y ya no necesito usar ningún otro método de control de natalidad.

Muy bien, le voy a avisar al cirujano.

History of Pregnancy and Family Planning

Mrs. López is pregnant with her fourth child and talks openly with her doctor in the consulting room.

Mrs. López	Dr. Fernández
Good day, doctor.	Good day, Ma'am. I have to ask you some questions about your history of pregnancy. Is this baby going to be your fourth?
Yes, God willing.	How do you feel today? Your weight hasn't increased much. Only 15 kilos. How many children do you have?
I already have two.	And the third one?
He died during delivery . . . a stillborn.	My deepest sympathy. Have you had a miscarriage or an abortion?
Neither one, I never have had an abortion, thank God.	Nor a cesarean operation either?
Exactly.	Do you want a natural childbirth?
No, I prefer local anesthesia or maybe a spinal puncture.	Ma'am, if you don't feel too bad, it may be a very easy delivery. I advise you

5. The Spanish term is **D.I.U. (dispositivo intrauterino)**.

6. Also, **atar** = *to tie.*

7. Figuratively, *union, tie.*

Bottle feed. Doctor, I have frequent pains, now. I don't feel very well.

Let's see . . . every five minutes, I believe.

to choose a local anesthesia. Do you want to breast or bottle feed the infant?

Hmm. (*He writes in his notebook.*) How frequent?

O.K. lie down and rest. I will call the nurse so she can be with you until the delivery.

Later, the registered nurse enters Mrs. López's room in order to take care of her before the delivery.

Nurse

Good afternoon, Ma'am, I have to prepare you and shave you.

Yes, to have a child, a little angel, is a miracle of creation.

Very well. Here you have a folder. Read it and if you don't understand it you can ask the doctor questions. O.K. At last, I'm finished. Now, I have to take your vital signs.

Very well, immediately. How do you feel?

Señora López

Good afternoon. Oh, me! It is such a bother but it is worth it if one wants to give birth to a baby.

Yes, I know (in agreement), but I want to know more about birth control.

Nurse, please, tell the doctor that I want to talk with him about these methods of birth control.

Better, much better.

The doctor enters:

Doctor

I have been told that you want to talk with me about the birth control methods, which are also referred to as family planning and contraception. Ma'am, family planning means that you can have the number of children when you want them.

One of them is the *Rhythm Method*. Every woman has a safe period each month when she can have sexual relations without becoming pregnant. A public health doctor can help you cal-

Sra. López

I know that it is a good idea to plan my times of pregnancy. Which are the methods of birth control?

culate when is the most probable time that you can become pregnant.

No, it isn't too safe. A method that is very safe is the *Pill*. It is taken by mouth. First the doctor has to examine you and then decide which pill best suits you.

Or, if you want, you can use the *Diaphragm and Jelly*.

It is a small safety device contraceptive of rubber. You have to put it inside of the vagina before having sexual relations. It is necessary to cover one side with jelly before inserting it.

No, not much. But if you want, you can use *Foam for Birth Control*.

The I.U.D. or Loop is an object of plastic that the doctor puts into the womb until you want to have children.

Well, the doctor makes a small incision in the abdomen in order to cut and tie off the tubes that lead to the ovaries from the womb.

Very well, I'll advise the surgeon.

Is this method very safe?

I don't like to take medicine.

What is the diaphragm?

Is it very bothersome?

Yes, I am acquainted with it. Before having sexual relations, I put this foam in the vagina and I don't take it out for at least six hours after having sexual relations. What is an I.U.D.?

And sterilization for women?

That is what I want. I want a tubal ligation. In this way I will never get pregnant and I will no longer need to use another method of birth control.

FRASES ÚTILES

¿Esta criatura va a ser la cuarta?

¿———————— quinta?
¿———————— sexta?

¿Ha tenido usted un aborto accidental?
¿————————————
provocado?

Is this baby going to be your fourth?
———————————— *fifth?*
———————————— *sixth?*

Have you had a miscarriage?

———————— *an abortion?*

¿——————————— una operación?

——————— an operation?

¿——————————— cesárea?

——————— a cesarean?

¿Prefiere un parto natural?

Do you prefer a natural childbirth?

¿——— la anestesia local?

——————— local anesthesia?

¿——— una raquídea?

——————— spinal (anesthesia)?

¿Tiene dolores?

Do you have pain?

Sí, tengo dolores frecuentes.

Yes, I have frequent pains.

——————————— cada quince minutos.

——————— pains every fifteen minutes.

——————————— cada cinco

——————————— five minutes.

———.

¿Va a tener un niño?

Are you going to have a baby?

¿——— dar a luz un niño?

——————————— give birth to a baby?

¿Quiere estar embarazada?

Do you want to be pregnant?

¿——————— encinta?

———————————————

Debe planificar sus embarazos.

You must plan your pregnancies.

¿Cuáles son los métodos de control de natalidad?

Which are the methods of birth control?

Uno de ellos es el de ritmo.

One of them is the rhythm method.

——————— la píldora.

——————— pill.

——————— el diafragma.

——————— diaphragm.

——————— el I.U.D.

——————— I.U.D.

NOTA CULTURAL

1. For centuries in the Hispanic countries, and also here more recently in the United States, the **partera** (*midwife*) has played a major role in the delivery of babies. Many people felt frightened to leave home and have their babies in **la Clínica** (*hospital*) believing that they would become sick if they entered a public place. This habit is changing with modern medicine and family planning.

Ejercicios de conversación

Conteste las preguntas siguientes:

1. ¿Cuáles son los cuatro métodos de control de natalidad?
2. ¿Cuál prefiere usted (si usted es mujer)? ¿Por qué?
3. ¿Qué hace la enfermera de la señora López?
4. ¿Ha tenido un aborto accidental la señora López?
5. ¿Qué le pasó?
6. ¿Ha aumentado de peso? ¿Cuánto?
7. ¿A quién tiene que avisar el doctor Fernández? ¿Por qué?
8. ¿Cuántos niños tiene la señora López?
9. ¿Con qué frecuencia son sus dolores?
10. ¿Qué clase de anestesia quiere?
11. ¿Quiere dar el pecho al niño?
12. ¿Qué opina la señora López acerca del parto?
13. ¿Cuáles son las maneras de expresar la planificación de familia?
14. ¿De todos los métodos de control de natalidad, ¿cuál es el más seguro?
15. ¿El menos seguro? ¿Por qué?
16. Explique el procedimiento de la operación de ligazón.
17. ¿Por qué no quiere tomar la píldora la señora López?
18. ¿Cuál método de control de natalidad ya conoce la señora?
19. ¿Cuál método usa un objeto de plástico?
20. ¿Cuál método requiere el uso de la jalea?

Situación y simulación

Write a conversation between a female patient and a doctor discussing the various methods of birth control. Make sure that you have your patient give all the reasons why she doesn't want any other method than the "rhythm method." Help her calculate her safe periods.

Go to the public health clinic in your city and see if any of the materials are published in Spanish. See if new material has appeared for the Hispanic community.

VOCABULARIO

SUSTANTIVOS

el aborto
la anestesia
el biberón
el consultorio
la criatura
el cuaderno
el diafragma
el dispositivo
el embarazo
la espuma
la fecha
la goma
el hule (*Mex.*), goma
la jalea
el lazo
la ligazón
la matrix
el milagro
la natalidad
el óvulo
la pastilla
el parto
la píldora
la presión
la raquídea
la regla
el ritmo
la sala de consulta

NOUNS

abortion, miscarriage
anesthesia
baby bottle
consulting room
infant, baby
notebook
diaphragm
safety device
pregnancy
foam
date
rubber
rubber
jelly
loop
ligature, bond, tie
womb
miracle
birth
ovary
pill
delivery
pill
blood pressure
spinal anesthesia
period (menstrual period)
rhythm
consulting room

VERBOS

aconsejar
afeitar
amarrar
atar
aumentar

VERBS

to advise
to shave
to tie up
to tie
to grow, increase

avisar — *to warn*
colocar — *to place*
convenir — *to be convenient*
dar el pecho — *to breast feed*
planificar — *to plan*
ponerse (encinta) — *to get pregnant*
quitar — *to take away, remove*
saber — *to know*
significar — *to mean*
terminar — *to finish*
valer — *to be worth*

ADJETIVOS

ADJECTIVES

embarazada, encinta — *pregnant*
fastidioso, -a — *bothersome*
provocado, -a — *provoked*

ADVERBIOS

ADVERBS

francamente — *openly*

FRASES ÚTILES

EXPRESSIONS

a salvo de — *safe from*
dar el pecho — *to breast feed*
sentido pésame — *deepest sympathy*
si Dios quiere — *God willing*
vale la pena — *it's worthwhile*
veamos . . . — *let's see . . .*

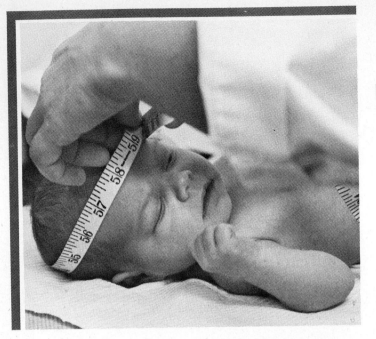

LA MATERNIDAD: II

DIÁLOGO

En la sala de partos

La señora Jiménez está en la sala de partos por primera vez y habla con la enfermera encargada.

Repita:

La enfermera	Sra. Jiménez
Señora Jiménez, ¿Se ha roto ya su bolsa de agua?	Sí, acaba de romperse.[1] Ay de mí. Tengo mucho dolor. ¿Voy a tener un parto muy difícil?

1. Also, **perder agua.**

Creo que no, pero si usted ya ha perdido su agua entonces el niño va a nacer. Voy a llamar al médico. No se preocupe, él ya viene. El parto empieza. ¡Puje,[2] señora, puje más!

Más tarde . . .

Despiértese, por favor. Ha tenido un niño normal.
Pronto, señora, muy pronto.

¡Ay, ay, ay, ay, el dolor es muy agudo!

Pesa nueve libras y dos onzas.

Al día siguiente:

¡Gracias a Dios! ¿Puedo ver al niño?

¿Cuánto pesa?

Dr. Fernández

Sra. Jiménez

Muy buenos días, señora. ¿Cómo están ustedes?
Usted debe llenar el certificado de nacimiento. Necesito su autorización. Firme aquí, por favor.

Muy bien, gracias.

¿Aquí? Muy bien. Doctor, ¿cuándo puedo usar el baño?

Dentro de unos días; por ahora, use el bacín. Ahora, es necesario secarle la leche porque no va a dar el pecho al bebé. La enfermera le va a poner una inyección y también una sonda. Ella me dijo que usted tiene unas preguntas acerca del cuidado natal. Tengo unos folletos que explican todo, pero usted ya sabe que es importante mantener al niño limpio, bañarle cada día y alimentarlo cada tres horas o según diga el doctor pediatra. También es muy importante saber cuándo el bebé esté enfermo, porque los bebés se pueden enfermar gravemente en muy poco tiempo.

¿Cuáles son algunas señas que indican una enfermedad seria?

2. **Empujar** = *to push with hands and arms;* **pujar** = *to push or strain (body).*

Primeramente, el estar muy tranquilo, el frotarse las orejas, el no querer comer y el llorar más de lo usual.

¿Cuándo debo llevar mi bebé al médico?

Muy bien, llévelo al médico sin demorar: si el niño tiene dos o tres de lo siguiente, diarrea, vómitos después de comer, tos constante, un marcado salpullido en la ingle, el cuerpo o la cara, y sobre todo una temperatura rectal de 101°F o axilar de 100°F y si tiene sangre en los excrementos.

Claro que sí, señora. Aquí tiene usted su nombre y teléfono y una tarjeta de cita para la clínica paciente-ambulante. Usted está dada de alta. ¿Quiere que llame a su esposo por teléfono?

¿Conoce usted a un buen pediatra? Quiero hacer una cita.

No, no gracias. Él acaba de llamarme por teléfono para decirme a que hora me va a recoger.

¡Que le vaya bien! Fue un gran placer.

Igualmente. Gracias.

In the Delivery Room

Mrs. Jiménez is in the delivery room for the first time, talking with the head nurse.

Nurse	Mrs. Jiménez
Mrs. Jiménez, has your water broken?	Yes, I just lost my water. Ay! I have a lot of pain. Am I going to have a difficult delivery?
I don't think so, but if you have already lost your water, then the baby is going to be born. I am calling the doctor. Don't worry, he is coming. The delivery begins. Push, Ma'am, push harder!	Ay! the pain is very sharp.

Later . . .

Wake up, please, you have a normal baby.

Soon, Ma'am, soon. He weighs 9 pounds and two ounces.

The following day . . .

Thanks be to God! Can I see the baby? How much does he weigh?

Dr. Fernández

Mrs. Jiménez

Good day, Ma'am. How are you all?
You ought to fill out the birth certificate. I need your authorization. Please sign here.

Very well, thank you.

Within a few days; for now, use the bedpan. Now, it is necessary to dry up your milk because you are not going to breast feed the baby. The nurse will give you an injection and also put in a catheter. She told me that you have some questions about baby care. I have some folders that explain a lot about care, but you know that it is important to keep the baby clean, bathe him each day and feed him every three hours or according to what the pediatrician says. Also it is very important to be able to know when the baby is sick, because babies can get sick very seriously in a short time.

Here? Very well. Doctor, when can I use the bathroom?

First, being very quiet, rubbing the ears, not wanting to eat and crying more than usual.

What are some of the signs that indicate a serious illness?

Very well, if the baby has two or three of the following, take him to the doctor without delay: diarrhea, vomiting all that he has eaten, a constant cough, a strong rash in the groin area, in the body or on the face and above all, a rectal temperature of 101°F or armpit temperature of 100°F and if he has blood in his stools.

When should I take my baby to the doctor?

Do you know a good pediatrician? I want to get an appointment with one (ask for an appointment).

Certainly, Ma'am. Here you have his name and telephone number and an appointment card for the out-patient clinic. You are discharged. Do you want me to call your husband?

No thanks. He just called me on the telephone to tell me what time he is coming to pick me up.

I hope it goes well for you. It was a great pleasure (to help you).

Same here! Thanks.

FRASES ÚTILES

¿Se ha roto su bolsa de agua?	*Is your water's bag broken?*
Sí, acaba de romperse.	*Yes, it has just broken.*
¿Voy a tener un parto difícil?	*Am I going to have a difficult delivery?*
¿_____ fácil?	*_____ an easy _____?*
¿_____ complicado?	*_____ a complicated _____?*
El niño va a nacer. El bebé _____. La criatura _____.	*The baby is going to be born.* *_____.* *_____.*
El niño va a nacer. _____ ha nacido. _____ nació.	*The baby is going to be born.* *_____ has been born.* *_____ was born.*
¿Puedo ver al niño? _____ pediatra? ¿Cuándo puedo usar el baño?	*Can I see the baby?* *_____ pediatrician?* *When can I use the bathroom?*
Usted debe limpiar al niño. _____ bañar _____. _____ alimentar _____.	*You must clean the baby.* *_____ bathe _____.* *_____ feed _____.*

¿Qué señas indican una enfermedad seria?	*What signs indicate a serious illness?*
El estar muy tranquilo. — frotarse las orejas. — no querer comer. — llorar mucho.	*By being very quiet.* *— rubbing his ears.* *— not wanting to eat.* *— crying a lot.*
Si el bebé tiene diarrea . . . ——————— vómitos . . . ——————— tos . . . ——————— salpullido . . . ——————— temperatura . . .	*If the baby has diarrhea . . .* *——————— is vomiting . . .* *——————— has a cough . . .* *——————— rash . . .* *——————— temperature . . .*
Entonces, debe llevarlo al médico inmediatamente.	*Then, you must take him to the doctor immediately.*

NOTA CULTURAL

1. An Hispanic person will often carry both his father's and his mother's names, e.g., **Luis López García: López** is his father's name and will be listed first in the telephone book and will be the surname for his children. **García** is his mother's name and is most often used for social identification (calling cards, etc., and to trace lineage). When **María Romero Díaz** marries **Luis**, she becomes **María Romero** (her father's name) **de López**. The couple's son, **Jesús**, will carry the name, **Jesús López Romero** (which will show that he descended from the mother's and the father's separate families).

Ejercicios de conversación

Conteste en español.

1. ¿Cómo es el dolor de la señora Jiménez?
2. ¿Qué le dice la enfermera que la señora haga?
3. ¿Da luz un niño o a una niña? ¿Cuánto pesa el bebé?
4. ¿Tiene un parto muy difícil la señora?

5. ¿Qué tiene que firmar la madre? ¿Por qué?
6. ¿Por qué tiene que secarle la leche a la señora?
7. En cuanto al cuidado natal ¿cuáles son los más importantes?
8. ¿Cuándo se debe llevara su bebé al médico?
9. ¿Cuáles son algunas señas que indican una enfermedad seria?
10. ¿Qué parte del cuerpo es la ingle?
11. ¿Qué quiere decir una tos constante?
12. ¿Qué le pide al doctor la señora Jiménez?
13. ¿Cómo se llama el médico que se especializa en el tratamiento de niños?
14. ¿Quién va a recoger a la señora?
15. ¿Qué le da el doctor a la señora para la clínica de pacientes ambulantes?

Situación y simulación

You are a head nurse giving natal care instructions to the mothers of newborns. Be sure to tell them to notice the signs of serious illness in babies. Ask if they are going to breast or bottle feed their babies, and make appointments for them at the out-patient clinics with the information provided in the Dialog.

PALABRAS COGNADAS

Read through the following forms, noting the cognate words. If there are no cognate words in English, then the word will appear in the vocabulary in the back of the book.

A V I S O   D E   S A L I D A

Del servicio de: _____ Cama No. _____

Diagnóstico de salida: _____

Operación: _____

Alta por: _____ Fecha _____ Hora _____

Nombre de la persona que recibe al enfermo: _____

Firma: _____ Fecha: _____

MEDICO TRATANTE   JEFE DEL SERVICIO

_____   _____
    (firma y clave)   (firma y clave)

Forma de ingreso y alta del paciente hospitalizado

SOLICITUD DE OPERACION

El enfermo _____ Edad _____ Sexo _____ NUM. DE REGISTRO _____
(APELLIDOS PATERNO Y MATERNO)

que ocupa la cama Núm. _____ del Servicio de _____
en la Unidad _____ deberá ser operado el día _____
de _____ de 19 ____ a las ____ horas _____

Diagnóstico pre-operatorio _____

Operación proyectada _____

Anestesia _____

Agréguese al instrumental: _____

Cirujano _____
(NOMBRE Y CLAVE)

1er. Ayudante _____
(NOMBRE Y CLAVE)

2do. Ayudante _____
(NOMBRE Y CLAVE)

3 er. Ayudante _____
(NOMBRE Y CLAVE)

Anestesista _____
(NOMBRE Y CLAVE)

Lugar _____ Fecha _____
(CIUDAD O POBLACION)

El Médico Jefe de Servicio _____
(Clave y firma)

Autorizo a los Médicos del Instituto Mexicano del Seguro Social para que efectúen las intervenciones quirúrgicas que sean necesarias para alivio o curación de mi padecimiento, en la inteligencia de que no desconozco los riesgos a que quedo sujeto por el procedimiento quirúrgico y anestésico.

_____ _____
FIRMA DEL PACIENTE   FIRMA DE PERSONA LEGALMENTE RESPONSABLE

Anverso de la forma de operaciones

Hallazgos quirúrgicos _____

Operación practicada _____

Describase la técnica de la operación _____

Diagnóstico Postoperatorio _____

Se remitieron para exámen histopatológico las siguientes piezas: _____

SUTURAS	MATERIAL EMPLEADO	NUM.	MARCA	CANTIDAD
Viscerales				
Serosas				
Oseas				
Musculares				
Aponeurosis				
Tejido Celular				
Piel o Mucosas				

Se canalizó con _____

Motivo _____

Accidentes _____

Estado Postoperatorio inmediato _____ Bueno ☐ Delicado ☐ Grave ☐ Muy grave ☐

Pulso _____ Respiraciones _____ Tensión Arterial ____ Mx. ____ Mn. ____

Medicación empleada durante la operación: _____

Fecha y hora _____ El Cirujano _____
(FIRMA Y CLAVE)

Reverso de la forma de operaciones

VOCABULARIO

SUSTANTIVOS

el agua	*waters*
el bebé	*baby*
la bolsa	*sac, bag*
la ingle	*groin area*
las orejas	*ears*
el pediatra	*pediatrician*
el salpullido	*rash*
la seña	*sign*
el turno	*medical appointment, turn*

NOUNS

VERBOS

acabar	*to have just finished*
alimentar	*to nourish*
bañar	*to bathe*
conocer	*to be acquainted with*
decir	*to say*
despertarse	*to awaken*
empezar	*to begin*
empujar	*to push (a door, etc.)*
explicar	*to explain*
frotarse	*to rub oneself*
llenar	*to fill (out)*
nacer	*to be born*
pedir	*to ask for (something)*
perder	*to lose*
preguntar	*to ask a question*
pujar (puje)	*to push, to strain*
recoger	*to pick up*
romper	*to break*
secar	*to dry*

VERBS

ADJETIVOS

agudo, -a	*sharp*
difícil	*difficult*
limpio, -a	*clean*
marcado, -a	*strong*

ADJECTIVES

FRASES ÚTILES

¡Gracias a Dios!	*Thanks be to God!*
Igualmente	*Same here.*

EXPRESSIONS

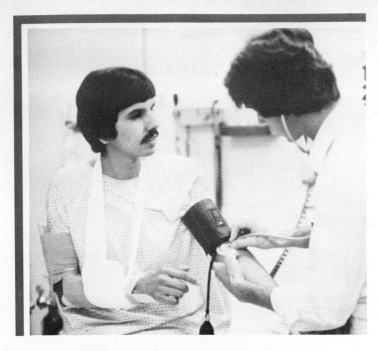

EN LA SALA DE EMERGENCIA

DIÁLOGO

El doctor Sánchez es el médico residente de la sala de emergencia de un gran hospital urbano, adonde vienen muchos pacientes latinos. Ahora está hablando con el herido que está en la camilla.

Repita:

Dr. Sánchez

¿Puede oírme?
Su auto chocó con otro y creo que usted tiene una fractura en el brazo izquierdo. Quiero que le

El Herido

Sí, le oigo bien. Pero ¿qué me pasó?

178

saquen unas radiografías. ¿Cómo se llama usted?

Me llamo Roberto Salazar, a sus órdenes.

¿Me permite examinarle? Primero, abra los ojos, bien; ahora, saque la lengua, bien . . . mmm ¿Toma drogas ahora?

¿Dónde le duele?

¿Sabe usted dónde está?

¿Sabe usted qué fecha es hoy?

Hoy es lunes.[1]

¿Tiene usted sueño?

¿Toma usted drogas?

No comprendo, no comprendo.

Todo el cuerpo y sobre todo el brazo.

Sí, en el hospital.

No, no estoy seguro.

Sí, sí, hoy es lunes . . .

Sí, tengo sueño y mucha sed.

Sí, tomo drogas, las anfetaminas y los rojos.

¿Cuál es la dosis?

¿Cuántos globos? Diez, doce al día, no recuerdo.

¿Cuánto tiempo puede estar sin tomar drogas?

Pues, ¿es usted drogadicto?

¿Ha tenido alguna vez la hepatitis?

A pesar de todo, quiero una muestra de su sangre. Después de terminar en el departamento de rayos-X, el técnico del laboratorio le va a sacar sangre. Espéreme en la sala de consultar y no salga del hospital sin avisarme porque creo que usted tiene la hepatitis, que es una enfermedad peligrosa y contagiosa.

No quiero ser indiscreto, pero estoy tratando de ver dónde y cómo usted ha contraído posiblemente la hepatitis. ¿Toma usted bebidas alcohólicas?

¿Cuántas veces a la semana?

No más de medio día.

Quizás sí, quizás no.

No, nunca.

¡Caramba!

Sí, de vez en cuando.

Tres, cuatro veces a la semana. Una lata de cerveza, quizás dos.

¿Cuánto toma usted? ¿Se inyecta la droga en la vena?

Sólo la cocaína.[2] Y nunca lo hago si la jeringuilla no está limpia.

¿Fuma?

¿Por qué no?

¿No fuma la droga?

¿Cigarrillos? Claro que no.

No quiero contraer el cáncer.

No, nunca.

1. Days of the week in Spanish are not capitalized.
2. Also, **la coca.**

La enfermera llama al doctor Sánchez porque una pareja lleva a una niña que parece dormida.

Dr. Sánchez	Los padres
Muy buenas, ¿qué le pasó a la niña?	Estaba jugando con sus muñecas en la cocina y se quemó en la estufa eléctrica. Vomitó y ahora está inconsciente.
Acuéstenla aquí, por favor en la mesa. Favor de esperar fuera de la sala . . . allí en el pasillo. Tengo que examinarla. Enfermera . . . venga acá, por favor.	Gracias, doctor.
Mas tarde . . .	
Está mejor. He limpiado la quemadura y ella está consciente ahora, parece muy débil y miedosa. Si eso pasa otra vez en la casa, sumerja el área quemada en agua fría o cúbrala con toallas mojadas en agua bastante fría. Cubra el área con una venda limpia y seca. Llévela inmediatamente al doctor.	Y doctor, ¿qué hago si la ropa se incendie?
Entonces, apague las llamas con una toalla o alfombra o un abrigo. Acueste a la niña en el suelo. Vaya apagando las llamas de la cabeza para abajo.	Y, ¿si la quemadura es causada por una sustancia química?
Lave las quemaduras con abundante agua fría.	Muchas gracias por todo, doctor Sánchez.
Fue un placer servirle. Ahora me llaman. La secretaria le va a ayudar a conseguir una cita con la clínica del pacientes-ambulantes. ¡Que le vaya bien!	

Una madre trae un niño con una fractura en la pierna. El doctor Sánchez habla con la enfermera y le da instrucciones acerca del tratamiento de los pacientes que se quedan en la sala de espera.

Dr. Sánchez	La enfermera Díaz
No sé si el niño tiene una fractura en la pierna izquierda o no. Quiero que le saquen unas radiografías.	
	Muy bien, y, si es solamente una torcedura, ¿qué debo hacer?
Dígale al niño que no se mueva. Llámeme cuando tenga las radiografías.	
	De acuerdo. El paciente cardíaco se mejora, ¿quiere hablar con él?
¿Cómo está él?	Sin duda, ha tenido un ligero ataque al corazón.
¿Ha llamado al equipo especializado en las enfermedades cardíacas?	
	Sí, sí, ya le han visto esta mañana. El paciente dice que siente dolor, más bien fuerte en el pecho y que se extiende hacia los hombros, el cuello y los brazos. Su pulso está acelerado.
¡Ay! Debo auscultarle y asegurarme que el corazón está latiendo normalmente. Con toda prisa, llame al doctor Hurtado, él tiene que estar en el hospital. Dígale que baje a la sala de emergencia, necesito consultar con él.	
	Muy bien, Dr. Sánchez.

ER—Emergency Room

Doctor Sánchez is the resident doctor in the emergency room of a large urban hospital where a lot of Hispanic patients come. He is talking now with an injured patient on a stretcher.

Dr. Sánchez	Wounded patient
Can you hear me?	Yes, I can hear me well. But, what happened to me?
Your car collided with another one and I believe that you have a fracture of the left arm. I want to have some x-rays of you. What is your name?	
	My name is Roberto Salazar, at your service.

Will you let me examine you? First, open
your eyes, good; now, stick out your
tongue, good; hmm, do you take drugs
now?

Where does it hurt?

Do you know where you are?

Do you know what today's date is?

Today is Monday.

Are you sleepy?

Do you take drugs?

What is the dosage?

How long can you go without taking
drugs?

Well, are you a drug addict?

Have you ever had hepatitis?

In spite of everything, I want a blood
specimen. After finishing in the x-ray
department, the technician from the
laboratory will draw your blood. Wait
for me in the consulting room and
don't leave the hospital without telling me because I believe that you have
hepatitis, which is a dangerous and
contagious disease.

I don't mean to be rude, but I am trying
to discover where and how you might
have gotten hepatitis. Do you take alcoholic beverages?

How many times a week?

How much do you drink?

Do you inject the drug in your vein?

Do you smoke?

Why not?

Do you smoke drugs?

I don't understand.

In every part of my body and above all
my arm.

Yes, in the hospital.

No, I'm not sure.

Yes, yes, today is Monday . . .

Yes, I am sleepy and very thirsty.

Yes, I take drugs, amphetamines and the
reds.

How many do I pop? Ten, eleven a day,
I don't remember.

No more than half a day.

Maybe yes, maybe no.

No, never.

Darn!

Yes, from time to time.

Three, four times a week.

A can of beer, maybe two.

Only cocaine. I never do it if the syringe
isn't clean.

Cigarettes? Certainly not.

I don't want to get cancer.

No, never.

**The nurse calls Dr. Sánchez because a couple is carrying in a little girl who appears
to be asleep.**

Dr. Sánchez	**The parents**
Good afternoon, what happened to the child?	She was playing with her dolls in the kitchen and burned herself on the electric stove. She vomited and she is unconscious now.

Lay her down here, please, on the table. Please wait outside of the room . . . there, in the hallway. I have to examine her. . . . Nurse . . . come here, please.

Thank you, doctor.

Later . . .

She is better. I have cleaned the burn and she is conscious now, she seems weak and fearful. If that happens again at home, submerge the burned area in cold water and cover it with damp (cold water) towels. Cover the area with a clean and dry bandage. Take her immediately to the doctor.

And, doctor, what do I do if her clothes catch on fire?

Then put out the flames with a towel or a rug or an overcoat. Lay the child on the ground. Go on by putting out the flames from head to foot.

And if the burn is caused by a chemical substance?

Wash the burns with a lot of water.

Thank you so much for everything, Dr. Sánchez.

It was a pleasure to service you. They are calling me now. The secretary will help you obtain the appointment with the out-patient clinic. I hope everything goes well for you!

A mother brings in a child with a fracture in the leg. Dr. Sánchez is talking with his nurse and giving her instructions about the treatment of the patients who are left in the waiting room.

Dr. Sánchez	**Nurse Díaz**
I don't know if the child has a fracture of the left leg or not. I want to have some x-rays of him.	
	Very well, and if it is only a sprain, what should I do?
Tell the child to avoid moving. Call me when you have the x-rays.	
	Agreed. The cardiac patient is getting better. Do you want to talk with him?
How is he?	Without a doubt, he has had a mild heart attack.
Have you called the team that specializes in cardiac illnesses?	
	Yes, yes, they have already seen him this morning. The patient says that he feels pain, generally strong in the

chest and that it extends to the shoulders, neck and arms. His pulse has accelerated.

Oh! I must listen to assure myself that his heart is beating normally. Hurry, call Dr. Hurtado, he has to be in the hospital. Tell him to come down to the emergency room, I need to consult with him.

Very well, Dr. Sánchez.

FRASES ÚTILES

¿Dónde está el herido?	*Where is the injured person (party)?*
Está en la sala de emergencia. _____ rayos-X. _____ camilla.	*He is in the emergency room.* *_____ X-rays _____.* *_____ stretcher.*
Tiene una fractura en el brazo. _____ la pierna. _____ cabeza.	*He has a fracture in the arm.* *_____ leg.* *_____ head.*
No quiere tomar medicinas. _____ drogas. _____ contraer la hepatitis. _____ el cáncer.	*He doesn't want to take medicine.* *_____ drugs.* *_____ get hepatitis.* *_____ cancer.*
¿Qué le pasó a la niña?	*What happened to the child?*
Ella se quemó. _____ vomitó. ____ está inconsciente.	*She burned herself.* *___ vomited.* *___ is unconscious.*
Usted debe limpiar la quemadura. _____ sumergir _____. _____ cubrir _____.	*You must clean the burn.* *_____ submerge _____.* *_____ cover _____.*

Con toda prisa . . .	*Hurry . . .*
Dése prisa . . .	
llame al equipo especializado.	*call the specialized team.*
_____ médico _____.	_____ *doctor.*
_____ a la enfermera encargada.[1]	_____ *head nurse.*

NOTA CULTURAL

1. The word **droguista** generally refers to the druggist. **El droguero** in street language (**el caló**) can mean either the pusher or the user. *Pharmacy* is expressed as **la farmacia, la droguería, la botica. El boticario, el farmacéutico** are the most frequently used words for druggist.

Ejercicios de conversación

Conteste en español a las preguntas siguientes.

1. ¿Qué le pasó al paciente, Roberto Salazar?
2. ¿Toma drogas el herido? ¿Qué clase?
3. ¿Cómo es la enfermedad, la hepatitis? ¿Es contagiosa?
4. ¿Por qué no quiere fumar cigarrillos Roberto?
5. ¿Qué tiene la niña que parece dormida?
6. Según el doctor Sánchez, ¿qué se debe hacer si la ropa de un niño o de otra persona se incendie?
7. ¿Tiene fractura or torcedura el niño? ¿Sabe el doctor?
8. ¿Por qué cree la enfermera que el paciente cardíaco ha tenido un ligero ataque al corazón?
9. ¿Cuáles son los síntomas?
10. ¿De qué quiere asegurarse el doctor Sánchez?

PALABRAS COGNADAS

Read through the information about high blood pressure presented by the American Heart Association on the following page. The words that have no English cognate appear in the vocabulary in the back of the book.

1. Also, **cabecera** (*head*).

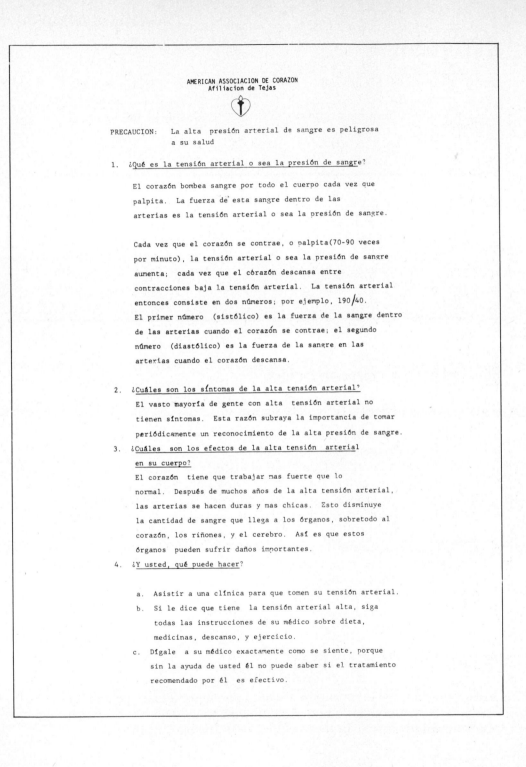

AMERICAN ASSOCIACION DE CORAZON
Afiliacion de Tejas

PRECAUCION: La alta presión arterial de sangre es peligrosa
              a su salud

1.   ¿Qué es la tensión arterial o sea la presión de sangre?

     El corazón bombea sangre por todo el cuerpo cada vez que
     palpita. La fuerza de esta sangre dentro de las
     arterias es la tensión arterial o sea la presión de sangre.

     Cada vez que el corazón se contrae, o palpita(70-90 veces
     por minuto), la tensión arterial o sea la presión de sangre
     aumenta; cada vez que el corazón descansa entre
     contracciones baja la tensión arterial. La tensión arterial
     entonces consiste en dos números; por ejemplo, 190/40.
     El primer número (sistólico) es la fuerza de la sangre dentro
     de las arterias cuando el corazón se contrae; el segundo
     número (diastólico) es la fuerza de la sangre en las
     arterias cuando el corazón descansa.

2.   ¿Cuáles son los síntomas de la alta tensión arterial?
     El vasto mayoría de gente con alta tensión arterial no
     tienen síntomas. Esta razón subraya la importancia de tomar
     periódicamente un reconocimiento de la alta presión de sangre.

3.   ¿Cuáles son los efectos de la alta tensión arterial
     en su cuerpo?
     El corazón tiene que trabajar mas fuerte que lo
     normal. Después de muchos años de la alta tensión arterial,
     las arterias se hacen duras y mas chicas. Esto disminuye
     la cantidad de sangre que llega a los órganos, sobretodo al
     corazón, los riñones, y el cerebro. Así es que estos
     órganos pueden sufrir daños importantes.

4.   ¿Y usted, qué puede hacer?

     a. Asistir a una clínica para que tomen su tensión arterial.
     b. Si le dice que tiene la tensión arterial alta, siga
         todas las instrucciones de su médico sobre dieta,
         medicinas, descanso, y ejercicio.
     c. Dígale a su médico exactamente como se siente, porque
         sin la ayuda de usted él no puede saber si el tratamiento
         recomendado por él es efectivo.

186

VOCABULARIO

SUSTANTIVOS

NOUNS

las anfetaminas	*amphetamines*
la alfombra	*rug*
la dosis	*dosage*
la estufa	*heater, stove*
la lengua	*tongue*
las llamas	*flames*
la fractura	*fracture*
la muñeca	*doll*
la pareja	*couple, pair*
la quemadura	*burn*
el suelo	*ground*
la toalla	*towel*
la torcedura	*sprain*

VERBOS

VERBS

apagar	*to put out*
auscultar	*to listen with a stethoscope, to auscultate*
avisar	*to warn, advise*
chocar	*to collide*
creer	*to believe*
curar	*to cure*
latir	*to beat*
lavar	*to wash*
oir	*to hear*
quemarse	*to get burned*
sacar	*to stick out (tongue)*
sumergir	*to submerge, dip*
ver	*to see*

ADJETIVOS

ADJECTIVES

debil	*weak*
fuerte	*strong*
indiscreto, -a	*rude*
ligero, -a	*light*
miedoso, -a	*fearful*
químico, -a	*chemical*
peligroso, -a	*dangerous*

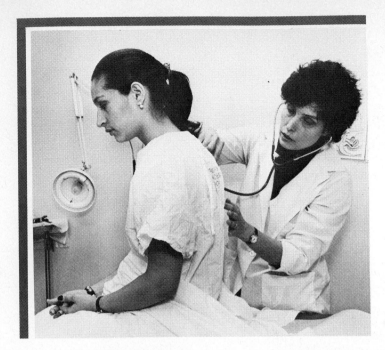

TERCERA PRUEBA

Preguntas acerca de la lección novena

Conteste en español.

1. ¿Adónde se debe ir para obtener la vacuna contra la polio?
2. ¿Por qué le aconseja a la señora la secretaria en vez del médico?
3. ¿Cuál división del centro de salud pública tiene informes sobre la vacuna?
4. ¿Sabe bien el inglés y el español la señora Valdéz?
5. Nombre algunos de los términos para explicar la planificación de la familia.
6. ¿Cuánto cuesta la vacuna en el centro de salud pública?
7. ¿Es drogadicto el esposo de la señora Valdéz?
8. ¿Por qué tiene miedo de llamar a la policía la señora Valdéz?
9. ¿Qué le pasó al señor Valdéz en su empleo?
10. ¿Cómo se llama el especialista que trata de las enfermedades mentales?

Preguntas acerca de la lección décima

Conteste en español.

1. Identifique los cuatro métodos de control de natalidad.
2. ¿Cuál prefiere usted, si usted es mujer? ¿Por qué?
3. ¿Cuál es la historia médica de la señora López? ¿Cuántas veces ha estado ella encinta?
4. ¿Qué opina la señora López acerca del parto?
5. ¿De todos los métodos de control de natalidad, cuál es el más seguro?
6. ¿Cuál es el menos seguro?
7. Explique el procedimiento de la operación de ligazón.
8. ¿Por qué no quiere la señora tomar la píldora?
9. ¿Quiere ella dar el pecho al niño?
10. ¿Ha tenido un aborto provocado la señora López?

Preguntas acerca de la lección once

Conteste en español.

1. ¿Cuáles son dos métodos de control de natalidad?
2. ¿Cuál método le parece a usted el mejor para una mujer joven? ¿Por qué?
3. ¿Cuál método es el menos seguro? ¿Por qué?
4. ¿Es difícil el procedimiento de la operación de ligazón?
5. ¿Es seguro el método de usar la píldora? De todos los métodos, ¿cuál es el más seguro?

Preguntas acerca de la lección doce

Conteste en español.

1. ¿De qué quiere asegurarse el doctor Sánchez?
2. ¿Por qué cree la enfermera de la sala de emergencia que el paciente cardíaco ha tenido un ligero ataque al corazón?
3. ¿Por qué se enoja el doctor Sánchez con Roberto Salazar?
4. ¿Qué opina el doctor Sánchez acerca del tratamiento de las quemaduras causadas por sustancias químicas?
5. ¿Tiene torcedura el niño?
6. ¿Toma drogas el herido?
7. ¿Cómo es la enfermedad, la hepatitis?
8. ¿Cómo se debe tratar la quemadura según el doctor Sánchez?
9. Según el doctor Sánchez ¿qué se debe hacer si la ropa de un niño o de otra persona se incendie?
10. ¿Qué tiene la niña que parece dormida?

APPENDIX

PARTS OF SPEECH

1. Nouns

A. General Guidelines

Nouns in Spanish have either masculine or feminine gender.

Most masculine nouns end in -*o*, and most feminine nouns end in -*a*. They form the plural by adding -*s*.

Examples:
el queso   los quesos
la enfermera   las enfermeras

Some nouns do not end in -*a* or -*o*, and their gender must be memorized. Nouns which end in the other vowels (mostly -*e*, with a few ending in -*i* and -*u*) form the plural by adding -*s*. Nouns which end in a consonant form the plural by adding -*es*.

Examples:
la calle   las calles
el ayudante   los ayudantes
el zaguán   los zaguanes
la enfermedad   las enfermedades

Most nouns which name a person or an occupation can have either masculine or feminine gender, depending on the sex of the person named.

Examples:
el cirujano / la cirujana
el abuelo / la abuela
el / la asistente
el / la paciente

Masculine singular nouns are preceded by the definite article *el;* masculine plural nouns are preceded by the definite article *los.* Feminine singular nouns are preceded by the definite article *la;* feminine plural nouns are preceded by the definite article *las. El, la, los,* and *las* are all translated in English as "the."

B. Irregular Nouns

Some Spanish nouns are irregular. For instance, certain nouns of Greek origin are masculine even though they end in *-a*.

Examples:
el síntom*a*
el diafragm*a*
el sistem*a*

Most nouns of foreign origin are masculine no matter their termination, e.g., *el test*, etc.

Many nouns which end in *-ma* and *-ta* show this irregularity and have the masculine gender.

Examples:
el problem*a*
el / la dentist*a*

C. Cognate Nouns

The meanings of many Spanish nouns will be extremely easy to learn because the nouns have English cognates (that is, the Spanish and English nouns share a common linguistic origin). These Spanish nouns therefore closely resemble their English counterparts.

In very many cases, a Spanish noun ending has a direct English equivalent. The following are some of the most common cognate noun endings, showing the Spanish endings and their English equivalents.

-ión = -ion
  Examples:

admis*ión*	admiss*ion*
expectorac*ión*	expectorat*ion*
inyecc*ión*	inject*ion*

-ancia, -encia = -ance, -ence
  Examples:

ambul*ancia*	ambul*ance*
import*ancia*	import*ance*
resist*encia*	resist*ance*

-ia, -ía = -ia, -y
  Examples:

difter*ia*	diphther*ia*
emergenc*ia*	emergenc*y*

famil*ia*	famil*y*
anatom*ía*	anatom*y*
cardiolog*ía*	cardiolog*y*

-ino, -ina = -in, -ine
Examples:

aspir*ina*	aspir*in*
margar*ina*	margar*ine*
intest*ino*	intest*ine*

-rio = -ry
Examples:

secreta*rio*	secreta*ry*
suposito*rio*	suposito*ry*

-ismo = -ism
Examples:

alcohol*ismo*	alcohol*ism*
botul*ismo*	botul*ism*

-ante, -ente, -ento = -ant, -ent
Examples:

ag*ente*	ag*ent*
desodor*ante*	deodor*ant*
departa*mento*	depart*ment*

-dad = -ty
Examples:

identi*dad*	identi*ty*
materni*dad*	materni*ty*

-sis, -lis = -sis, -lis
Examples:

análi*sis*	analy*sis*
diagno*sis*	diagno*sis*

-itis = -itis
Examples:

artr*itis*	arthr*itis*
burs*itis*	burs*itis*

PALABRAS COGNADAS

INFINITIVES

ENGLISH

INFINITIVOS

SPANISH

ENGLISH	SPANISH
to absorb	absorber
to accept	aceptar
to acquire	adquirir
to affirm	afirmar
to adjust	ajustar
to alienate	alienar
to alter	alterar
to amputate	amputar
to analyze	analizar
to annul	anular
to appreciate	apreciar
to arrest	arrestar
to articulate	articular
to authorize	autorizar
to balance	balancear
to calm	calmar
to cause	causar
to circulate	circular
to coagulate	coagular
to compensate	compensar
to communicate	comunicar
to concede	conceder
to concentrate	concentrar
to conclude	concluir
to conserve	conservar
to consider	considerar
to consist	consistir
to constipate	constipar
to consult	consultar
to contaminate	contaminar
to contain	contener
to contract	contraer
to control	controlar
to converse	conversar
to convert	convertir
to cost	costar
to cure	curar
to debilitate	debilitar
to decide	decidir
to declare	declarar

ENGLISH	SPANISH
to depend	depender
to describe	describir
to discover	descubrir
to disinfect	desinfectar
to destroy	destruir
to determine	determinar
to diagnose	diagnosticar
to digest	digerir
to dilate	dilatar
to discuss	discutir
to diminish	disminuir
to dissolve	disolver
to distinguish	distinguir
to distribute	distribuir
to divide	dividir
to eliminate	eliminar
to sterilize	esterilizar
to evacuate	evacuar
to evaluate	evaluar
to examine	examinar
to exist	existir
to explore	explorar
to facilitate	facilitar
to form	formar
to fracture	fracturar
to function	funcionar
to imagine	imaginar
to include	incluir
to indicate	indicar
to infect	infectar
to inform	informar
to inhibit	inhibir
to immunize	inmunizar
to inoculate	inocular
to inspect	inspeccionar
to interest	interesar
to interpret	interpretar
to investigate	investigar
to maintain	mantener
to masticate	masticar
to masturbate	masturbar
to note	notar
to observe	observar
to obstruct	obstruir
to occur	ocurrir
to offend	ofender
to omit	omitir

ENGLISH	SPANISH
to operate	operar
to urinate	orinar
to penetrate	penetrar
to perceive	percibir
to permit	permitir
to practice	practicar
to precipitate	precipitar
to preoccupy	preocupar
to prepare	preparar
to prevent	prevenir
to proceed	proceder
to progress	progresar
to prohibit	prohibir
to prolong	prolongar
to pronounce	pronunciar
to propagate	propagar
to propose	proponer
to protect	proteger
to protest	protestar
to provoke	provocar
to project	proyectar
to purify	purificar
to recommend	recomendar
to recognize	reconocer
to recuperate	recuperar
to reduce	reducir
to refer	referir
to relate	relatar
to remedy	remediar
to renovate	renovar
to repair	reparar
to repeat	repetir
to represent	representar
to resent	resentir
to resolve	resolver
to respect	respetar
to respire	respirar
to restore	restaurar
to resuscitate	resucitar
to result	resultar
to resume	resumir
to retire	retirar
to revise	revisar
to select	seleccionar
to separate	separar
to suffer	sufrir
to suppurate	supurar

ENGLISH	SPANISH
to suspend	suspender
to transmit	transmitir
to ulcerate	ulcerar
to use	usar
to utilize	utilizar
to ventilate	ventilar
to visit	visitar
to vomit	vomitar
to vote	votar

ENDINGS: -ion
TERMINACIONES: -ión

ENGLISH	SPANISH
action	acción
administration	administración
admission	admisión
alienation	alienación
alimentation	alimentación
alteration	alteración
hallucination	alucinación
amplification	amplificación
application	aplicación
articulation	articulación
association	asociación
attention	atención
authorization	autorización
calcification	calcificación
cauterization	cauterización
certification	certificación
cession	cesión
circulation	circulación
coagulation	coagulación
commission	comisión
comparison	comparación
complication	complicación
compression	compresión
communication	comunicación
concentration	concentración
condition	condición
conservation	conservación
consideration	consideración
constipation	constipación
constitution	constitución

ENGLISH	SPANISH
construction	construcción
contamination	contaminación
contraction	contracción
contraception	contracepción
conversation	conversación
convulsion	convulsión
deception	decepción
decision	decisión
declaration	declaración
defecation	defecación
depression	depresión
description	descripción
desertion	deserción
malnutrition	desnutrición
deterioration	deterioración
determination	determinación
digestion	digestión
direction	dirección
discretion	discreción
discussion	discusión
distribution	distribución
division	división
duration	duración
education	educación
elevation	elevación
elimination	eliminación
emotion	emoción
eruption	erupción
station	estación
sterilization	esterilización
evacuation	evacuación
evaluation	evaluación
evasion	evasión
evolution	evolución
expectation	expectación
expectoration	expectoración
explication	explicación
exploration	exploración
explosion	explosión
extraction	extracción
ejaculation	eyaculación
fecundation	fecundación
fibrillation	fibrilación
flexion	flexión
formation	formación
friction	fricción
function	función

ENGLISH	SPANISH
gestation	gestación
hospitalization	hospitalización
hypertension	hipertensión
hyperventilation	hiperventilación
hypotension	hipotensión
hypoventilation	hipoventilación
identification	identificación
illusion	ilusión
incision	incisión
incubation	incubación
indecision	indecisión
indication	indicación
indigestion	indigestión
indisposition	indisposición
infection	infección
inflammation	inflamación
information	información
infraction	infracción
inhalation	inhalación
immersion	inmersión
immunization	inmunización
inoculation	inoculación
inspection	inspección
installation	instalación
institution	institución
instruction	instrucción
interaction	interacción
interpretation	interpretación
interruption	interrupción
intoxication	intoxicación
investigation	investigación
injection	inyección
irritation	irritación
lesion	lesión
limitation	limitación
lotion	loción
locomotion	locomoción
mastication	masticación
masturbation	masturbación
menstruation	menstruación
moderation	moderación
mortification	mortificación
nutrition	nutrición
observation	observación
obsession	obsesión
obstruction	obstrucción
occupation	ocupación

ENGLISH	SPANISH
omission	omisión
operation	operación
palpitation	palpitación
perception	percepción
portion	porción
position	posición
prostration	postración
preoccupation	preocupación
preparation	preparación
presentation	presentación
prevention	prevención
privation	privación
profession	profesión
prohibition	prohibición
promotion	promoción
propensity	propensión
protection	protección
provision	provisión
projection	proyección
pulsation	pulsación
ration	ración
radiation	radiación
reaction	reacción
recreation	recreación
recuperation	recuperación
reduction	reducción
reflection	reflexión
refraction	refracción
region	región
rehabilitation	rehabilitación
relation	relación
religion	religión
repetition	repetición
reputation	reputación
resolution	resolución
respiration	respiración
restriction	restricción
resuscitation	resucitación
retention	retención
revision	revisión
revolution	revolución
salivation	salivación
satisfaction	satisfacción
section	sección
secretion	secreción
selection	selección
separation	separación

ENGLISH	SPANISH
session	sesión
signification	significación
situation	situación
solution	solución
suggestion	sugestión
suppuration	supuración
tension	tensión
temptation	tentación
traction	tracción
transformation	transformación
transfusion	transfusión
transmission	transmisión
trepanation	trepanación
ulceration	ulceración
union	unión
variation	variación
ventilation	ventilación
vision	visión

ENDINGS:
-ance, -ence, -ia, -y

TERMINACIONES:
-ancia, -encia, -ia

ENGLISH	SPANISH
abstinence	abstinencia
acromegaly	acromegalia
adolescence	adolescencia
allergy	alergia
ambulance	ambulancia
analgesia	analgesia
anemia	anemia
anesthesia	anestesia
anorexia	anorexia
anuria	anuria
arrogance	arrogancia
assistance	asistencia
asthenia	astenia
atrophy	atrofia
autopsy	autopsia
biopsy	biopsia
clemency	clemencia
competency	competencia
conscience	conciencia
constancy	constancia
convalescence	convalescencia

ENGLISH	SPANISH
decency	decencia
deficiency	deficiencia
dementia	demencia
diathermy	diatermia
diphtheria	difteria
discrepancy	discrepancia
dyspepsia	dispepsia
distance	distancia
dystrophy	distrofia
eclampsia	eclampsia
efficiency	eficiencia
elegance	elegancia
embolism	embolia
emergency	emergencia
eminence	eminencia
epilepsy	epilepsia
essence	esencia
spice	especia
euphoria	euforia
eugenics	eugenesia
euthanasia	eutanasia
evidence	evidencia
excellence	excelencia
existence	existencia
experience	experiencia
family	familia
pharmacy	farmacia
flatulence	flatulencia
phobia	fobia
frequency	frecuencia
hemophilia	hemofilia
hemorrhage	hemorragia
hernia	hernia
hydrophobia	hidrofobia
hydrotherapy	hidroterapia
hysteria	histeria
idiosyncrasy	idiosincracia
ignorance	ignorancia
importance	importancia
incontinence	incontinencia
independence	independencia
indigence	indigencia
indulgence	indulgencia
infancy	infancia
imminence	inminencia
instance	instancia
insufficiency	insuficiencia

ENGLISH	SPANISH
interference	interferencia
laparoscopy	laparoscopia
leukemia	leucemia
malaria	malaria
memory	memoria
menopause	menopausia
negligence	negligencia
neuralgia	neuralgia
neurasthenia	neurastenia
orthopedics	ortopedia
patience	paciencia
permanence	permanencia
polycythemia	policitemia
potency	potencia
presence	presencia
prominence	prominencia
rabies	rabia
reference	referencia
residence	residencia
resistance	resistencia
resonance	resonancia
septicemia	septicemia
sufficiency	suficiencia
tendency	tendencia
therapy	terapia
tolerance	tolerancia
toxemia	toxemia
transcendence	transcendencia
transparency	transparencia
uremia	uremia
urgency	urgencia
vehemence	vehemencia
violence	violencia

ENDINGS: -y

TERMINACIONES: - ía

ENGLISH	SPANISH
anatomy	anatomía
anesthesiology	anestesiología
anomaly	anomalía
bacteriology	bacteriología
biology	biología
bronchopneumonia	bronconeumonía
calorie	caloría
cardiology	cardiología

ENGLISH	SPANISH
surgery	cirugía
citizenry	ciudadanía
colectomy	colectomía
company	compañía
accounting	contaduría
courtesy	cortesía
dermatology	dermatología
dysentery	disentería
ecology	ecología
empathy	empatía
endocrinology	endocrinología
infirmary	enfermería
epidemiology	epidemiología
episiotomy	episiotomía
pharmacology	farmacología
physiology	fisiología
gastroenterology	gastroenterología
geography	geografía
geriatrics	geriatría
gynecology	ginecología
hematology	hematología
hypochondria	hipocondría
hysterectomy	histerectomía
engineering	ingeniería
immunology	inmunología
laparotomy	laparotomía
lobectomy	lobectomía
mastectomy	mastectomía
microbiology	microbiología
myopia	miopía
neonatology	neonatología
neurology	neurología
odontology	odontología
ophthalmology	oftalmología
optometry	optometría
orthodontics	ortodontología
osteopathy	osteopatía
otorhinolaryngology	otorrinolaringología
parasitology	parasitología
pathology	patología
pediatrics	pediatría
pleurisy	pleuresía
police	policía
proctology	proctología
psychology	psicología
psychiatry	psiquiatría
pneumonia	pulmonía

ENGLISH	SPANISH
radiography	radiografía
radiology	radiología
roentgenology	roentgenología
sympathy	simpatía
sociology	sociología
technology	tecnología
tracheotomy	traqueotomía
urology	urología
vasectomy	vasectomía
zoology	zoología

ENDINGS: -ic, -ical

TERMINACIONES: -ico

ENGLISH	SPANISH
alcoholic	alcohólico
anaphylactic	anafiláctico
analgesic	analgésico
analytic	analítico
antibiotic	antibiótico
antispasmodic	antiespasmódico
antiseptic	antiséptico
antitetanic	antitetánico
aortic	aórtico
bubonic	bubónico
characteristic	característico
Catholic	católico
clinic	clínico
cosmetic	cosmético
cubic	cúbico
diabetic	diabético
ectopic	ectópico
emetic	emético
barbaric	barbárico
spasmodic	espasmódico
physical	físico
genetic	genético
mechanical	mecánico
narcotic	narcótico
orthopedic	ortopédico
paralytic	paralítico
plastic	plástico
prophylactic	profiláctico
pubic	púbico
public	público
rheumatic	reumático

ENGLISH	SPANISH
rhythmic	rítmico
technical	técnico
therapeutic	terapeútico
tetanic	tetánico
tubal	tubárico
uric	úrico

ENDINGS: -ry

TERMINACIONES: -rio

ENGLISH	SPANISH
adversary	adversario
agrarian	agrario
ambulatory	ambulatorio
anniversary	aniversario
circulatory	circulatorio
commentary	comentario
compensatory	compensatorio
consulting (office)	consultorio
contrary	contrario
criterion	criterio
dictionary	diccionario
dormitory	dormitorio
exploratory	exploratorio
functionary	funcionario
funerary	funerario
gregarious	gregario
hereditary	hereditario
laboratory	laboratorio
lavatory	lavatorio
mystery	misterio
necessary	necesario
ordinary	ordinario
ovary	ovario
preparatory	preparatorio
primary	primario
regulatory	regulatorio
revolutionary	revolucionario
rudimentary	rudimentario
sanatorium	sanatorio
sanitary	sanitario
secretary	secretario
solitary	solitario
suppository	supositorio
territory	territorio
transitory	transitorio

ENGLISH	SPANISH
various	vario
veterinary	veterinario
vibratory	vibratorio

ENDINGS: -in, -ine   ## TERMINACIONES: -ina, -ino

ENGLISH	SPANISH
Achromycin	acromicina
adrenaline	adrenalina
amphetamine	anfetamina
angina	angina
aspirin	aspirina
calamine	calamina
cholesterol	colesterina
curtain	cortina
discipline	disciplina
Dramamine	dramamina
ephedrine	efedrina
endocrine	endocrina
scarlet fever	escarlatina
streptomycin	estreptomicina
strychnine	estricnina
estrauterine	extrauterino
gamma globulin	gamaglobulina *or* globulina gamma
gasoline	gasolina
gelatin	gelatina
glycerin	glicerina
insulin	insulina
intestine	intestino
intrauterine	intrauterino
margarine	margarina
medicine	medicina
melamine	melamina
mescaline	mescalina
mine	mina
office	oficina
urine	orina
penicillin	penicilina
protein	proteína
quinine	quinina
resin	resina
routine	rutina
saccharin	sacarina
sardine	sardina
tetramycin	tetramicina

ENGLISH	SPANISH
toxin	toxina
vagina	vagina
Vaseline	vaselina
vitamin	vitamina

ENDINGS: -ism

TERMINACIONES: -ismo

ENGLISH	SPANISH
activism	activismo
albinism	albinismo
alcoholism	alcoholismo
altruism	altruismo
anachronism	anacronismo
aneurysm	aneurismo
anglicism	anglicismo
asceticism	ascetismo
astigmatism	astigmatismo
baptism	bautismo
botulism	botulismo
conventionalism	convencionalismo
cretinism	cretinismo
dramatization	dramatismo
egotism	egoismo
embolism	embolismo
strabismus	estrabismo
fatalism	fatalismo
favoritism	favoritismo
feudalism	feudalismo
humanism	humanismo
humorousness	humorismo
illusionism	ilusionismo
intellectualism	intelectualismo
mechanism	mecanismo
metabolism	metabolismo
mysticism	misticismo
mongolism	mongolismo
occultism	ocultismo
optimism	optimismo
patriotism	patriotismo
pessimism	pesimismo
professionalism	profesionalismo
rickets	raquitismo
regionalism	regionalismo
rheumatism	reumatismo
symbolism	simbolismo

ENGLISH	SPANISH
sinapism	sinapismo
somnambulism	sonambulismo
vandalism	vandalismo

ENDINGS: -ous

TERMINACIONES: -oso

ENGLISH	SPANISH
ambitious	ambicioso
anxious	ansioso
harmonious	armonioso
cancerous	canceroso
contagious	contagioso
copious	copioso
curious	curioso
defective	defectuoso
delicious	delicioso
desirous	deseoso
envious	envidioso
spacious	espacioso
studious	estudioso
famous	famoso
fibrous	fibroso
furious	furioso
generous	generoso
glorious	glorioso
gracious	gracioso
impetuous	impetuoso
industrious	industrioso
ingenious	ingenioso
intravenous	intravenoso
marvelous	maravilloso
melodious	melodioso
meticulous	meticuloso
mysterious	misterioso
monstrous	monstruoso
morbid	morboso
mucous	mucoso
nervous	nervioso
prodigious	prodigioso
religious	religioso
suspicious	sospechoso
talented	talentoso
verbose	verboso
vigorous	vigoroso

ENDINGS: -ant, -ent

TERMINACIONES: -ante, -ente

ENGLISH	SPANISH
abundant	abundante
agent	agente
ambulant	ambulante
arrogant	arrogante
assistant	asistente
brilliant	brillante
sedative	calmante
competent	competente
complacent	complaciente
conscious	consciente
constant	constante
convalescent	convaleciente
correspondent	correspondiente
current	corriente
decent	decente
deficient	deficiente
demented	demente
disinfectant	desinfectante
deodorant	desodorante
different	diferente
diligent	diligente
distant	distante
efficient	eficiente
stimulant	estimilante
student	estudiante
excellent	excelente
frequent	frecuente
gallant	galante
ignorant	ignorante
impatient	impaciente
impertinent	impertinente
important	importante
incoherent	incoherente
incompetent	incompetente
independent	independiente
infant	infante
imminent	inminente
instant	instante
interesting	interesante
intermittent	intermitente
latent	latente
patient	paciente
permanent	permanente
pertinent	pertinente

ENGLISH	SPANISH
potent	potente
present	presente
president	presidente
Protestant	protestante
recent	reciente
referring	referente
regent	regente
repugnant	repugnante
resident	residente
servant	sirviente
solvent	solvente
sufficient	suficiente
tolerant	tolerante
turgid	turgente
urgent	urgente
vacant	vacante
vehement	vehemente

ENDINGS: -ent

TERMINACIONES: -ento

ENGLISH	SPANISH
accompaniment	acompañamiento
apartment	apartamento
compartment	compartimiento
condiment	condimento
consent	consentimiento
corpulent	corpulento
department	departamento
discovery	descubrimiento
deterioration	deterioramiento
document	documento
establishment	establecimiento
excrement	excremento
firmament	firmamento
fomentation	fomento
fragment	fragmento
function	funcionamiento
impediment	impcdimcnto
implement	implemento
instrument	instrumento
lament	lamento
ligament	ligamento
liniment	linimento
medication	medicamento
moment	momento

ENGLISH	SPANISH
monument	monumento
movement	movimiento
procedure	procedimiento
recognition	reconocimiento
refinement	refinamiento
regiment	regimiento
requirement	requerimiento
resentment	resentimiento
rudiment	rudimento
section	seccionamiento
sentiment	sentimiento
somnolent	soñoliento
talent	talento
temperament	temperamento
torment	tormento
treatment	tratamiento

ENDINGS: -ble ## TERMINACIONES: -ble

ENGLISH	SPANISH
acceptable	aceptable
agreeable	agradable
amiable	amable
applicable	aplicable
comparable	comparable
communicable	comunicable
conservable	conservable
considerable	considerable
countable	contable
controllable	controlable
credible	creíble
disagreeable	desagradable
digestible	digestible
disposable	disponible
durable	durable
educable	educable
emotional	emocionable
stable	estable
fallible	falible
flexible	flexible
impassable	impasible
impossible	imposible
improbable	improbable
incomparable	incomparable

ENGLISH	SPANISH
incommunicable	incomunicable
uncontrollable	incontrolable
incorrigible	incorregible
incredible	increíble
incurable	incurable
indicatable	indicable
indigestible	indigestible
uneducable	ineducable
unstable	inestable
immobile	inmovible
unobservable	inobservable
inoperable	inoperable
insensible	insensible
inseparable	inseparable
unserviceable	inservible
unsupportable	insoportable
unreasonable	irrazonable
irresistible	irresistible
irritable	irritable
laudable	laudable
maintainable	mantenible
movable	movible
notable	notable
observable	observable
obtainable	obtenible
operable	operable
passable	pasable
possible	posible
potable	potable
presentable	presentable
probable	probable
reasonable	razonable
removable	removible
resistible	resistible
responsible	responsable
sensible	sensible
serviceable	servible
sociable	sociable
soluble	soluble
supportable	soportable
sufferable	sufrible
terrible	terrible
tractable	tratable
usable	usable
variable	variable
visible	visible
vulnerable	vulnerable

ENDINGS: -ty

TERMINACIONES: -dad

ENGLISH	SPANISH
amiability	amabilidad
amenity	amenidad
animosity	animosidad
abnormality	anormalidad
atrocity	atrocidad
calamity	calamidad
capacity	capacidad
charity	caridad
cavity	cavidad
clarity	claridad
community	comunidad
continuity	continuidad
quality	cualidad
debility	debilidad
deformity	deformidad
density	densidad
difficulty	dificultad
durability	durabilidad
infirmity	enfermedad
stability	estabilidad
sterility	esterilidad
eternity	eternidad
facility	facilidad
faculty	facultad
familiarity	familiaridad
femininity	feminidad
flexibility	flexibilidad
formality	formalidad
fragility	fragilidad
generality	generalidad
generosity	generosidad
gentility	gentilidad
gravity	gravedad
ability	habilidad
hospitality	hospitalidad
humanity	humanidad
impossibility	imposibilidad
improbability	improbabilidad
incapacity	incapacidad
identity	identidad
instability	inestabilidad
immobility	inmovilidad
immunity	inmunidad
insensibility	insensibilidad
intensity	intensidad

ENGLISH	SPANISH
invisibility	invisibilidad
irritability	irritabilidad
legality	legalidad
liberty	libertad
maternity	maternidad
morality	moralidad
mobility	movilidad
nationality	nacionalidad
naturalness	naturalidad
necessity	necesidad
nervousness	nerviosidad
neutrality	neutralidad
obesity	obesidad
opportunity	oportunidad
partiality	parcialidad
popularity	popularidad
possibility	posibilidad
priority	prioridad
probability	probabilidad
regularity	regularidad
responsibility	responsabilidad
sanity	sanidad
security	seguridad
sensibility	sensibilidad
similarity	similaridad
solemnity	solemnidad
solidarity	solidaridad
university	universidad
vanity	vanidad
versatility	versatilidad
viscosity	viscosidad
visibility	visibilidad
vitality	vitalidad

ENDINGS: -sis, -lis

TERMINACIONES: -sis, -lis

ENGLISH	SPANISH
acidosis	acidosis
alkalosis	alcalosis
amebiasis	amebiasis
analysis	análisis
anuresis	anuresis
arteriosclerosis	arterioesclerosis
avitaminosis	avitaminosis
brucellosis	brucelosis

ENGLISH	SPANISH
cyanosis	cianosis
cirrhosis	cirrosis
chlorosis	clorosis
diagnosis	diagnosis
dose	dosis
elephantiasis	elefantiasis
sclerosis	esclerosis
halitosis	halitosis
hypnosis	hipnosis
hypochondriasis	hipocondriasis
hypothesis	hipótesis
lordosis	lordosis
mononucleosis	mononucleosis
necrosis	necrosis
paralysis	parálisis
paresis	paresis
prognosis	prognosis
prosthesis	prótesis
psychoanalysis	psicoanálisis
psychosis	psicosis
psoriasis	psoriasis
syphilis	sífilis
synthesis	síntesis
thesis	tesis
phthisis	tisis
torticollis	tortícolis
trichinosis	triquinosis
thrombosis	trombosis
turberculosis	tuberculosis

ENDINGS: -itis   ## TERMINACIONES: -itis

ENGLISH	SPANISH
appendicitis	apendicitis
arthritis	artritis
bronchitis	bronquitis
bursitis	bursitis
cystitis	cistitis
colitis	colitis
conjunctivitis	conjuntivitis
dermatitis	dermatitis
diverticulitis	diverticulitis
encephalitis	encefalitis
encephalomyelitis	encefalomielitis
endocarditis	endocarditis

ENGLISH	SPANISH
enteritis	enteritis
scleritis	escleritis
sclerotitis	esclerotitis
phlebitis	flebitis
gastritis	gastritis
gingivitis	gingivitis
hepatitis	hepatitis
iritis	iritis
laryngitis	laringitis
mastoiditis	mastoiditis
meningitis	meningitis
metritis	metritis
myocarditis	miocarditis
osteomyelitis	osteomielitis
otitis	otitis
pancreatitis	pancreatitis
parotitis	parotiditis, parotitis
pericarditis	pericarditis
peritonitis	peritonitis
pyelitis	pielitis
poliomyelitis	poliomielitis
prostatitis	prostatitis
retinitis	retinitis
rhinitis	rinitis
sinusitis	sinusitis
tonsillitis	tonsilitis
vaginitis	vaginitis

NUMBERS AND MISCELLANEOUS

NUMBERS	NUMERALS	NÚMEROS
one	1	uno
two	2	dos
three	3	tres
four	4	cuatro
five	5	cinco
six	6	seis
seven	7	siete
eight	8	ocho
nine	9	nueve
ten	10	diez
eleven	11	once

NUMBERS	NUMERALS		NÚMEROS
twelve	12		doce
thirteen	13		trece
fourteen	14		catorce
fifteen	15		quince
sixteen	16		dieciséis, diez y seis
seventeen	17		diecisiete, diez y siete
eighteen	18		dieciocho, diez y ocho
nineteen	19		diecinueve, diez y nueve
twenty	20		veinte
twenty-one	21		veintiuno, veinte y uno
twenty-two	22		veintidós, veinte y dos
twenty-three	23		veintitrés, veinte y tres
twenty-four	24		veinticuatro, veinte y cuatro
twenty-five	25		veinticinco, veinte y cinco
twenty-six	26		veintiséis, veinte y seis
twenty-seven	27		veintisiete, veinte y siete
twenty-eight	28		veintiocho, veinte y ocho
twenty-nine	29		veintinueve, veinte y nueve
thirty	30		treinta
forty	40		cuarenta
fifty	50		cincuenta
sixty	60		sesenta
seventy	70		setenta
eighty	80		ochenta
ninety	90		noventa
one hundred	100		cien, ciento
two hundred	200		doscientos, -as
three hundred	300		trescientos, -as
four hundred	400		cuatrocientos, -as
five hundred	500		quinientos, -as
six hundred	600		seiscientos, -as
seven hundred	700		setecientos, -as
eight hundred	800		ochocientos, -as
nine hundred	900		novecientos, -as
one thousand	1,000	1.000	mil
one million	1,000,000	1.000.000	un millón

ORDINAL NUMBERS		NÚMEROS ORDINALES	
first	1st	primer, primero, -a	1°, 1ª
second	2nd	segundo, -a	2°, 2ª
third	3rd	tercer, tercero, -a	3°, 3ª
fourth	4th	cuarto, -a	4°, 4ª
fifth	5th	quinto, -a	5°, 5ª

ORDINAL NUMBERS

sixth	6th
seventh	7th
eighth	8th
ninth	9th
tenth	10th

NÚMEROS ORDINALES

sexto, -a	6°, 6ª
séptimo, -a	7°, 7ª
octavo, -a	8°, 8ª
noveno, -a	9°, 9ª
décimo, -a	10°, 10ª

MONTHS / MESES

January	enero
February	febrero
March	marzo
April	abril
May	mayo
June	junio
July	julio
August	agosto
September	septiembre
October	octubre
November	noviembre
December	diciembre

DAYS OF THE WEEK / DÍAS DE LA SEMANA

Sunday	el domingo
Monday	el lunes
Tuesday	el martes
Wednesday	el miércoles
Thursday	el jueves
Friday	el viernes
Saturday	el sábado

SEASONS OF THE YEAR / ESTACIONES DEL AÑO

spring	la primavera
summer	el verano
fall, autumn	el otoño
winter	el invierno

CARDINAL POINTS / PUNTOS CARDINALES

north, northern	el norte, septentrional
south, southern	el sur, meridional
east, eastern	el este, oriental
west, western	el oeste, occidental

TIEMPO, ESTACIONES, MESES Y DÍAS DE LA SEMANA

tiempo	*time*
hora	*hour*
segundos	*seconds*
minutos	*minutes*
media hora	*half-hour*
mediodía	*noon*
medianoche	*midnight*
anoche	*last night*
hoy	*today*
esta mañana	*this morning*
esta tarde	*this afternoon*
esta noche	*this evening, tonight*
ayer	*yesterday*
anteayer	*day before yesterday*
la mañana	*tomorrow*
pasado mañana	*day after tomorrow*
el día	*day*
los días	*days*
la semana	*week*
el mes	*month*
los meses	*months*
el año	*year*
el año bisiesto	*leap year*
el siglo	*century*
el año pasado	*last year*
el año venidero	*next year*
el año próximo	*next year*
la semana entrante	*next week*
el día siguiente	*the following day*
el día de trabajo	*working day*
el día feriado	*working day*
el día de fiesta	*holiday*
las vacaciones	*holidays*

THE STATES OF MEXICO AND THEIR ABBREVIATIONS

Aguascalientes-Ags.
Baja California-B.C.
Campeche-Camp.
Chiapas-Chis.
Chihuahua-Chih.
Coahuila-Coah.
Colima-Col.
Distrito Federal-D.F.
Durango-Dgo.
Guanajuato-Gto.
Guerrero-Gro.
Hidalgo-Hgo.
Jalisco-Jal.
México-Mex.
Michoacán-Mich.
Morelos-Mor.

Nayarit-Nay.
Nuevo León-N.L.
Oaxaca-Oax.
Puebla-Pueb.
Querétaro-Qto.
Quintana Roo (no abbreviation)
San Luis Potosí-S.L.P.
Sinaloa-Sin.
Sonora-Son.
Tabasco-Tab.
Tamaulipas-Tamps.
Tlaxcala-Tlax.
Veracruz-Ver.
Yucatán-Yuc.
Zacatecas-Zac.

OCCUPATIONS

ENGLISH	SPANISH
agent	agente
artist	artista
aviator	aviador
ballplayer	pelotero
barber	peluquero, barbero
blacksmith	herrero
bookkeeper	tenedor de libros
book seller	librero
bootblack	limpiabotas, bolero
butcher	carnicero
carpenter	carpintero
cattleman	ganadero
chauffeur	chofer, chófer
chicken raiser	gallinero
clerk	dependiente
conductor	conductor
constable	alguacil
cook	cocincro
cotton grower	algodonero
cowboy	vaquero
customs agent	agente de aduana, aduanero

ENGLISH	SPANISH
dairyman	lechero
dancer	bailador, bailarina
dentist	dentista
director	director
doctor	doctor, médico
driver	muletero (horses), cochero (coach)
druggist	boticario, droguista
engineer	ingeniero
farmer	hacendado, agricultor
fisherman	pescador
gardener	jardinero
guide	guía
harvester	cosechero
hatmaker	sombrerero
inventor	inventor
irrigator	regador
jeweler	joyero
laborer	jornalero, trabajador, labrador
lawyer	abogado, licenciado
machinist	maquinista
mailcarrier	cartero
manufacturer	fabricante
mason	albañil
merchant	comerciante
mechanic	mecánico
midwife	partera
miller	molinero
miner	minero
musician	músico
nurse	enfermera
obstetrician	partero
official	oficial
painter	pintor
peddler	comerciante ambulante, buhonero
picker (cotton)	piscador
pilot	piloto
plasterer	emplastador
plumber	plomero
planter	plantador, sembrador
porter	portero, cargador
priest	cura, sacerdote, padre
promoter	promotor
rancher	ranchero
sailor	marinero
seller	vendedor
servant	mozo, sirviente, criado
seamstress	costurera

ENGLISH	SPANISH
sharecropper	mediero
shepherd	pastor, borrequero
sheriff	alguacil, policía
shoemaker	zapatero
soldier	soldado
stenographer	taquígrafo
surgeon	cirujano
tailor	sastre
teacher	profesor, maestro
tinsmith	hojalatero
usher	conserje, acomodador
valet	camarero
waiter	mozo, mesero, camarero
washerwoman	lavandera
watchmaker	relojero
wet nurse	nodriza
woodworker (cabinetmaker)	ebanista
worker	trabajador, obrero

2. Verbs

A. General Guidelines

The infinitive form, or name, of a Spanish verb can be readily recognized by the presence of one of the three infinitive endings, *-ar*, *-er*, or *-ir*. The *-ar*, *-er*, or *-ir* ending on a verb indicates not only the infinitive form, but also the class to which the verb belongs. All Spanish verbs belong to one of the three classes.

Examples:

oper*ar*	*to operate*
com*er*	*to eat*
escrib*ir*	*to write*

The part of the verb before the infinitive ending is called the verb's *stem*.

Examples:

operar = *oper-* (stem) + -ar (infinitive ending)
comer = *com-* (stem) + -er (infinitive ending)
escribir = *escrib-* (stem) + -ir (infinitive ending)

As will be explained further below, Spanish verbs form their different meanings and tenses by adding endings to their stems and/or by using helping verbs. The endings added to verb stems usually differ slightly depending on the verb's class (*-ar*, *-er*, or *-ir*).

Verbs in Spanish are either regular or irregular. Regular verbs have stems which remain unchanged, and their meanings are formed by adding standard sets of endings to the stems or by using helping verbs. Irregular verbs, which will be discussed below, either show a stem change in some of their forms, or use something other than the standard set of endings to form some of their meanings. In general, though, you should assume that a verb is regular unless you learn otherwise.

Some Spanish verbs are *reflexive* in some or all of their meanings. That is, they express an action which in some way reflects back upon the subject. These verbs are usually written with *-se* following the infinitive ending.

Examples:

quedar*se*   *to stay*
poner*se*   *to put on*
sentir*se*   *to feel*

When conjugated, these reflexive verbs are preceded by a reflexive pronoun which matches the verb's subject.

Examples:

Yo *me* quedo aquí.   *I stay here.*
Usted *se* pone la bata.   *You are putting on the gown.*
La señora *se* siente enferma.   *The lady feels sick.*

The reflexive pronoun is often not directly expressed in translating such reflexive constructions into English.

B. Cognate Verbs

The meanings of many Spanish verbs will be extremely easy to learn because the verbs have English cognates (that is, the Spanish and English verbs share a common linguistic origin). These Spanish verbs therefore closely resemble their English counterparts.

Examples:

amputar   *amputate*
sufrir   *suffer*
vomitar   *vomit*

C. Regular Verbs: Present Tense

The Spanish present tense can have several loose translations which are equivalent both to the English present tense and to the English constructions formed by the helping verb *to be* plus the present participle and by the helping verb *to do* plus the infinitive. The examples show several equally valid English translations for the Spanish present tense.

Examples:

yo hablo	*I talk, I am talking, I do talk*
usted come	*you eat, you are eating, you do eat*
ella escribe	*she writes, she is writing, she does write*

The following are the endings which are added to the verb stems of the three classes of Spanish verbs to form their meanings in the present tense.

-AR Verbs		-ER Verbs		-IR Verbs	
-o	-amos[1]	-o	-emos	-o	-imos
-as }		-es }		-es }	
-a }	-an[2]	-e }	-en	-e }	-en

Examples:

hablar (infinitive)

hablo	*I talk*	hablamos	*we talk*
hablas	*you (singular) talk*		
habla	*he/she talks, you (singular) talk*	hablan	*they/you (plural) talk*

comer (infinitive)

como	*I eat*	comemos	*we eat*
comes	*you (singular) eat*		
come	*he/she eats, you (singular) eat*	comen	*they/you (plural) eat*

escribir (infinitive)

escribo	*I write*	escribimos	*we write*
escribes	*you (singular) write*		
escribe	*he/she writes, you (singular) write*	escriben	*they/you (plural) write*

Singular and plural formal commands are formed by adding the following endings to the three classes of verbs.

-AR Verbs		-ER Verbs		-IR Verbs	
-e	-en	-a	-an	-a	-an

---

1. Listen for sounds identifying the subject of the verb: yo *-o*, tú *-s*, nosotros *-mos*, ellos, ellas-*n*. Learn to train your ear.

2. Third-person plural is plural form for **tú, usted, ustedes, él, ella, ellos** and **ellas.**

Examples:

hable	*talk*	(addressed to *you*, singular)
hablen	*talk*	(addressed to *you*, plural)
coma	*eat*	(addressed to *you*, singular)
coman	*eat*	(addressed to *you*, plural)
escriba	*write*	(addressed to *you*, singular)
escriban	*write*	(addressed to *you*, plural)

(An informal Spanish command form also exists, but it is customarily reserved for use among relatives and close friends and is therefore inappropriate for hospital and medical settings, which are considered relatively formal.)

Commands involving reflexive verbs are formed as described above, except that the reflexive pronoun -*se* is added to the command form and an accent is placed on the third syllable from the end.[1]

Examples:

quédese	*stay*
póngase	*put on*

D. Irregular Verbs: Present Tense

Spanish has many irregular verbs. Learning them is facilitated, however, by the fact that there are a number of common irregularities in which an entire group of verbs all show the same pattern of irregularity. There are, in fact, very few totally irregular verbs that do not follow one of the commonly encountered patterns of irregularity.

In two such groups of verbs that are irregular in the present tense, a vowel that appears in the stem of the infinitive changes before the present-tense endings are added—with the exception of the "we" form, for which the stem does not change. These are called stem-changing verbs. The present-tense endings themselves are not affected by this irregularity; however, the endings are the same as for regular -*ar*, -*er*, and -*ir* verbs.

In the first of these two groups of stem-changing verbs, the stem vowel -*o* changes to -*ue*.

---

1. An accent is required where stress would normally fall—which is often the third syllable from the end.

Examples:

poder (infinitive)   **doler** (infinitive)

puedo	podemos	duelo	dolemos
puedes		dueles	
puede	pueden[2]	duele	duelen

In the second of the two groups of stem-changing verbs, the stem vowel *-e* changes to *-ie.*

Examples:

querer (infinitive)   **sentirse** (infinitive)

quiero	queremos[3]	me siento	nos sentimos
quieres		te sientes	
quiere	quieren	se siente	se sienten

Some verbs only partly follow one of the patterns of irregularity described above, showing the stem changes only in some of their forms.[4]

Example:

tener (infinitive)

tengo	tenemos
tienes	
tiene	tienen

Other verbs are not irregular in their stems, but show unpredictable irregularities that simply must be memorized.

Examples:

padecer (infinitive)   **ir** (infinitive)

padezco	padecemos	voy	vamos
padeces		vas	
padece	padecen	va	van

E. Present Perfect Tense

In Spanish as in English, the present perfect is a compound tense, in which the present-tense forms of *haber* (*to have*) are used as a helping verb with the past participle of another verb.

---

2. These are sometimes easy to remember because their form resembles a shoe, e.g., shoe verbs.

3. Notice that the *nosotros* form will always resemble the infinitive.

4. The third class (III) (E > I) of stem-changing verbs has been omitted on this level.

Examples:

he vomitado	*I have vomited*
he perdido	*you have (or he/she has) lost*

The first element of the past-perfect construction, the verb *haber,* is irregular and is conjugated as follows in the present tense:

he	*I have*	hemos	*we have*
has	*you (singular) have*		
ha	*he/she has, you (singular) have*	han	*they/you (plural) have*

The second element of the past-perfect construction, the past participle, is formed by adding the following endings to the verb stems of the three classes of verbs.

-AR Verbs	*-ER Verbs*	*-IR Verbs*
-ado	*-ido*	*-ido*

Many Spanish verbs have irregular past participles which must be learned individually. As with other Spanish linguistic irregularities, however, there are groups of past participles which have similar irregularities, making them easier to remember.

Examples:

he puesto	*I have put*
ha escrito	*he (or she) has (or you have) written*
han dicho	*they (or you, plural) have said*
hemos hecho	*we have done*

F. Future Tense Using *Ir a* + Infinitive

In Spanish as in English, the future can be formed as a compound tense by using present-tense forms of *ir* ("to go") as a helping verb with the infinitive of another verb.

Examples:

voy a dormir	*I am going to sleep*
van a andar	*they (or you, plural) are going to walk*

Ir is an irregular verb; its present-tense conjugation was shown in item I.2.E above.

In addition to the *ir a* + infinitive construction, Spanish also has a future tense that does not use a helping verb and is equivalent to the English future tense.

G. Verbs that Present Special Problems

ser and *estar*

Ser and *estar* are both irregular verbs, which are conjugated as follows in the present tense.

ser (infinitive)		**estar** (infinitive)	
soy	somos	estoy	estamos
eres		estás	
es	son	está	están

Ser and *estar* are both translated "to be," but they differ in the *sense* of their meaning. *Ser* indicates "to be" in the sense of identification, time, origin, or permanent condition; *estar* indicates "to be" in the sense of position, location, or a temporary condition.

Examples:

SER

identification	Este señor **es** el paciente.
	(*This gentleman is the patient.*)
time	La operación **es** a las cuatro.
	(*The operation is at four o'clock.*)
origin	**Soy** de México.
	(*I am from Mexico.*)
permanent condition	**Es** alérgica a la leche.
	(*She is allergic to milk.*)

ESTAR

position or location	La medicina **está** en la mesa.
	(*The medicine is on the table.*)
temporary condition	**Estoy** muy enferma.
	(*I am very sick.*)
Soy loco vs. Estoy loco	**Estoy** loco por . . .
	(*I'm crazy—temporary—about*)

Common expressions with ESTAR

Estar de   to be temporarily performing action indicated by noun:

Estoy de paseo.
de pie.
de prisa.
de viaje.
de vuelta.
de buen humor.

Estar con   to be with a person or to be in a state:

Estoy con fiebre.
gripe.
ellos.

Estar a	to be at a certain day of the week:

¿A cuántos estamos?   Estamos a lunes.
                        Estamos a quince de marzo.

to be a certain price.
El carro está a mil dólares.

Estar para	to be about to do something or to be ready for something:

Estoy para comer.   Trabajo para Aetna.
No está para bromas.
¿Está usted para ir de viaje?

Estar por	to be in favor of:

¿Está usted por terminar el trabajo?
El médico está por amputar la pierna.

Telling time is commonly expressed with SER.

¿Qué hora es?   Es la una.
                  Son las dos.

- *hace* in time expressions

Two of the idiomatic translations of *hace* ("it makes") are "ago" and "for" when used with expressions of time. *Hace* can refer to action that was begun and completed in the past (the "ago" translation) or to action that began in the past and continues into the present (the "for" translation). The second verb in the sentence must be in the past tense to convey the idea of *ago*.

Examples:

Eso pasó hace dos horas.	*That happened two hours ago.* (Literally, *"It makes two hours [since] that happened."*)
Hace dos horas que estoy aquí.	*I have been here for two hours.* (Literally, *"It makes two hours that I am here."*)

- *hay*

Hay is a special, irregular form of the verb *haber*. It is impersonal (that is, it does not refer to a specific subject) and is translated "there is" or "there are." It is particularly useful for forming descriptions.

Examples:

Hay un paciente en la sala de emergencia.	*There is a patient in the emergency room.*
Hay dos píldoras en el plato.	*There are two pills on the plate.*

- verbs taking an indirect object construction (*doler, gustar*)

Some expressions which are formed in English by a subject-verb-direct object (I like dessert) or by a possessive pronoun-noun-verb (His arm hurts) are formed in Spanish by an indirect object pronoun-verb-subject construction. Such Spanish expressions are usually translated very loosely.

Examples:

Me gusta postre.	*I like dessert.* (Literally, *"The dessert is pleasing to me."*)
Me gustan las enfermeras.[1]	*I like the nurses.* (Literally, *"The nurses are pleasing to me."*)
Le duele el brazo.	*His arm hurts.* (Literally, *"The arm is painful to him."*)
Me duelen los pies.	*My feet hurt.* (Literally, *"The feet are painful to me."*)

3. Adverbs

Many Spanish adverbs are formed by adding the ending *-mente* to the feminine singular form of an adjective.

Examples:

rápido	rápidamente
tranquilo	tranquilamente
frecuente[2]	frecuentemente
general[2]	generalmente

Other adverbs do not follow the pattern of adding *-mente* and must simply be learned individually.

Examples:

quizás	*perhaps*
durante	*during*
casi	*almost*

4. Adjectives

A. General Guidelines

Unlike English adjectives, all Spanish adjectives match[3] the nouns they modify in number (i.e., singular or plural). Spanish adjectives which end in

---

1. When referring to liking a person, many Spanish speakers will use the expression **caer bien** or **mal** (*to fall well*), e.g., **Me caen bien las enfermeras.** *I like the nurses.* **Me caen mal.** *I don't like them.*

2. Note that there is no gender form for adjectives ending in *e* or in a consonant. Therefore, *mente* is attached to the entire neuter form.

3. agree with

-*o* will also match the nouns they modify in gender (i.e., masculine or feminine). Spanish adjectives end in either vowels or consonants, with those ending in vowels forming their plurals by adding -*s* and those ending in consonants forming their plurals by adding -*es*.

Examples:

amarillo (*yellow*)
  la píldor*a* amarill*a*
  las cápsul*as* amarill*as*
  el líquid*o* amarill*o*

fuerte (*strong*)
  el paciente fuerte
  las pacient*es* fuert*es*

peor (*worse*)
  el peor problema
  las peor*es* situacion*es*[4]

In Spanish as in English, one group of adjectives is formed from the past participles of verbs and is often translated "-ed."

Examples:

curar	*to cure*
curado	*cured*
admitir	*to admit*
admitido	*admitted*
perder	*to lose*
perdido	*lost*

To form the past participle, take off the vowel + *r*, add *ado* to *ar verbs*, *ido* to *er, ir verbs*. Adjectives formed from the past participles follow the rules for other Spanish adjectives ending in -*o* (i.e., they match the nouns they modify in both number and gender).

The definite articles (*el, la, los,* and *las*) and the indefinite articles (*un, una, unos,* and *unas*) are also adjectives. The Spanish definite and indefinite articles, unlike their English counterparts, match the nouns they modify in both number and gender.

Examples:

el médico	*the doctor*
los líquidos	*the liquids*
la enfermera	*the nurse*
las comidas	*the meals*

4. **Mejor** (*better*); **peor** (*worse*) precedes the noun it modifies.

un departamento	*a department*
unos accidentes	*some accidents*
una semana	*a week*
unas pacientes	*some patients*

B. Cognate Adjectives

The meanings of many Spanish adjectives will be extremely easy to learn because the adjectives have English cognates (that is, the Spanish and English adjectives share a common linguistic origin). These Spanish adjectives therefore closely resemble their English counterparts.

In very many cases, a Spanish adjective ending has a direct English equivalent. The following are some of the most common cognate adjective endings, showing the Spanish endings and their English equivalents.

-ico = -ic, -ical

Examples:

alcohól*ico*	alcohol*ic*
antisépt*ico*	antisept*ic*
mecán*ico*	mechan*ical*

-rio = -ry

Examples:

ambulato*rio*	ambulato*ry*
necesa*rio*	necessa*ry*
preparato*rio*	preparato*ry*

-oso = -ous

Examples:

contagi*oso*	contagi*ous*
fibr*oso*	fibr*ous*
intraven*oso*	intraven*ous*

-ante, -ente = -ant, -ent

Examples:

excel*ente*	excell*ent*
protest*ante*	Protest*ant*
import*ante*	import*ant*

-ble = -ble

Examples:

incura*ble*	incura*ble*
posi*ble*	possi*ble*
varia*ble*	varia*ble*

5. Pronouns

In Spanish as in English, pronouns are used in place of nouns in sentences. Pronouns may take the place of the subject (that which performs the action stated in the verb), the indirect object (that which indirectly receives the action of the verb), and the direct object (that which directly receives the action of the verb). The following are the three groups of pronouns and some examples of their use.

SUBJECT PRONOUNS

yo	*I*
tú	*you (informal, singular)*
él	*he*
ella	*she*
usted	*you (formal, singular)*
ellos	*they (masculine)*
ellas	*they (feminine)*
ustedes	*you (formal, plural)*

Examples:

Yo estoy enfermo.	*I am sick.*
Usted busca el zaguán.	*You are looking for the lobby.*
Ellas toman las píldoras.	*They (feminine) take the pills.*

INDIRECT OBJECT PRONOUNS

me	*to me*
te	*to you (informal, singular)*
le	*to him, to her, to you (formal, singular)*
nos	*to us*
les	*to them (masculine or feminine), to you (formal, plural)*

Examples:

La enfermera me trae la medicina.	*The nurse brings me the medicine.*
El dolor le molesta.	*The pain bothers him (or her, or you).*
El paciente les escribe una carta.	*The patient writes a letter to them (or to you).*

DIRECT OBJECT PRONOUNS

me	*me*
te	*you (informal, singular)*
lo	*him, it, you (formal, masculine singular)*
la	*her, it, you (formal, feminine singular)*

nos	us
los	them (masculine), you (formal, masculine plural)
las	them (feminine), you (formal, feminine plural)

You will notice that Spanish has several ways of saying *you: tú* and *usted. Tú*, the informal form, is reserved for use with family members and close friends and is therefore not dealt with in this book. *Usted*, the formal form, is more commonly used in hospital and medical settings, which are considered relatively formal. You, however, will hear the *tú* form used by your Spanish speaking colleagues. It is preferable to wait until you are invited to use the familiar form.

6. Prepositions

Spanish prepositions are used in approximately the same way as English prepositions in sentence constructions.

Many Spanish prepositions are used and translated exactly like their English counterparts.

Examples:

| El médico viene *con* la enfermera. | The doctor comes *with* the nurse. |
| Ella tiene un dolor encima del corazón. | She has a pain *over* her heart. |

There are a number of cases, however, where several English meanings are expressed by a single Spanish preposition.

Examples:

El doctor llega *de* la sala de emergencia.	The doctor arrives *from* the emergency room.
Es la medicina *de* la paciente.	It is the patient's medicine (the medicine *of* the patient).
La paciente pone la medicina en la boca.	The patient puts the medicine *in* her mouth.
El técnico deja la orden en la mesa.	The technician leaves the order *on* the table.

The following is a list of the most commonly used prepositions:

a	to
de	of, from, about
con	with
para	to, for
entre	between, among

en	*in, into, on*
bajo	*under*
sobre	*over*
hasta	*until*
hacia	*towards*
sin	*without*
excepto	*except*
detrás	*behind*
debajo	*under*
cerca	*near*
ante	*before*
desde	*since*
según	*according to*

In still other cases, Spanish uses an entirely different preposition to express a particular meaning than would be used in English, or Spanish uses a preposition that would not appear at all in English (and which is therefore omitted when translating such Spanish constructions).

One common example of the Spanish use of a preposition that is not required in English is the personal preposition *a* which appears before a direct or indirect object to indicate that the object is a person.

Examples:

El técnico trae a la paciente.	The technician brings the patient.
El técnico trae la silla de ruedas.	The technician brings the wheelchair.

SYNTAX

In Spanish as in English, statements are formed by a subject, a verb, and a complement.

Examples:

subject	verb	complement
Mi nombre	es	Juan.
(*My name*	*is*	*Juan.*)
El señor	se siente	enfermo.
(*The gentleman*	*feels*	*sick.*)

To make such a statement negative, simply add *no* before the verb.

Examples:

Mi nombre *no* es Juan.	My name is *not* Juan.
El señor no se siente enfermo.	The gentleman does *not* feel sick.

VOCABULARY

A

a at, to, toward; **— menudo** often;
   — veces at times
abajo underneath
abierto (a) open
abdomen (*m*) abdomen
aborto (*m*) miscarriage;
   — voluntario abortion
abrigarse to cover up
abrigo (*m*) overcoat
abril (*m*) April
abrir to open; **abra** (*imperative*) open
abuelo (*m*) grandfather
acabar to have just finished
accite (*m*) oil
acerca de about, with regard to
acercarse to get close
ácido (a) acid
aconsejar (de) to advise
acordar(se) to remember
acostar(se) to lie down; **acuéstese**
   (*imperative*) lie down
¡adelante! come in!
adelgazar to lose weight
además besides
aderezo (*m*) salad dressing
adicto (*m*) addict
adjuntar to attach
admitido (a) admitted
adormecer to deaden
afeitar(se) to shave (oneself)
afuera (*adv*) outside
agente (*m*) agent; **— de**
   seguros insurance agent
agosto (*m*) August
agua (*m*) water
aguantar to stand (put up with)
agudo(a) sharp
ahihado (*m*) godson
ahora (*adv*) now
aireacondicionado (*m*) air conditioning

aislamiento (*m*) isolation
ajo (*m*) garlic
al to the; **— año** per year;
   — frente forward; **— menos** at
   least; **— través de** across, over
albaricoque (*m*) apricot
alergía (*f*) allergy
algo something
alguno (a) some
alimentar to nourish
almohada (*f*) pillow
almuerzo (*m*) lunch
alto (a) high, tall; **¡alto!** halt!; **dar de**
   —a discharged
alumbramiento (*m*) delivery
alzar to lift
allí (*adv*) there
ama de casa (*f*) housewife
amable kind
amarillo (a) yellow
amarrar to tie up
amígdalas (*f pl*) tonsils
amígdalitis (*f*) tonsillitis
amigo (*m*) friend
análisis (*m*) test
analizador (*m*) analyzer
ananá (*f*) pineapple
andador (*m*) walker
andar to walk
anestesia (*f*) anesthesia
anfetaminas (*f pl*) amphetamines
anillo (*m*) ring (I.U.D. ring)
ano (*m*) anus
ansiedad (*f*) anxiety
anteayer day before yesterday
antes (*adv*) before
año (*m*) year
aorta (*f*) aorta
apagar to turn off, to put out (a light)
aparato (*m*) system, equipment;
   — intrauterino (*m*) I.U.D.
apartamento (*m*) apartment

239

apellido (*m*) surname
apenas (*adv*) barely
apéndice (*m*) appendix
apendicitis (*f*) appendicitis
apetito (*m*) appetite
apio (*m*) celery
apósito (*m*) dressing
apretar (ie) to tighten
aprovecharse de to profit by
apurarse to be in a hurry
aquí (*adv*) here
arañar to scratch
arañazo (*m*) scratch
archivo (*m*) records
armazón (*f*) framework
arreglar to arrange
arriba (*adv*) up
arrojar to throw; to throw up
arroz (*m*) rice
arteria (*f*) artery
articulaciones (*f pl*) joints
ascensor (*m*) elevator
así (*adv*) like this, this way
asma (*f*) asthma
asustarse to get scared
ataque (*m*) attack; **— al
    cerebro** stroke; **— al corazón** heart
    attack
atar to tie
atender to look after
atendiente (*m or f*) attendant, helper
atentamente (*adv*) attentively
atragantarse to choke
atraso (*m*) setback
atún (*m*) tuna
audífono (*m*) hearing aid
aumentar to increase
aún (*adv*) even
ausculator to listen with a stethoscope
avisar to warn
aviso (*m*) warning
axila (*f*) armpit
ayer (*adv*) yesterday
ayuda (*f*) help
ayudante (*m or f*) helper
ayudar to help
azúcar (*m*) sugar
azul (*m*) blue
azuloso (a) bluish

B

bacín (*m*) bedpan, basin
bajar to go down, descend; **— de
    peso** to lose weight; **bájese**
    (*imperative*) get down
bajo (a) short
balanceado (a) balanced
banco de sangre (*m*) blood bank
bandeja (*f*) tray
bañadera (*f*) bathtub
bañarse to bathe oneself
baño (*m*) bathroom
barato (a) cheap
barbilla (*f*) chin
barbiturato (*m*) barbiturate
barriga (*f*) abdomen
barrio (*m*) neighborhood, subdivision
bastante (*adv*) enough
bata (*f*) robe, hospital gown
bazo (*m*) spleen
bebé (*m or f*) baby
bebida (*f*) drink
biberón (*m*) baby bottle
bidé, bidet (*m*) bidet
bien (*adv*) well
boca (*f*) mouth; **— abajo** head down
    (on stomach); **— arriba** head up
bodega (*f*) warehouse; grocery store
bolígrafo (*m*) ballpoint pen
bolsa (*f*) sac, bag
bostezar to yawn
botón (*m*) button
brazo (*m*) arm
brécol, brocolí (*m*) broccoli
bronquios (*m*) bronchial tubes
bueno (a) good
buzón (*m*) mailbox

C

cabecera (*f*) head (of bed, etc.)
cabello (*m*) hair
cabeza (*f*) head
cada (*adj*) each, every
cadera (*f*) hip
caer(se) to fall (down)
café (*m*) coffee; brown

cafetín (*m*)   cafeteria
caja (*f*)   box; cash register;
   — torácica   thoractic cavity
cajero (*m or f*)   cashier
calambre (*m*)   cramp
calcetines (*m*)   socks
calcio (*m*)   calcium
calcificado (a)   calcified
cálculo (*m*)   stone;
   — biliares   gallstones;
   — reñales   kidney stones
caldo (*m*)   broth (soup)
calefación (*f*)   heat (heating system)
calentura (*f*)   fever
caliente (*adj*)   hot
calmante (*m*)   tranquilizer
calmar(se)   to calm down; **cálmese**
   (*imperative*)   calm down
calor (*m*)   heat; **tener —**   to be hot
calzoncillos (*m*)   men's shorts
calzones (*m*)   panties
calle (*f*)   street
cama (*f*)   bed
camarones (*m pl*)   shrimp
cambiar   to change
cambio (*m*)   change
camilla (*f*)   stretcher
camillero (*m or f*)   orderly
caminar   to walk
camino (*m*)   walkway, road, pathway
camisa (*f*)   shirt
campanilla (*f*)   uvula, epiglottis
campo (*m*)   field, range
cáncer (*m*)   cancer
cansado (a)   tired
cansancio (*m*)   tiredness
capellán (*m*)   chaplain
capilar (*m*)   capillary
cápsula (*f*)   capsule
carbohidratos (*m*)   carbohydrates
cardiopulmonar (*m or f*)
   cardiopulmonary; **resucitador —**
   cardiopulmonary resuscitator
carne (*f*)   meat; **— asada**   roast beef;
   — de puerco   pork; **— de res**   beef
caro (a)   expensive
carpintero (*m*)   carpenter
carta (*f*)   letter
cartílago (*m*)   cartilage

casa (*f*)   house
casado (a)   married
casi (*adv*)   almost
caso (*m*)   case
catarro (*m*)   cold
catéter (*m*)   catheter
católico (a)   Catholic
cebolla (*f*)   onion
cédula (*f*)   identification card
ceja (*f*)   eyebrow
cena (*f*)   dinner, evening meal
centígrado (*m*)   centigrade
centímetro (*m*)   centimeter
centro (*m*)   center; **al —**   downtown
cepillo (*m*)   brush
cerca (*adv*)   close
cercano (a)   close
cerebro (*m*)   brain
cereza (*f*)   cherry
cerrado (a)   closed
cerrar   to close
cerveza (*f*)   beer
ciego (a)   blind
ciento (*m*)   one hundred; **por —**   per
   cent
cilindro (*m*)   cylinder
cintura (*f*)   waist
cinturón (*m*)   belt
circular   to circle, rotate; **circule**
   (*imperative*)   circle or rotate
ciruela (*f*)   plum; **— pasa**   prune
cirugía (*f*)   surgery
cirujano (*m*)   surgeon
cita (*f*)   date, appointment
ciudad (*f*)   city
ciudadano (*m*)   citizen
claro (a)   clear
claro (*adv*)   clearly, sure
clave (*f*)   key; code
clínica (*f*)   clinic, hospital; **— de
   reposo**   nursing home; **— de
   paciente ambulante**   outpatient
   clinic
clínico (a)   clinical
cloro (*m*)   Clorox; bleach
cobija (*f*)   blanket
cocido (a)   cooked
cocina (*f*)   kitchen
coctel (*m*)   cocktail

codo (*m*) elbow
coles de Bruselas (*m*) Brussels sprouts
colonia (*f*) colony, district, neighborhood
color de rosa pink
colapso nervioso (*m*) nervous breakdown
colesterol (*m*) cholesterol
colocar to place
columna vertebral (*f*) spine
comer to eat
comerciante (*m or f*) businessman, businesswoman
comezón (*f*) itching
comida (*f*) meal
compañero (*m or f*) companion; — **de cuarto** roommate
como (*adv*) since; **¿cómo?** (*interr*) how?; — **no** sure
cómodo (a) comfortable
compañía de seguros (*f*) insurance company
comprar to buy
comprender to understand
con (*prep*) with
conmigo with me
condado (*m*) county
conejo (*m*) rabbit; **examen de —** rabbit test
conocer to become acquainted with
conocimiento (*m*) consciousness
conseguir to get
consejo (*m*) advice
consultar to consult
consultorio (*m*) consulting room
contado (al —) cash
contar (ue) to count, to tell
contento (a) happy
conteo (*m*) count (blood)
contra (*prep*) against
contracepción (*f*) conception; **anticontracepción** birth control preventative
convenir to be convenient
corazón (*m*) heart
corbata (*f*) necktie
cordero (*m*) lamb
corpiño (*m*) bra
corral (*m*) playpen

correo (*m*) mail
correos (*m*) post office
correr to run
cortado (a) cut
cortadura (*f*) cut
cortar to cut
cosa (*f*) thing
costilla (*f*) rib
coyuntura (*f*) joint
craneo (*m*) cranium
creer to believe
crema (*f*) cream, ointment
creatura (*f*) infant, baby
cruzar to cross
cuadra (*f*) block
cuadrado (a) square
cuál which, what
cualquier any
cuando (*adv*) when
cuánto (a) (*adj*) how many, how much; — **tiempo** how much time
cuarto (a) quarter
cuarto (*m*) room; — **de baño** bathroom; — **de niños** nursery; — **de vestir** dressing room; — **doble** double room; — **sencillo** single room
cubrir to cover
cuchara (*f*) spoon
cucharada (*f*) tablespoon
cucharadita (*f*) teaspoon
cuchilla de afeitar (*f*) razor blade
cuchillo (*m*) knife
cuaderno (*m*) notebook
cuello (*m*) neck; — **de la matriz** (*m*) cervix
cuenta (*f*) bill
cuerpo (*m*) body
cuidado (*m*) care; — **intensivo** intensive care
cuidadosamente carefully
cuidar to care for
¡cuidado! look out!
cuidarse to take care of oneself
cumplir (con) to comply, carry out
cuna (*f*) cradle
cunero (*m*) nursery
cuña (*f*) bedpan

cuñado (*m or f*) brother-in-law
cura (*m*) priest
cura (*f*) cure
curado (a) cured
curar to heal
curita (*f*) Band-aid

CH

chaleco (*f*) vest
chaqueta (*f*) jacket
chata (*f*) bedpan
cheque (*m*) check; — **de viajero** traveler's check
chicharos (*m*) peas
chocar to run into, collide
choque (*m*) wreck, shock
chuleta (*f*) chop; — **de puerco** pork chop
chupar to suck; **chupe** (*imperative*) suck
chupeta (*f*) pacifier

D

dar to give; — **de alta** to discharge; — **de mamar** to nurse; — **el pecho**, —**se vuelta** to turn over
datíl (*m*) date (fruit)
de (*prep*) from, of; — **prisa** in a hurry; — **vez en cuando** from time to time
debajo (de) under
deber ought to, should; to owe
débil weak
debilidad (*f*) weakness
decaído (a) crestfallen
decir to say, to tell
dedo (*m*) finger; — **del pie** toe
defecar to defecate
debribrilador (*m*) defibrillator
dejar (de) to cease, to stop, to leave
del from the (*contraction*)
delante (de) in front of
delgado (a) thin
demasiado (a) too much
demora (*f*) delay

demorar to delay
dentadura (*f*) denture
dentista (*m or f*) dentist
departamento (*m*) department
dependiente (*m or f*) clerk
depósito (*m*) warehouse
deprimido (a) depressed
derecho (*m*) law; right
 a la derecha (*f*) to the right (direction)
derrame (*m*) stroke
desagradable unpleasant
desangrarse to bleed profusely
desastre (*m*) disaster
desayunar(se) to eat breakfast
desayuno (*m*) breakfast
descansar to rest; **descanse** (*imperative*) rest
descanso (*m*) rest, rest area
descremado (a) skimmed; **leche —a** skimmed milk
describir to describe
desde (*prep*) from
desear to desire
desecho (*m*) discharge
deshidratado (a) dehydrated
desmayarse to faint
desmayo (*m*) fainting spell
despacio (*adv*) slowly
despedir to say goodbye
despertarse to wake up
después (*adv*) later; — **de** (*prep*) after
desventaja (*f*) disadvantage; **tener —to** be handicapped
determinar to determine
detrás de (*prep*) in back of
día (*m*) day
diafragma (*m*) diaphragm
diagnóstico (*m*) diagnosis
diario (*m*) newspaper
diariamente daily
diarrea (*f*) diarrhea
diente (*m*) tooth
dieta (*f*) diet
dietista (*m or f*) dietician
difícil difficult
dificultad (*f*) difficulty
difteria (*f*) diphtheria
dinero (*m*) money

Dios   God; **si — quiere**   God willing
dirección (*f*)   address
dirigirse   to go to
disco (*m*)   disc; **— calcificado**   calcified
   disc; **— desplazado**   herniated disc
disponible (*m or f*)   available
dispositivo (*m*)   device;
   — intrauterino   I.U.D.
distrofía muscular (*f*)   muscular
   dystrophy
divorciado (a)   divorced
doblar   to bend; **doblarse**   to turn
   oneself over; **dóblese**
   (*imperative*)   turn over
doble   double
docena (*f*)   dozen
dólar (*m*)   dollar
doler   to ache
dolor (*m*)   pain; **— agudo**   sharp pain;
   — expulsivo   expulsive pain; **— de
   parto**   labor pain;
   — quemante   burning pain;
   tener —   to be in pain
donde (*adv*)   where; **¿adónde?**
   (*interrog*)   to where?
domicilio (*m*)   home address
dorado (a)   golden
dormido (a)   asleep
dormir   to sleep
dósis (*f*)   dosage
dracma (*m*)   dram
droga (*f*)   drug
drogadicto (*m*)   drug addict
ducha (*f*)   shower
duele (doler)   it hurts; **me duele**   it
   hurts me
dulce (*m or f adj*)   sweet
durante (*adv*)   during
durar   to last
durazno (*m*)   peach
duro (a)   hard

E

edad (*f*)   age
edificio (*m*)   building
efectivo (a)   effective; **en —**   cash
eficaz (*m or f*)   effective

ejercicio (*m*)   exercise
ejote (*m*)   green bean
él (*pronoun*)   he
el (*article*)   the
electrocardiograma
   (*m*)   electrocardiogram
elegir   to choose
elevadora (*f*)   elevator
elote (*m*)   corn on the cob
ella (*pronoun*)   she
embarazada   pregnant
embarazo (*m*)   pregnancy
embolia (*f*)   embolism
embriagado (a)   intoxicated
emergencia (*f*)   emergency; **sala de —**
   emergency room
empeor   worse
empezar (ie)   to begin
empleo (*m*)   job, employment
empujar   to push
en (*prep*)   in, into; **— caso de**   in case
   of; **— espera** (*adv*)   awaiting;
   — frente (*prep*)   in front of;
   — seguida (*adv*)   immediately
enagua (*f*)   slip
encantado (a)   delighted
encantar   to delight, to charm
encargado (a)   person in charge,
   guardian
encargar   to be in charge
encender   to light
encerrar   to encircle
encías (*f*)   gums
encinta   pregnant; **ponerse —**   to
   become pregnant
enero (*m*)   January
enfermedad (*f*)   illness
enfermera (*m or f*)   nurse
enfermería (*f*)   nursing
enfermo (a)   sick
enfisema (*f*)   emphysema
enojado (a)   angry
ensalada (*f*)   salad
ensuciar   to dirty, to defecate
enterarse (ie)   to be informed of
entierro (*m*)   burial
entonces (*adv*)   then
entrada (*f*)   entrance;
   — principal   main entrance

entrar to enter
entrepierna (*f*) crotch
enyesar to put in a plaster cast
equipo (*m*) equipment, team
equivocado (a) wrong
eructar to belch
eructo (*m*) belch
erupción (*f*) rash
escalera (*f*) stairway, ladder
escalfado (a) poached
escalofrío (*m*) chill
escarlatina (*f*) scarlet fever
escoger to choose
escribir to write
escuchar to listen
eso that
esófago (*m*) esophagus
espacio (*m*) space, blank
español (*m*) Spanish language
español (ola) Spanish
espalda (*f*) back
espárrago (*m*) asparagus
especializado (a) specialized
espejo (*m*) mirror
esperanza (*f*) hope
esperar to wait, to hope
espinaca (*f*) spinach
esplín (*m*) spleen
esposo (*m or f*) spouse
espuma (*f*) foam
esputo (*m*) sputum, saliva
esqueleto (*m*) skeleton
esta, este (*dem adj*) this
está (estar) is
estado (*m*) state; **— crítico** critical
  condition
estampilla (*f*) stamp
estar to be
estimado (a) esteemed
estirar to stretch
estómago (*m*) stomach
estricto (a) strict
estuche (*m*) case
estufa (*f*) heater; stove
etiqueta (*f*) label
evacuación (*f*) bowel movement
evitar to avoid
exactamente exactly
examinar to examine

excremento (*m*) excrement
excusado (*m*) toilet
exigente (*m or f*) demanding
expectoración (*f*) expectoration,
  sputum
explicar to explain

F

fábrica (*f*) factory
fácil (*m or f adj*) easy
facilmente easily
falda (*f*) skirt
Falopio Fallopian
falta (*f*) lack; **— de aire** (*f*) shortness
  of breath
fallecido (a) expired, deceased
fallo cardíaco (*m*) cardiac arrest
farmacia (*f*) pharmacy
fastidioso (a) bothersome
febrero (*m*) February
fecha (*f*) date; **— de nacimiento**
  (*f*) birthdate
feliz (*m or f*), **felices** (*pl*) happy
feo (a) ugly
feto (*m*) fetus
fibra (*f*) fiber
fibrosis quística (*f*) cystic fibrosis
fiebre (*f*) fever; **— amarilla** yellow
  fever; **— reumática** rheumatic fever
fijarse (en) to notice; **fíjese**
  (*imperative*) look, notice
firma (*f*) signature
firmar to sign; **firme aquí**
  (*imperative*) sign here
fisioterapia (*f*) physiotherapy
flema (*f*) phlegm
flor (*f*) flower
florero (*m*) vase
folleto (*m*) folder
fondo (*m*) slip, bottom
formulario (*m*) form; **— de**
  admisión admissions form
fosfato (*m*) phosphate
fractura (*f*) fracture
fracturar to break
francamente frankly
franco (a) frank
frase (*f*) sentence

frazada (*f*) blanket
fresco (a) cool
frecuentemente frequently
frente (*m*) forehead
fresa (*f*) strawberry
frijoles (*m*) beans
frío (*m*) cold; **estar —** to be cold
  (thing); **tener —** to be cold (person)
frito (a) fried; **papas — as** french
  fries
frotarse to rub oneself
frotis (*m*) smear; **— de
  Papanicolaou** Pap smear
fruta (*f*) fruit
fuerte (*m or f adj*) strong
fumar to smoke; **no —** no smoking
funcionar to function, work, run
funda (*f*) pillowcase

G

galleta (*f*) cookie, cracker
ganar to gain, to win
garantizar to guarantee
garganta (*f*) throat
gas (*m*) gas, flatulence
gemelos (*m pl*) twins
genitales (*m pl*) genitals
gente (*f*) people
gerente (*m or f*) manager
germen (*m*) germ
girar to turn, rotate; **gire**
  (*imperative*) turn, rotate
globo (*m*) globe; **— del ojo** eyeball
glóbulo corpuscle; **— blanco** white
  corpuscle; **— rojo** red corpuscle
golpe (*m*) blow, contusion
goma (*f*) rubber
gordo (a) fat, thick
gorro (*m*) cervical cap
grado (*m*) degree
grasa (*f*) fat
gratis (*m or f adj*) free
gratuito (a) free of charge
gripe (*f*) flu
gris (*m or f*) grey
gritar to yell
grito (*m*) scream
grueso (a) thick

guajalote (*m*) turkey (*Mex.*)
guardar to keep; **— cama** to stay in
  bed
guardarropa (*f*) closet
guía (*f*) guide
guisantes (*m*) peas
gustar to be pleasing, to like
gusto (*m*) pleasure

H

habichuela (*f*) green bean
hablar to speak
hacer to do, to make; **haga**
  (*imperative*) make; **hace calor** it is
  hot (weather)
hacia (*adv*) toward;
  — abajo downward;
  — adelante forward;
  —atrás backward
hambre (*f*) hunger; **tener —** to be
  hungry
hamberguesa (*f*) hamburger
hasta (*adv*) until
hebreo (a) Hebrew
helado (*m*) ice cream
hemorragia (*f*) bleeding
hemorroides (*f pl*) hemorrhoids
herida (*f*) incision, wound
herido (a) wounded; **— de
  bala** gunshot wound
hermana (*f*) sister, nun
hermano (*m*) brother
hermoso (a) beautiful
hervido (a) boiled
hervor (*m*) heartburn
hielo (*m*) ice
hierro (*m*) iron
hígado (*m*) liver
hija (*f*) daughter
hijastro (*m*) stepson
hijo (*m*) son
hijos (*m pl*) children
hinchado (a) swollen
hinchazón (*f*) swelling
hispanoparlante (*m or f*) Spanish-
  speaking person
hoja (*f*) leaf (page)

hombre (*m*) man; — **de negocios** businessman
hombro (*m*) shoulder
hongos (*m pl*) mushrooms
hora (*f*) hour, time; **¿Qué — es?** what time is it?; **¿a qué —** at what time?
horario (*m*) schedule
hormigueo (*m*) tingling
hospedado (a) lodged (have a place to stay)
hospital (*m*) hospital
hospitalización (*f*) hospitalization
hoy today
hueso (*m*) bone
huevo (*m*) egg; — **frito** fried egg; — **hervido** poached egg; — **revueltos** scrambled eggs
hule (*m*) (*Mex.*) rubber

I

ictericia (*f*) jaundice
identidad (*f*) identity
igual equal, same
impreso (*m*) printed matter
incapacidad (*f*) disability
incómodo (a) uncomfortable
incubadora (*f*) incubator
inclinarse to bend
indicarse to indicate
infancia (*f*) childhood; **enfermedades de —** childhood diseases
infarto (*m*) infarct
ingle (*f*) groin
inglés (*m*) English language
inglés (esa) (*adj*) English
ingresar to be admitted
injerto (*m*) graft
inmunización (*f*) immunization
inodoro (*m*) toilet
interno (*m or f*) intern
intestino (*m*) intestine; — **grueso** large intestine; — **delgado** small intestine
intrauterino (a) intrauterine; **dispositivo —** (*m*) intrauterine device (IUD)

introducir to introduce
inyección (*f*) injection
ir to go; —**se** to go away
izquierda (*f*) left

J

jabón (*m*) soap
jalea (*f*) jelly
jamón (*m*) ham
jaqueca (*f*) headache (migraine)
jarabe (*m*) syrup
jefe (*m or f*) chief
jerinquilla (*f*) syringe
jugo (*m*) juice; — **de ciruela pasa** prune juice; — **de tomato** tomato juice; — **de naranja** orange juice; — **de uva** grape juice
julio (*m*) July
junio (*m*) June
justillo (*m*) bra

L

labio (*m*) lip
laboratorio (*m*) laboratory
lado (*m*) side; **al —** beside, next to; **ponerse de —** to turn on one's side
lámpara (*f*) lamp
laparoscopía (*f*) laparoscopy
lapicera (*f*) ballpoint pen
lápiz (*f*) pencil
laringe (*f*) larynx
lástima (*f*) shame, pity
lastimado (a) injured
latido (*m*) heartbeat
latir to throb
lavamanos (*m sing*) lavatory
lavandería (*f*) laundry
lavándulo (a) lavender
lavar to wash; —**se** to wash oneself; —**se los dientes** to brush one's teeth
laxante (*m*) laxative
lazo (*m*) loop
le (*indef pron*) to him, to her, to you (*polite*)

leche (*f*) milk
lechuga (*f*) lettuce
leer to read
legal legal
legumbre (*f*) vegetable
lejos (*adv*) far away
lengua (*f*) tongue, language
lentamente slowly
lentes (*m pl*) lenses; — **de contacto** contact lenses
letra (*f*) print
levantar to raise; —**se** to get up; **levántese** (*imperative*) get up; —**se la manga (subirse)** to roll up one's sleeves
ley (*f*) law
libra (*f*) pound
licensia (*f*) license; — **de manejar** driver's license
licor (*m*) liquor
ligero (a) light
lima (*f*) lime
limpiar to clean; —**se** to clean oneself
línea (*f*) line
litro (*m*) liter
loco (a) crazy
locura (*f*) insanity
luchar to fight
lucidez (*f*) sanity
lugar (*m*) place
luz (*f*) light; **encender la** — to turn on the light; **apagar la** — to turn off the light

LL

llamar to call; **llámeme** (*imperative*) call me; —**se** to be named; — **a la puerta** to knock on the door
llave (*f*) key
llenar to fill, to fill out
llevar to wear, to carry
llorar to cry

M

madre (*f*) mother
madrina (*f*) godmother

maestro (*m or f*) teacher
malestar (*m*) discomfort
maleta (*f*) suitcase
maligno (a) malignant
mamografía mammograph
mandar to send
mandíbula (*f*) jaw
manga (*f*) sleeve
manta (*f*) blanket, bedspread
mantener to maintain; **mantenga** (*imperative*) maintain
mantenimiento (*m*) maintenance
mantequilla (*f*) butter
manzana (*f*) apple
mañana (*f*) tomorrow; **de la —, hasta** — until tomorrow
maquillaje (*m*) makeup
máquina (*f*) machine
máquina de afeitar shaver
marcapasos (*m sing*) pacemaker
marearse to get dizzy
mareo (*m*) dizziness
marido (*m*) husband
más (*adv*) more, most
masaje (*m*) massage
masticar to chew; **mastique** (*imperative*) chew
matrix (*f*) womb
mayo (*m*) May
mayor major; older; adult
mayoría (*f*) majority
me (*pronoun*) me
mécanico (*m or f*) mechanic
médula (*f*) medulla
medias (*f pl*) hose
medio (a) middle; half
medianoche (*f*) midnight
mediodía (*m*) noon
médico (a) medical
médico (*m or f*) doctor
medir (i) to measure; **¿Cuánto mide?** how tall are you (he, she)?
mejilla (*f*) cheek
mejor (*adv*) better
mejorarse to get better; **¡que se mejore!** get better!
menor younger; minor
menos (*adv*) less
menstruación (*f*) menstruation
mente (*f*) mind

merienda (*f*)   tea (snack)
mes (*m*)   month; **al —**   per month
método (*m*)   method
microbio (*m*)   germ
miedo (*m*)   fear; **tener —**   to be afraid
milagro (*m*)   miracle
mirar   to look at
mitad (*f*)   half
mojado (a)   damp
molestar   to bother
molestia (*f*)   trouble, pain
moneda (*f*)   coin
morado (a)   brown
morado (*m*)   bruise
morder (ue)   to bite
mordida de serpiente   snakebite
moretón (*m*)   bruise
morir (ue)   to die
mortificado (a)   worried
mover(se) (ue)   to move; **no se mueve**
   (*imperative*)   don't move
muchacha (*f*)   girl
muchacho (*m*)   boy
mucho (a)   much, a lot
mueble (*m*)   piece of furniture
muerte (*f*)   death
muerto (*m*)   dead person
muerto (a)   dead
muestra (*f*)   sample, specimen
mujer (*f*)   woman, wife; **— de**
   negocios   businesswoman
muleta (*f*)   crutch
mundo (*m*)   world
muñeca (*f*)   wrist; doll
músculo (*m*)   muscle
muslo (*m*)   thigh
muy (*adv*)   very

N

nacer   to be born
nacido   born; **recien —**   newborn
nacimiento (*m*)   birth; **fecha de —**
   date of birth
nada   nothing; **de —**   don't mention it
nalgas (*f* pl)   buttocks
naranja (*f*)   orange (fruit)
naranjado (a)   orange (color)
nariz (*f*)   nose
nasal   nasal; **fosa —** (*f*)   nostril

natalidad (*f*)   birth
náusea (*f*)   nausea
necesario (a)   necessary
necesitar   to need
negro (a)   black
nervio (*m*)   nerve
nervioso (a)   nervous
neurólogo (*m or f*)   neurologist
ninguna   not one, not any
nivel (*m*)   level
niña (*f*)   little girl, child
niño (*f*)   little boy, child
niños (*m pl*)   little children
nieto (*m*)   grandson
noche (*f*)   night
nombre (*m*)   name
notificar   to notify
noviembre (*m*)   November
novio (*m or f*)   sweetheart, steady,
   bridegroom
nuca (*f*)   nape
nudillos (*m*)   knuckles
nuera (*f*)   daughter-in-law
número (*m*)   number
nuevo (a)   new
nunca (*adv*)   never

O

o   or
obscuro (a)   dark
obrar   to work; to have a bowel
   movement
octubre (*m*)   October
ocupación (*f*)   occupation
ocurrir   to happen
oficina (*f*)   office
oído (*m*)   inner ear
ohalá   I hope so
ojo (*m*)   eye
olor (*m*)   odor
ombligo (*m*)   navel
onda (*f*)   wave
operación (*f*)   operation; **sala de —**
   operating room
operar   to operate
opresión (*f*)   tightness
orden (*f*)   order
ordenar   to order

oreja (*f*) outer ear
órgano (*m*) organ
orina (*f*) urine
orinal (*m*) urinal
orinar to urinate
orzuelo (*m*) sty
otra vez again
otro (a) other, another
ovarios (*m pl*) ovaries
ovulación (*f*) ovulation
ovulo (*m*) ovule
oxígeno (*m*) oxygen

P

paciente (*m or f adj*) patient
padecer (zc) to suffer
padrastro stepfather
padre (*m*) father
padrino (*m*) godfather
pagar to pay; **— al contado, en efectivo** pay in cash; **— a plazos** to charge
pagos (*m pl*) payment, fees
país (*m*) country
pareja (*f*) pair
párese stand up
paleta (*f*) bedpan; shoulderblade; popsicle
paludismo (*m*) malaria
pan (*m*) bread
pañuelo de papel (*f*) tissue paper
papa (*f*) potato
papel (*m*) paper; **— higiénico** toilet paper
papera (*f*) goiter
paperas (*f pl*) mumps
par (*m*) pair
para (*prep*) for, in order to
pararse to stand
pardo (a) brown
parar to stop
parche (*m*) dressing, patch
parentesco (*m*) relationship (kinship)
pariente (*m or f*) relative
paro cardíaco (*m*) cardiac arrest
parótidas (*f pl*) parotid glands
parotiditis (*f*) mumps
párpado (*m*) eyelid

parto (*m*) childbirth;
   — cesáreo Cesarean birth;
   — natural natural childbirth
pasado (a) (*adj*) past
pasado (*m*) past
pasar to happen, to pass; **¿qué —?** what's happening?; **¿qué le — ?** what's happening to you (to him, to her)?
pasillo (*m*) hallway
pasta de dientes (*f*) toothpaste
pastel (*m*) pie
pastilla (*f*) tablet
patata (*f*) potato
pato (*m*) bedpan; duck
pavo (*m*) turkey
pecho (*m*) chest; **dar el —** to breast feed
pediatra (*m or f*) pediatrician
pedir (i) to ask for; **— prestado** to borrow
peinar to comb
peine (*m*) comb
peligro (*m*) danger
peligroso (a) dangerous
pelo (*m*) hair
pena (*f*) pain (emotional); **¡qué —!** what a pain, pity
pene (*m*) penis
penicilina (*f*) penicillin
pensar to think
pentotal de sodio (*m*) sodium pentothal
peor worse
pequeño (a) little, small
pepino (*m*) cucumber
pera (*f*) pear
perder to lose
perdido (a) lost
perineo (*m*) perineum
periódico (*m*) newspaper
periódo period (menstrual)
periósteo (*m*) periosteum
permitir to allow
permiso (*m*) permission; **con —** with (your) permission
pero but
persona (*f*) person
personal (*m*) personnel
pesado (a) heavy, boring

pesar to weigh; **¿cuánto pesa usted?** how much do you weigh?
pescado (*m*) fish
peso (*m*) weight
pestaña (*f*) eyelash
pezón (*m*) nipple
picar to itch; **me pica** it itches; **¿le pica?** does it itch?
picazón (*f*) itching
pie (*m*) foot; **— de la cama** foot of the bed
piel (*f*) skin; fur
pierna (*f*) leg
píldora (*f*) pill
pimienta (*f*) pepper
pinchar to prick, puncture
pinza (*f*) pliers; forceps; **— de cejas** tweezers
piña (*f*) pineapple
pisar to step on
piso (*m*) floor of building
placa (*f*) plate; **— de rayos X** X-ray plate, picture
planificación (*f*) planning; **— de familia** family planning
planificar to plan
plástico (a) plastic; **cirugía —** (*f*) plastic surgery
plátano (*m*) banana
plato (*m*) dish
platillo (*m*) saucer
plazo: a — on terms, on credit
pluma (*f*) pen
población (*f*) population, town
pobre (*m or f adj*) poor
pobrecito (*m*) poor thing
poco (a) few
poder to be able
policía (*f*) police
póliza (*f*) policy; **— de seguros** insurance policy
pollo (*m*) chicken; **— frito** fried chicken; **— asado** baked chicken
pomada (*f*) salve
pomelo (*m*) grapefruit
poner to place, to put; to turn on; **—se** to put on; **—se de lado** to turn on one's side; **—se de acuerdo** to agree on; **—se encenta** to get pregnant

por (*prep*) for, through; **— ciento** per cent; **— favor** please; **— lo tanto** therefore; **— supuesto** of course
poros (*m pl*) pores
porque (*conj*) conjunction
¿por qué? why?
positivo (a) positive
postilla (*f*) scab
postiza (*f*); **dentura —** false teeth
postre (*m*) dessert
potable: agua — drinking water
preescolar (*m or f adj*) preschool
preguntar to ask a question
preocupado (a) worried
preocuparse de to worry about
preparar to prepare
presentar to introduce
presilla (*f*) clip
presión (*f*) pressure; **— alta** high blood pressure; **— arterial** blood pressure; **— baja** low blood pressure; **— de la sangre** blood pressure
previo (a) previous
primero (a) first; **—os auxilios** (*m pl*) first aid
primo (a) (*m or f*) cousin
privado (a) private
privar deprive
probar to try, to test; to taste
problema (*m*) problem
promesa (*f*) promise
prometer to promise
proteína (*f*) protein
protestante (*m or f*) Protestant
provocado (a) provoked
pronto (*adv*) soon
prueba (*f*) test
psiquiatra (*m or f*) (*also spelled* **siquiatra**) psychiatrist
puedo (poder) I can
puerco (*m*) pork
pues (*adv*) well
puerta (*f*) door, port
pujar to push; **¡puje!** (*imperative*) push (down)!
pujo (*m*) expulsive contraction
pulgada (*f*) inch
pulgar (*m*) thumb

pulmón (*m*) lung
pulmotor (*m*) iron lung
pulmonía bronquial
   (*f*) bronchopneumonia
pulsación (*f*) pulsation, beat
pulsera (*f*) bracelet; **— de**
   identificación identification bracelet
pulso (*m*) pulse
punto (*m*) stitch; dot, period
puño (*m*) fist
purgante (*m*) purgative, laxative
pupila (*m*) pupil
pus (*m*) pus

Q

que (*conj*) that, which; **¿qué?** what?
quebrado (a) broken
quebrar to break
quedar(se) to stay
quemadura (*f*) burn
quemante burning
quemar(se) to burn (oneself)
querer to want; **te quiero** I love you;
   — decir to mean
querido (a) dear, sweetheart
queso (*m*) cheese
quien who
quijada (*f*) jaw
químico (a) chemical
quinto (a) fifth
quitar(se) to take away, to remove; to
   take off
quizás perhaps

R

rábano (*m*) radish
radiografía (*f*) X-ray
radiólogo (*m*) radiologist
radioterapia (*f*) radiotherapy
raíz (*f*) root
rapidamente rapidly
raquídea (*f*) spinal anesthesia
rascar(se) to scratch oneself
rasurar to shave
rato (*m*) a little while

rayos-X X-ray
razón (*f*) right, correct; **tener —** to be
   right, correct
receta (*f*) prescription
recibir to receive
recibo (*m*) receipt
recomendar to recommend
reconocimiento (*m*) examination
recoger to pick up
recto (*m*) rectum
recuento (*m*) blood count
recurso (*m*) resource
referirse a to refer to
refresco (*m*) refreshment
refuerzo (*m*) booster
regla (*f*) menstrual period; rule
regalo (*m*) gift; **tienda de —** gift shop
registro (*m*) registry
región (*f*) region
regresar to return
relaciones sexuales (*f* pl) sexual
   relations
relajar to relax
reloj (*m*) watch
repente; de — suddenly
requerir to require
requesón (*m*) cottage cheese
repollo (*m*) cabbage
residente (*m or f*) resident
resfrió (*m*) cold
resolver to resolve
respirar to breathe
respuesta (*f*) reply
resucitador cardiopulmonar
   (*m*) cardiopulmonary resuscitator
resultado (*m*) result
resume (*m*) summary
revista (*f*) magazine
riñon (*m*) kidney
ritmo (*m*) rhythm
rosbif (*m*) roast beef
rojo (a) red
ropa (*f*) clothing
romper to break
roto (a) broken
rubéola (*f*) German measles
rubrica (*f*) heading
ruído (*m*) noise
rutinario (a) routine

S

sábana (f)   sheet
saber   to know (a fact)
sabor (m)   taste
sacar   to take out; to take a picture
sacarina (f)   saccharine
sacerdote (m)   priest
sal (f)   salt
sala (f)   room
salchicha (f)   sausage
salida (f)   exit
saliva (f)   saliva
salsa picante (f)   hot sauce
salud (f)   health
salvar   to save
 a salvo de   safe from
sanar   to heal, recover
sangrar   to bleed
sangre (f)   blood
sarampión (m)   measles
sé (saber)   I know
secar   to dry
seco (a)   dry
sed (f)   thirst; tener —   to be thirsty
seguir   to follow
 la siguiente   the following
sígame   follow me
según   according to
segundo (a)   second
seguro (m)   insurance
seguro (a)   certain
seguro social   Social Security
seleccionar   to select
sello (m)   stamp
semana (f)   week
semejante   similar
sencillo (a)   simple
senos (m pl)   breasts
sentarse (ie)   to sit down; siéntese
 (imperative)   sit down
sentir(se)   to feel; lo siento   I'm sorry;
 mi sentido pésame   my deepest
 sympathy
señal (f)   sign
señalado (a)   indicated
septiembre (m)   September
ser   to be
serio (a)   serious

servilleta (f)   napkin;
 — sanitaria   sanitary napkin
si   if
sí   yes
siempre   always
sien (f)   temple
sífilis (f)   syphilis
significar   to mean, to signify
signos vitales (m pl)   vital signs
silla (f)   chair; — de ruedas
 (f)   wheelchair
silleta (f)   bedpan
sin (prep)   without
síntoma (m)   symptom
sistema (m)   system; — venoso   venous
 system
sitio (m)   place
sobaco (m)   armpit
sobre (m)   envelope
sobre (prep)   over, above
sobrino (a)   nephew, niece
¡socorro!   help!
solicitante (m or f)   applicant
solo (adv)   only
solo (a)   alone
soltero (a)   bachelor, single person
sonda (f)   catheter, probe
sordo (a)   deaf; dull (pain)
sótano (m)   basement
su (adj)   his, her, yours (pol), theirs
subir   to go up; súbase (imperative)   go
 up; súbase la manga
 (imperative)   roll up your sleeve
sudor (m)   sweat
suegra (f)   mother-in-law
suero (m)   IV serum
suerte (f)   luck; tener —   to be lucky;
 ¡buena —!   good luck!
suficiente   sufficient
sufrir   to suffer
suicidarse   to commit suicide
sujetar   to hold
suyo (a) (adj)   yours, his, hers, theirs

T

tableta (f)   tablet
talón (m)   heel

tamaño (*m*)   size
también   also
tanto (a)   so much
tapar   to cover
tapete (*m*)   paper (examination) table cover
tampón (tapón) (*m*)   tampon
taza (*f*)   saucer
tazón (*m*)   emesis basin
tarde (*f*)   afternoon; **buenas —**   good afternoon
tarde (*adv*)   late
tarjeta (*f*)   card
técnico (a) (*m or f*)   technician
tejido (*m*)   tissue
teléfono (*m*)   telephone
televisora (*f*)   television
temblor (*m*)   twitching
temprano (a)   early
temprano (*adv*)   early
tenedor (*m*)   fork
tener   to have; **— cuidad**   to be careful; **— sed**   to be thirsty; **— que**   to have to
terapeútica (*f*)   therapy
tercero (a)   third
terminar   to finish
termómetro (*m*)   thermometer
ternera (*f*)   veal
testículos (*m pl*)   testicles
tiempo (*m*)   time, weather
timbre (*m*)   bell
tía (*f*)   aunt
tío (*m*)   uncle
tiroides (*f*)   thyroid
toalla (*f*)   towel
tobillos (*m pl*)   ankles
tocino (*m*)   bacon
todavía (*adv*)   yet, still
tomar   to take, to eat (drink)
tórax (*m*)   thorax
torcedura (*f*)   sprain
torcer (ue)   to twist
toronia (*f*)   grapefruit
tortilla (*f*)   omelette
tos (*f*)   cough; **— ferina** (*f*)   whooping cough
toser   to cough
trabajo (*m*)   work

trabajar   to work
traer   to bring; **traígame** (*imperative*)   bring me
tragar   to swallow; **trague** (*imperative*)   swallow
tranquilixante (*m*)   tranquilizer
tráquea (*f*)   trachea
trastorno (*m*)   disturbance, problem
tratamiento (*m*)   treatment
tratar   to try
tripas (*f*)   guts
tuberculina (*f*)   tuberculine
tuberculosis (*f*)   tuberculosis
tubo (*m*)   tube; system
tumor (*m*)   tumor
turno (*m*)   turn; **— de día**   day shift; **— de noche**   night shift

U

úlcera (*f*)   ulcer
últimamente   lately
último (a)   last
unidad (*f*)   unity; **— de cuidados intensivos**   intensive care unit (ICU)
uretra (*f*)   urethra
úrico   uric
urólogo (*m*)   urologist
usar   to use
útero (*m*)   uterus
útil   useful
usted (*pron*)   you (*polite*)

V

vacío (a)   empty
vacuna (*f*)   vaccine
vacunado (a)   vaccinated
vagina (*f*)   vagina
válvula (*f*)   valve
valer   to be worth
varocena (*f*)   chicken pox
vario (a)   various
vasija (*f*)   basin
vaso (*m*)   glass; **— sanguíneo**   blood vessel; **— capilar**   capillary
vecino (*m or f*)   neighbor

vegetal (*m*)   vegetable
vejiga (*f*)   bladder
vello (*m*)   body hair
vena (*f*)   vein
vendaje (*m*)   bandage
vender   to sell
vesícula (*f*)   gall bladder
vestíbulo (*m*)   vestibule, lobby
vestidor (*m*)   dressing room
vestuario (*m*)   dressing room
ver   to see
verdadero (a)   truly
verde (*m or f*)   green
vez (*f*)   time
vida (*f*)   life
viejo (a)   old
vino (*m*)   wine
virar   to turn one's head
viruela (*f*)   smallpox
visita (*f*)   visit; **horas de —**   visiting hours
vivir   to live

volverse (ue)   to turn over;
  —loco (a)   to go crazy
vomitar   to vomit
voltearse   to turn oneself over
voluntad (*f*)   willpower, will

Y

y   and (**e** *before words beginning with* **i** *or* **hi**)
ya (*adv*)   already
yerno (*m*)   son-in-law
yeso (*m*)   plaster cast
yo (*subj pronoun*)   I
yogur (*m*)   yogurt

Z

zanahoria (*f*)   carrot